# ANCIENT GR
# THOUGHT

Ancient Greece was a place of tremendous political experiment and innovation, and it was here too that the first serious political thinkers emerged. Using carefully selected case studies, Professor Cartledge investigates the dynamic interaction between ancient Greek political thought and practice from early historic times to the early Roman Empire. Of concern throughout are three major issues: first, the relationship of political thought and practice; second, the relevance of class and status to explaining political behaviour and thinking; and, third, democracy – its invention, development and expansion, and extinction, prior to its recent resuscitation and even apotheosis. In addition, monarchy in various forms and at different periods, and the peculiar political structures of Sparta, are treated in detail over a chronological range extending from Homer to Plutarch. The book provides an introduction to the topic for all students and non-specialists who appreciate the continued relevance of ancient Greece to political theory and practice today.

PAUL CARTLEDGE is A. G. Leventis Professor of Greek Culture at Cambridge University and a Fellow of Clare College. He has published extensively on Greek history over several decades, including *The Cambridge Illustrated History of Ancient Greece* (1997, new edition 2002), *Sparta and Lakonia: A Regional History 1300–362 BC* (new edition 2001) and *Alexander the Great: The Hunt for a New Past* (2004, revised edition 2005).

# KEY THEMES IN ANCIENT HISTORY

EDITORS

## P. A. Cartledge
*Clare College, Cambridge*

## P. D. A. Garnsey
*Jesus College, Cambridge*

Key Themes in Ancient History aims to provide readable, informed and original studies of various basic topics, designed in the first instance for students and teachers of classics and ancient history, but also for those engaged in related disciplines. Each volume is devoted to a general theme in Greek, Roman or, where appropriate, Graeco-Roman history, or to some salient aspect or aspects of it. Besides indicating the state of current research in the relevant area, authors seek to show how the theme is significant for our own as well as ancient culture and society. By providing books for courses that are oriented around themes it is hoped to encourage and stimulate promising new developments in teaching and research in ancient history.

## Other books in the series

*Death-ritual and social structure in classical antiquity*, by Ian Morris
978 0 521 37465 1 (hardback), 978 0 521 37611 2 (paperback)

*Literacy and orality in ancient Greece*, by Rosalind Thomas
978 0 521 37346 3 (hardback), 978 0 521 37742 3 (paperback)

*Slavery and Society at Rome*, by Keith Bradley
978 0 521 37287 9 (hardback), 978 0 521 37887 1 (paperback)

*Law, violence, and community in classical Athens*, by David Cohen
978 0 521 38167 3 (hardback), 978 0 521 38837 5 (paperback)

*Public order in ancient Rome*, by Wilfried Nippel
978 0 521 38327 1 (hardback), 978 0 521 38749 1 (paperback)

*Friendship in the classical world*, by David Konstan
978 0 521 45402 5 (hardback), 978 0 521 45998 3 (paperback)

*Sport and society in ancient Greece*, by Mark Golden
978 0 521 49698 8 (hardback), 978 0 521 49790 9 (paperback)

*Food and society in classical antiquity*, by Peter Garnsey
978 0 521 64182 1 (hardback), 978 0 521 64588 1 (paperback)

*Banking and business in the Roman world*, by Jean Andreau
978 0 521 38031 7 (hardback), 978 0 521 38932 7 (paperback)

*Roman law in context*, by David Johnston
978 0 521 63046 7 (hardback), 978 0 521 63961 3 (paperback)

*Religions of the ancient Greeks*, by Simon Price
978 0 521 38201 4 (hardback), 978 0 521 38867 2 (paperback)

*Christianity and Roman society*, by Gillian Clark
978 0 521 63310 9 (hardback), 978 0 521 63386 4 (paperback)

*Trade in classical antiquity*, by Neville Morley
978 0 521 63279 9 (hardback), 978 0 521 63416 8 (paperback)

*Technology and culture in Greek and Roman antiquity*, by Serafina Cuomo
978 0 521 81073 9 (hardback), 978 0 521 00903 4 (paperback)

*Law and crime in the Roman world*, by Jill Harries
978 0 521 82820 8 (hardback), 978 0 521 53532 8 (paperback)

*The social history of Roman art*, by Peter Stewart
978 0 521 81632 8 (hardback), 978 0 521 01659 9 (paperback)

*Asceticism in the Graeco-Roman world*, by Richard Finn OP
978 0 521 86281 3 (hardback), 978 0 521 68154 4 (paperback)

# ANCIENT GREEK POLITICAL THOUGHT IN PRACTICE

PAUL CARTLEDGE

CAMBRIDGE
UNIVERSITY PRESS

CAMBRIDGE UNIVERSITY PRESS
Cambridge, New York, Melbourne, Madrid, Cape Town, Singapore, São Paulo, Delhi

Cambridge University Press
The Edinburgh Building, Cambridge CB2 8RU, UK

Published in the United States of America by Cambridge University Press, New York

www.cambridge.org
Information on this title: www.cambridge.org/9780521455954

First published 2009

Printed in the United Kingdom at the University Press, Cambridge

*A catalogue record for this publication is available from the British Library*

*Library of Congress Cataloguing in Publication data*
Cartledge, Paul.
Ancient Greek political thought in practice / Paul Cartledge.
p. cm. – (Key themes in ancient history)
Includes bibliographical references and index.
ISBN 978-0-521-45455-1 (hardback : alk. paper)
1. Political science – Greece – History – To 1500. I. Title.
JC73.C368 2009
320.01 – dc22 2008055928

ISBN 978-0-521-45455-1 hardback
ISBN 978-0-521-45595-4 paperback

*To the memory of*
Moses Finley *(1912–1986)*
*and*
Pierre Vidal-Naquet *(1930–2006)*

# Contents

# *Preface*

'The next remove must be to the study of politics; to know the beginning, end, and reasons of political society.'

(John Milton, 'Of education', 1644)

John Milton was born almost exactly 400 years ago as I write this preface. Paraphrasing Wordsworth, I should say that his spirit at least is still living at this hour. A powerful renascence is currently under way in the practice of political theory and the study of its history, as an academic subject lying on the interdisciplinary margins between philosophy, history and social thought. Within the frame of this academic renascence and the pragmatic political concerns associated with it, the Greeks' pioneering and fundamental role in the Western political tradition is universally recognised. General books on democracy typically start with a ritual obeisance to the ancient Greeks; a few (Dunn 2006, for conspicuous example) even attempt to do something like justice to the ancient Greeks' – very different – kind of democracy. Newer still is the reappraising of the potential contemporary reference and relevance of ultimately Greek ideas, especially those of democracy, with its axiomatic components of freedom and equality (see in particular Barber 1984, Euben, Wallach and Ober 1994, and chapter 11, below). For political theory can entertain also the legitimate ambition to affect the world outside the academy (e.g. Held 1991; Tuck 1991).

The present study is a historian's book, as befits the series in which it appears. Professional ancient philosophers, experts in the 'great thinkers' from Solon and Democritus on through to Sphaerus and Plutarch, may regret the general lack of close reading of texts or close contextualisation (or both) (but see appendix II), and, even more perhaps, the incompetence where such is essayed. If historians may be too prone to despise or dismiss as irrelevant the philosophical niceties, however, most professional philosophers in my experience are not usually as well versed, or as passionately interested, in the history – social, economic and cultural as well as narrowly political – conditioning political thought as they arguably should be.

Hence the present attempt to combine the two, placing 'ideas in context' (to borrow the title of another Cambridge University Press series), in the manner advocated in chapter 1. I am, moreover, as interested in ordinary-language, everyday political thought as I am in high-flown political theory. The thoughts, however inchoate or inarticulate, of the mass rather than the theories of the elite will be what predominantly engages me here – in contrast to an earlier book (Cartledge 2002), in which Aristotle was featured centrally and very prominently as a uniquely valuable witness to Greek theoretical ideas of, among other things, citizenship, gender and slavery. I shall thus be concerned especially with the practical relevance of ordinary Greeks' thoughts to collective, above all revolutionary, action. What has been well called 'man's double-edged capacity to reason and make speech concerning the advantageous, the just, and the good' (Rahe 1992: 229) will therefore be only one part of my story. On the other hand, it hardly needs to be spelled out that any treatment of any conception of Greek political thought is throughout conditional upon the nature of the available evidence – a ticklish methodological issue that is explicitly faced head-on in chapter 1 (but see also Cartledge 1998).

Among the usual *Key Themes* series audience of colleagues and students in especially classics, classical studies, history, and social and political sciences, my target audience specifically includes the young – in defiance of Aristotle's strictures about not trying to teach political theory to them (*Nicomachean Ethics* 1095a2–6; cf. 1142a11–12, 1181a9–12; but see 1179b7–8). The ancient Greek world or worlds that I shall be covering stretch(es) across a span of about 1,000 years in time, and in space from central Asia to western Europe. Of course, during that period and area there were several major political changes; indeed, it is an important part of the purpose of this book to chart, explain or at least contextualise some of them. Besides the changes and differences, however, this ancient Greek world as a whole shared certain common features that made it in several fundamental respects quite alien to our own: the size of the political units, the nature and levels of technology, the place and function of religion, the exclusion of non-citizens, including women, and – not least by any means – the practice and ideology of slavery (Cartledge 2002: ch. 6).

One of my major *historiographical* aims therefore is to draw attention to and do some justice to this alienness. On the other hand, the small scale and deeply political nature of the Greek *polis*, including a high dosage of intense self-criticism and reflexivity, make it potentially not only a theatre of ideas but also a school of civil prudence. It is precisely because we have chosen to adopt the ancient Greeks as our political ancestors by labelling as 'democracy' our own preferred mode of self-government (and all too often the mode chosen for governing or at least controlling others) that I shall be keeping on the alert throughout for 'interference' between ancient and modern political thinking and action.

In evidentiary *scope* the discussion will range from the Homeric shield of Achilles (chapter 3) to Plutarch's pamphlet 'Advice on public life' (chapter 10). The former, an imaginary artefact commissioned from the Greeks' craftsman god Hephaestus by Achilles's divine mother Thetis and lovingly described in the *Iliad* (Book 18), was cunningly tricked out with images of two 'cities', one at peace, one at war; this was at or near the inception of the novel, real-life Greek state form, the *polis* (chapter 2). Plutarch's advisory tract was composed for a Greek or hellenophone readership under the high Roman Empire almost 1,000 years later, by which time the significance of the *polis* as a self-governing power unit had shrunk drastically, although it retained symbolic appeal as a focus of primary socialisation and communal solidarity, especially through the medium of shared public religious ritual.

There will inevitably be some attention paid to the major political-philosophical works of the fourth century BCE, above all those of Plato and Aristotle (see especially chapter 8). Plato at least seems to have relatively little direct connection to practical politics, however, and this is partly, I am sure, because his powerfully original and intellectual ideas were unlikely to strike a chord with the mass of ordinary Greeks (for whom he expressed some distaste, if not contempt). Aristotle's thought, by contrast, was far more practical and pragmatic, and is indispensably informative on the nature of ancient Greek conceptions of politics and the political. Even so, there are several very good reasons for proceeding beyond the usual late fourth-century BCE terminus of studies of Greek politics and political thought into the Hellenistic era. My two are as follows. First, that this was an era when Sparta, always a source of fascinated political reflection by outsiders, made a – second – direct and positive contribution to major political change and thinking (chapter 9). Second, that the writers and thinkers of the last three 'Hellenistic' centuries BCE include members of new philosophical schools or movements, some of whose members were committed to translating political ideas into practice, and a major historian, Polybius of Megalopolis, who made political thinking central to his analysis and explanation of the rise of Rome to 'world' power.

Cynics and Stoics will therefore get a look-in in their own right (and 'write'), but Rome as such will feature only as backdrop to the essentially Greek political thought of Polybius and of Plutarch. Although the Roman reception of Greek ideas ('Graecia Recepta', rather than Horace's 'Graecia Capta' – narrative VI), was crucial to the early-modern and modern reception (or, usually, rejection) of Greek-style democracy (chapter 11), there is not the space to do justice to a properly contextualised reading of Roman political thought, above all that of Cicero (who, astonishingly, managed to translate, both literally and metaphorically, the thought of his Greek sources into an alien '*res*-publican' context).

Clare College, Cambridge, 1 September 2008

# *Acknowledgements*

The present book is, in a strong sense, a Cambridge product. It is broadly, and now somewhat remotely, based on the undergraduate lectures I have delivered periodically from the 1980s on within the History faculty's course in the history of political thought from the Greeks to John Locke. It is hoped that students taking this course, as also those pursuing Cambridge's interfaculty (classics, history, social and political sciences) MPhil in political thought and intellectual history, and indeed all undergraduates and postgraduates enrolled in similar programmes throughout the English-speaking world, not to mention their instructors, will find it as stimulating and helpful – and problematic – to read as I have found it to write.

The book is dedicated to the memory of two great scholars and teachers, great mutual friends and comrades, both of whom had a special interest in the political thought of the ancient Greeks.

Moses Finley (1912–1986) was my immediate predecessor and inspiration in this as in so many other aspects of my teaching and research at Cambridge, and my continuing role model as an informed, critical and accessible public communicator far beyond the boundaries of the discipline of classics and, indeed, of the university as an institution. It is very good to know that Professor Daniel Tompkins of Temple University, Philadelphia, has in hand a major study of the 'early' Finley, while Mohammad Nafissi's 2005 book is a clear sign of Finley's continuing influence and inspiration outside classics and ancient history.

Pierre Vidal-Naquet (1930–2006) was the living embodiment of the marriage of political theory and practice. Seeing himself as a public intellectual in the direct line of descent from Voltaire and Zola, he suffered in his career for being unwilling to keep silent on what he considered to be cases of monstrous political injustice, whether in colonial Algeria or metropolitan France. Together with the late Jean-Pierre Vernant, he was principally responsible for placing the 'Paris School' of cultural historians and literary critics of ancient Greece centrally on the map of world classical scholarship, and through his connections with such equally committed scholars in other disciplines as Cornelius Castoriadis he maintained the high profile of classics and ancient history within the broad field of 'les sciences humaines'.

Among the living, I have learned most from my present and former Cambridge colleagues, including, most notably, my series co-editor Peter Garnsey and Malcolm Schofield, a constant source of support and stimulation (not least in most generously reading through an entire penultimate draft with his usual acuity of insight); and from (in alphabetical order) Annabel Brett, Patricia Crone, Nick Denyer, John Dunn, Pat Easterling, Raymond Geuss, Simon Goldhill, Geoff Hawthorn, Istvan Hont, Michael Ignatieff, Melissa Lane (who also very kindly read and most helpfully commented upon a near-final draft of the whole), Aleka Lianeri, Geoffrey Lloyd, Robin Osborne, Garry Runciman, David Sedley, Quentin Skinner, Gareth Stedman Jones, Richard Tuck, Robert Wardy and James Warren; and from my former PhD students Matt Edge, Lene Rubinstein, Joanne Sonin and Stephen Todd.

I should like also to record my deep appreciation of the stimulation provided by both the writings and the conversation in friendship of colleagues in universities outside Cambridge, especially Ryan Balot (Washington University, St Louis), Janet Coleman (London School of Economics), François Hartog (École des Hautes Études en Sciences Sociales, Paris), Karl Hölkeskamp (Cologne), Phillip Mitsis (New York University), Josh Ober (Stanford, formerly Princeton), Pauline Schmitt (Paris, Sorbonne), Rolf Schneider (Munich) and Ellen Wood (formerly York University, Toronto), and by all those – too many to list by name – from eastern as well as western Europe, and from across the Atlantic, who participated in a colloquium entitled 'The Greek revolution' co-organised by Geoffrey Lloyd and me at Darwin College, Cambridge, in May 1992.

Finally, since this book has been rather long in the gestation, it should be noted that earlier versions of these particular chapters have been published as, or were delivered as, the following:

Chapter 1: Cartledge 1996b, 1998.

Chapter 2: Cartledge 1996b, 2000a.

Chapter 5: Cartledge 2007. A German version has also been published as Cartledge 2008: ch. 1.

Chapter 7: Versions of this chapter were delivered, first, in March 2006 as the Dabis Lecture in the Department of Classics, Royal Holloway, University of London (I am most grateful to Professor Jonathan Powell and his colleagues for their invitation, instruction and hospitality); next, in May 2006, at the University of Heidelberg, at the kind invitation of Professors Tonio Hölscher and Joseph Maran (see Cartledge 2008: ch. 3); and, thirdly, in September 2006 as my inaugural lecture as founding Hellenic Parliament Global Distinguished Professor in the Theory and History of Democracy, New York University.

Chapter 9: A much-abbreviated version was delivered in a panel at the annual meeting of the American Philological Association, Boston, January 2005. On utopianism, see also Cartledge 1996a.

In addition to those mentioned by name above, I am most grateful to the relevant conference convenors and book editors for making my contributions possible.

# *Timeline*

(All dates are BCE [before the Common Era] unless otherwise stated; many are approximate, especially those pre-500.)

| | |
|---|---|
| 1600–1100 | **Late Bronze Age** |
| 1300 | Acme of Mycenaean (Late Bronze Age Greek) kingdoms |
| 1184 | Fall of Troy (traditional) |
| 1100 | End of Mycenaean political dispensation |
| 1100–800 | **Dark Age** |
| 1000 | Migrations east to Ionia and Asia Minor |
| 975 | Lefkandi 'hero' burial |
| 950/900 | Spartan king lists (adjusted) begin |
| 775 | Migrations west to south Italy begin |
| 735 | Migrations west to Sicily begin |
| 750–500 | **Archaic Era** |
| ?700 | Homer |
| 700–670 | Spartan political reform ('*rhêtra*', Lycurgus) |
| 660 | First stone temple of Apollo, Corinth |
| 650 | Archilochus, Tyrtaeus |
| 640 | Tyrannies at Corinth, Sicyon, Megara |
| 600 | Sappho, Alcaeus |
| 594 | Solon |
| 585 | *Floruit* of Thales |
| 570 | Birth of Cleisthenes |
| 570–550 | Anaximander, Anaximenes of Miletus |
| 559 | Cyrus II founds Persian Empire |
| 545 | Rule at Athens by tyrant Peisistratus |
| 540 (–522) | Tyranny of Polycrates on Samos |
| 525 | Pythagoras (originally of Samos) politically active in south Italy |

| 522 (–486) | Darius I of Persia |
|---|---|
| 520 (–468) | Simonides the Praise-singer active |
| 510 | Hippias tyrant of Athens overthrown |
| 508/7 | Democracy at Athens: revolution of Cleisthenes |
| 500–323 | **Classical Era** |
| 500 | Heracleitus of Ephesus, Hecataeus of Miletus |
| 499 (–494) | Ionian Revolt |
| ?493 | Birth of Pericles |
| 490 | Battle of Marathon |
| 486 (–465) | Xerxes of Persia |
| ?484 | Births of Herodotus, Protagoras |
| 480 | Invasion of Xerxes: Battles of Thermopylae, Salamis |
| 479 | Battles of Plataea, Mycale |
| 478 | Delian League formed |
| 475–450 | Earliest extant political theory |
| 472 | Aeschylus's *Persians* |
| 469 | Births of Socrates, Democritus (approximately) |
| 463 | Democracy at Syracuse |
| 462/1 | Democratic Reforms of Ephialtes and Pericles |
| 460 (–445) | 'First' Peloponnesian War |
| ?460 | Birth of Thucydides |
| 447 (–432) | Building of the Parthenon |
| 440–439 | Revolt of Samos |
| 430s | Protagoras, Anaxagoras in Athens |
| 431 (–404) | Peloponnesian War |
| 429 | Death of Pericles |
| 427 | Gorgias visits Athens; birth of Plato, Xenophon |
| ?425 | Publication of Herodotus's *Histories* |
| ?420 | Birth of Epaminondas |
| 411 | First Oligarchic counter-revolution at Athens |
| 410 | Democracy restored at Athens |
| 405 (–367) | Tyranny of Dionysius I of Syracuse |
| 404 | Defeat of Athens by Sparta (with Persia) in Peloponnesian War |
| 404/3 | Thirty Tyrants' junta at Athens |
| 403 | Restoration of democracy at Athens; General Amnesty |
| 401/0 | 'Ten Thousand' Greek mercenaries hired by Cyrus the Younger, Persian pretender |
| ?400 | Death of Thucydides |
| 399 | Trial and death of Socrates |

| | |
|---|---|
| 395 (–386) | Corinthian War: Sparta (with Persia) defeats Greek coalition |
| 387 | Plato visits Syracuse |
| 386 | King's Peace (also known as Peace of Antalcidas) |
| ?385 | Plato founds Academy at Athens |
| 384 | Births of Aristotle, Demosthenes |
| 379/8 | Liberation of Thebes from Sparta |
| 378 | Refoundation (democratic) of Boeotian federal state, foundation of Second Athenian Sea-League |
| 377 (–353) | Mausolus Satrap of Caria |
| 371 | Battle of Leuctra |
| 369 | Foundation of Messene |
| 368 | Foundation of Megalopolis |
| 367 | Death of Dionysius I; Plato visits Syracuse again |
| 362 | Battle of Mantinea; death of Epaminondas |
| 359 | Accession of Philip II of Macedon |
| 357 (–355) | Social War: Athens defeated by allies |
| 356 | Birth of Alexander |
| 356 (–346) | Third Sacred War |
| 353–351 | Mausoleum constructed at Halicarnassus |
| 347 | Death of Plato |
| 343 | Aristotle tutors Alexander at Mieza |
| 338 | Battle of Chaeronea; foundation of League of Corinth |
| 336 | Assassination of Philip II, accession of Alexander |
| ?335 | Aristotle founds Lyceum at Athens, composes *Politics* (330s/320s) |
| 334 | Alexander begins Asia campaign |
| 331 | Alexander founds Alexandria (Egypt); Battle of Gaugamela |
| 327 | Death of Callisthenes |
| 324 | Exiles Decree |
| 323 | Death of Alexander the Great |
| 323 (–281) | Wars of Successors |
| 323/2 | Lamian War |
| 323 (–30) | **Hellenistic Era** |
| 322 | Deaths of Demosthenes, Aristotle, Athenian democracy; Theophrastus heads Lyceum |
| 316 | Death of Olympias |
| 309 (–265) | Areus I of Sparta |
| 305 | Antigonus, Ptolemy I and Seleucus I become 'kings' |

| | |
|---|---|
| 301 | Battle of Ipsus: Kingdoms of Antigonids, Ptolemies, Seleucids |
| 300 | Ptolemy I founds Museum and Library at Alexandria; Zeno founds 'Stoic' school at Athens |
| 290 | Aetolian League |
| 281 | Battle of Corupedium; Seleucus I takes over Asia Minor |
| 280 | Achaean League |
| 287–146 | **Middle Roman Republic** |
| 267 (–262) | Chremonidean War |
| 244–241 | Agis IV of Sparta |
| 235–222 | Cleomenes III of Sparta |
| ?235 | Sphaerus advises Cleomenes |
| 196 | Flamininus declares Greece 'free' |
| 167 (–150) | Polybius held hostage in Italy |
| 146–27 | **Late Roman Republic** |
| 146 | Achaean War: Greece falls to Rome, Corinth sacked |
| 133, 121 | Murders of Tiberius and Gaius Gracchus |
| 106 | Cicero born |
| 55 (–43) | Cicero's political theory |
| 49 | Civil war |
| 44 | Assassination of Julius Caesar |
| 31 | Battle of Actium: Octavian (later called Augustus) defeats Mark Antony |
| 30 | Deaths of Antony and Cleopatra: Rome completes absorption of Hellenistic Greek world |
| 27 BCE – CE 330 | **Roman Imperial Era** |
| 27 | Augustus founds Principate, Greece made a province of Roman Empire |
| CE 14 | Death of Augustus |
| ?46 | Birth of Plutarch |
| 60 (–230) | 'Second Sophistic' |
| 68 | Death of Nero |
| 70 | Law on the Imperial Power of Vespasian |
| ?120 | Death of Plutarch |
| 307(–337) | Reign of Constantine (sole emperor 324–337) |
| 330–1453 | **Byzantine Era** |
| 330 | Dedication of Constantinople |
| 391 | Library at Alexandria destroyed |
| 393 | Olympic Games terminated |

| | |
|---|---|
| 476 | End of Roman Empire in West |
| 529 | Emperor Justinian closes Academy in Athens |
| 1204 | Sack of Constantinople (Fourth Crusade) |
| 1397 | Classical Greek learning migrates west to Italy from Constantinople |
| 1453 | Fall of Constantinople to Sultan Mehmet II the Conqueror |
| 1453– | **Post-Byzantine/Renaissance and Modern Eras** |
| 1494 (–1515) | Printed editions of classical texts at Venice by Aldus Manutius |
| 1891 | First modern edition of (?Aristotle's) *Athenian Constitution* |
| 2000 | Publication of *The Cambridge History of Greek and Roman Political Thought* (eds. C. J. Rowe and M. Schofield) |
| 2005 | Publication of Copenhagen Polis Centre's *An Inventory of Archaic and Classical Poleis* (eds. M. H. Hansen and T. H. Nielsen) |

# CHAPTER I

# Meaning in context: how to write a history of Greek political thought

What experience and history teach is this – that people and governments never have learned anything from history, or acted on the
principles deduced from it.

> (Georg Wilhelm Friedrich Hegel, *Philosophy of History*
> [Philosophie der Geschichte], 1822–1831)

> [M]an
> Equal, unclassed, tribeless, and nationless,
> Exempt from awe, worship, degree, the king
> Over himself.
> (Percy Bysshe Shelley, *Prometheus Unbound*, 1820)

It is not hard to find quotations from major politicians to justify the
importance of any study of the history of political thought. 'The principles
of freedom and the topics of government . . . will always be interesting to
mankind so long as they shall be connected in Civil Society' was how
George Washington put it (*ap.* Rahe 1992: 581; see Thomas Jefferson *ap.*
Rahe 1992: 709). Modern students are just a little more disenchanted,
perhaps, or disabused, yet even the severest critics, whether they realise
it or not, are performing an agenda prescribed over 2,400 years ago by
Socrates, as reported by his best-known and most brilliant student Plato:
'The unexamined life is not worth living for a human being' (*Apology* 38A).

There is, however, a major difficulty or set of major difficulties in writing
a 'history' – in any continuous or seamless sense – of political thought.
Suppose, for example, that we choose (as recommended by John Pocock
in 1962) to try to write a history of political discourse, including or even
privileging rhetoric in its particular discursive contexts, as opposed to a
history of more abstracted political thinking. It would still be questionable
whether we really can reconstruct all the mentalities, paradigms, traditions, ideologies and languages of discourse available to any given society
in any given context (Rahe 1992: 12). Alternatively, suppose that we were
to adopt – as I think we should – a strictly contextualised approach that

reads texts in their original dialogue with each other as well as with our own contemporary modes of discourse (Skinner 1969): this mode of 'Skinnerism' too has its critics (Rahe 1992: 916 n. 7), both for its choice of particular texts (set well below the level of the loftiest) and for the use it makes of them. Some critics are, of course, never satisfied.

EVIDENCE

Touching any history of political thinking or thought – as opposed to more or less high theory – in ancient Greece, we historians are hard up against certain unbudgeable or uncircumventable obstacles. There was no prose 'literature' anywhere in Greece before the second half of the sixth century, and none that survives earlier than the second half of the fifth. On the other hand, there is a very considerable compensation for that echoing silence. If we may paraphrase a famous quotation from Shelley and turn it on its head, early Greek poets from Homer (*c.* 700) to Pindar (518– 446) were the 'acknowledged legislators of the word'. They were not just arbiters of elegance and taste but articulators, often enough controversially so, of ideologies and moral values. That was especially true of the Athenian Solon (*fl. c.* 600), who combined poetry and politics in the most practical way imaginable (chapter 4). A very special class of poets is constituted by the writers of Athenian tragedy, an officially recognised competitive vehicle of both religious reflection and mundane entertainment at Athens from at least 500 BCE. Theirs could be an explicitly didactic genre, though necessarily an indirect, analogical medium for commenting on current political affairs or ideas, since with very rare exceptions tragedy's plots were taken ultimately from the 'mythical' past of gods and heroes. (The one great exception is the *Persians* of Aeschylus: see narrative III.)

Formal written prose had been invented and published from *c.* 550 on (Anaximenes, Anaximander of Miletus), but it hits us with a thump only a century later, in the third quarter of the fifth century. Placed side by side, the magnum opus of Herodotus's *Histories* and the short, sharp shock of the so-called Old Oligarch's vitriolic pamphlet on the contemporary democratic *Politeia* of the Athenians (appendix II) together illustrate the extreme range of literary expression available both then and to us today. Contemporary Sophists (as defined in chapter 6) wrote and published small-circulation tracts, as well as teaching individually and giving epideictic (show-off display) performances before large audiences. Their writings are mostly lost, however, and it is usually hard to know what to make of the isolated 'fragments' attributed by later, often hostile commentators to the likes of

Protagoras and Democritus (contemporaries, and both, intriguingly, from Abdera in northern Greece). Nevertheless, the Old Oligarch, Herodotus, and – above all – Herodotus's great successor Thucydides are all clearly Sophist-influenced if not necessarily Sophist-inspired.

Some would say that Greek political theory properly so-called was invented by Plato. I would beg to disagree (for the reasons advanced in chapter 6). Still, allowance has to be made for his towering genius, complemented by that of his greatest pupil, Aristotle (chapter 8). Thereafter, the extant tradition is again spotty and lacunose, until we reach Cicero and Plutarch (chapter 10), in, respectively, the last century BCE and the first/second CE. Polybius (c. 200–120), however, in emulation of Thucydides, practised a theoretically self-conscious and politically specific sort of historiography, often enough in sharply critical reaction against predecessors whom he despised. One of those, the third-century Athenian Phylarchus, has a special relevance to the practical utopianism of mid/late-third-century BCE Sparta (chapter 9).

On top of the more or less literary sources in poetry and narrative prose, we have a number of inscribed prose documents that betray political ideology. At Athens, indeed, there was a recognised connection between published official documentation on stone or bronze and the practice (and theory) of democracy: to take a local as opposed to 'national' example, the honorific inscriptions of the fourth century BCE set up in the Athenian demes (constituent wards of the *polis* of Athens) celebrated and sought to encourage further *philotimia* (ambitious civic do-gooding) and other such qualities of the admirable man and citizen.

Besides the various kinds of written evidence, there is also the mute evidence of archaeology. For example, the ideological programmes of great public monuments such as the Parthenon speak louder than, if not always as distinctly as, the words of a written text (Castriota 1992; Buitron-Oliver, 1993; Hedrick and Ober, 1993). Major public statuary too can make a political point: the statues of the 'Tyrannicides' at Athens leap to the mind – or would if they had survived (the bronze originals of c. 500 BCE were removed to Susa by Persian Great King Xerxes in 480 and replaced in 477; we have access only to Roman marble copies of the latter). So too does the combined figure by Praxiteles' father Cephisodotus showing the goddess Wealth holding the infant goddess Peace a century and a quarter later. Humbler political messages could also be inscribed, literally or figuratively, on painted pottery (Neer 2002) or sculpted on funerary or votive reliefs. Town planning too has its political implications. The very layout of a whole town (on the egalitarian 'gridiron' plan ascribed to the fifth-century BCE Milesian theoretician Hippodamus, author of the earliest known political treatise: see chapter 9), or the inegalitarian design of a private house, or the inclusivity or exclusivity of a city's graveyard – all these urban plans are making explicit or implicit political statements, of a more or less consciously ideological character. I shall attempt to exploit appropriately all these different kinds of evidence.

PROBLEMATICS

Of special concern throughout will be the following three problematics. First, the relationship of theory and practice – or *theôria* and *praxis*. Greek *theôria* had at its root the notion of sight, but it branched out to include both what we would call cultural sightseeing (Solon of Athens, Herodotus) and religious pilgrimage (for example, participation in official delegations to the Olympic Games). *Praxis* is the agent noun of a verb *prattein*, which also gave rise to the abstract phrase *ta pragmata*, literally 'doings' and hence 'transactions' or 'business', but also specifically political business, the business of government. To be politically active was 'to have a share in *ta pragmata*' (chapter 2), and that was considered in Greek antiquity to be a wholly good thing. On the other hand, *neôtera pragmata*, 'too new transactions', were thought unambiguously bad.

Hegel (epigraph) was surely too sceptical or cynical about the impact of political thinking on practice: does not the revolutionary political success of the 'philosophies' of communism and Nazism count, decisively if also sadly, against him? A career such as that of Martin Heidegger, though, whose philosophically motivated political engagement with Nazism ironically blinded him to the real nature of events, does neatly illustrate how complex the relationship between human thought and political reality can be (Rahe 1992: 795 n. 22; see Macintyre 1983). One particular, foundational aspect of that problem will be addressed in chapter 5, dealing with the origins of democracy and democratic thinking: how far may that usefully be classified as a political 'revolution', and, if so, was it in any sense caused by political thought, theory or philosophy?

The second main problematic is the relevance of class (however defined) and/or status to explaining political behaviour. This has its direct correlates in ancient Greek thinking and vocabulary. In ancient Greek culture, from highest to lowest, the habit of binary polarisation – seeing everything in terms of either black or white, with no shades of grey between, or reducing complex social phenomena to two mutually exclusive and jointly exhaustive constituents – was deeply engrained (Cartledge 2002). In socio-political analysis Aristotle was the greatest theoretician of ancient Greek citizen politics; we note that ultimately – in the last analysis – he found most fruitful a binary polar classification of citizens as either rich or poor (though he was well aware that there were both moderately rich and moderately poor citizens). He based this governing taxonomic dichotomy on real life – that is, on the ownership and exploitation of property, including especially land and slaves. Quantitatively translated, that dichotomy could be expressed in another way as the distinction and opposition of the (elite) few and the many or the mass.

A further refinement suggests that the archetypal or underlying model organising classical Greek thought and mentality regarding politics was the polar opposition of slavery and freedom. Nonetheless, within the citizen body, however differently defined from city to city, the relevant polarity was more typically expressed qualitatively, as by Aristotle, as rich against poor. The leading Roman political theorist Cicero (in his *De Officiis*, or *On Duties*) went far further and argued that it was actually the main business of government, as well as the main cause of the origins of states, to protect private property. Many ancient Greeks, sometimes the majority, disagreed violently, however: this was indeed a principal cause of what the Greeks rather puzzlingly at first sight called *stasis* (literally a 'standing', so a standing-apart and a standing-against, or civil faction, at the limit civil war).

The third major problematic to be addressed here is the history or histories of ancient Greek democracy: of special concern will be its invention (in the late sixth century BCE at Athens, according to the story told by me in chapter 5), development and expansion, and extinction, in antiquity, prior to its relatively very recent (nineteenth-century CE) resuscitation and even apotheosis. If there was ever a 'Greek revolution' in politics, it was the invention of democracy (and democratic political theory) and its extension, thanks largely to Athens' role as imperial capital and 'city hall of Wisdom' (Plato's phrase in the *Protagoras*, 337e), such that in Aristotle's day democracy was one of the two most prevalent constitutional forms in the Hellenic world. Not long after Aristotle's death, however, democracy had been snuffed out first in its birthplace, then throughout the Greek world, with the rare and isolated lingering exception, such as Rhodes.

Of all the many political systems devised by men since the coming of the state (in the sense of some form of organised political community), democracy has always had the fiercest critics and opponents. Aristotle and Plato were themselves not the least of them, but their mentor in this as in many other ways was Socrates (469–399). It is a conventional view that

Socrates paid too high a price and suffered a gross injustice when he was condemned to death by his own democratic Athens. At any rate, no history of political thought in the ancient Greek world can afford to bypass the trial of Socrates in 399 BCE: as a paradigm of free thought – or political subversion – on public trial, it continues to have the deepest resonance for Western liberal political thought and practice (see chapter 7). Nevertheless, the major problem of getting at the 'democratic beliefs of ordinary men' (Brunt 1993: 389) must always remain.

For Cicero and his contemporary Romans, democracy was no more than an unpleasant memory, and, indeed, until as recently as two centuries ago 'democracy' remained a dirty word in refined political society, despite or because of the American and French Revolutions. One of the founding fathers of the United States, Alexander Hamilton (a product of a long and intense engagement with Greek and the classics), wrote: 'No friend to rational liberty can read without pain and disgust the history of the commonwealths of Greece . . . a constant scene of the alternate tyranny of one part of the people over the other, or of a few usurping demagogues over the whole' (1781; see Rahe 1992: 585, 953 n. 115). Today, in the sharpest possible contrast, we are all democrats (if not necessarily party-card-carrying Democrats). We may well ask: how come? One – too simple but poignantly accurate – answer is that the term 'democracy' has become etiolated to the point of meaninglessness, in contrast to its original, full-blooded sense or senses of 'people power'.

EQUALITY

To conclude this opening methodological chapter, I take as a test case the problem of equality in ancient Greek theory and practice. (It could equally have been freedom: see below.) What Raymond Aron (1972: 87–8) nicely calls 'the democratic gospel of equality' has never been more insistently or globally preached than it is today. Equality of what, however, and for whom? Can humans ever be, really, equal, or is the best that can be achieved to treat equally those deemed to be relevantly equal?

All of us, presumably – whether we are ancient historians, political philosophers or just plain citizens – are mainly interested in explaining, or understanding, the ways in which political concepts are negotiated through discourse and implemented in institutional or other forms of practice. Both in ancient and in modern democratic discourse, equality seems to be one of the two most fundamental of these concepts (the other being freedom). Because language is constituted in political action, however, and political action in turn conditions or determines language, there is a dialectic – or more often a tension – between political theory (or ideology) and political praxis. This is especially likely to be so in an antagonistic, zero-sum political culture such as that (or, rather, those) of classical Greece. It follows that we should expect the meanings of a core concept such as equality to be especially unstable, and to become extraordinarily hotly contested in situations of civil strife or outright civil war. Thucydides' famous account of the civil war on Corcyra (see further below) neither confounds nor disappoints that expectation.

One useful way of approaching this infinitely delicate topic is constructive comparison, both within ancient Greece and between ancient Greece and other political communities. For some scholars, the aim of comparison is to discover the universal. For disciples of the 'Cambridge School' of 'conceptual history', on the contrary, among whom I should count myself, comparison ought rather to emphasise particularity and above all difference (cf., as applied to a different topic, Cartledge 1985). In the present case, at all events, it is hoped that comparison will serve, first, to make us 'clearer about features of our own social and political environment, features whose very familiarity may make it harder for us to bring them into view' (Miller 1990: 427); and, second, to help us specify the peculiarities of ancient Greek constructions of equality by contrasting the set of meanings then potentially available to political actors with the range available today.

In the first place, then, we must ask what kinds of equality were at stake in reference to ancient Greek politics, and within what value system. Negatively, we are not dealing here with the – or a – liberal sense of the equality of individual rights against the State. Even if the Greeks did recognise a notion of individual autonomy, they did not have the fortune to know the separately instituted 'State' in any post-Hobbesian sense, and they did not construe the individual in a modern, oppositional way (see further chapter 2). Ancient Greek claims to equality can therefore only be said to have, at most, implied an appeal to rights in our sense. Nor is the equality of all humankind in the sight of God at issue, nor, finally, is there any question here of sexual or gender equality.

Positively, there were basically two kinds of meanings of equality in question in classical Greece. First, and most broadly, there was political (or civic) equality. That meant equality of status and respect within the conceptual framework of the Greeks' normative socio-political system of polarised hierarchy. Insofar as the Greek citizen was by definition male not female, free not slave, native insider not stranger or outsider, and adult not a child, he was equal to all other citizens, and deserving therefore of equal respect, privilege, consideration and treatment. Aristotle advanced a peculiarly strong – that is, peculiarly exclusive and exclusionist – version of this equalitarian notion of citizenship (Cartledge 2002). By implication, Greeks, especially those Greeks who considered themselves democrats, operated with some idea of equality of opportunity. All relevant citizen contestants in the (too often literally) life-and-death race of public, political action ideally should start from behind the same line and run across a more or less level playing field. As Aristotle for one was well aware, however, inequalities of birth (aristocrat against commoner, *agathos* against *kakos*) and, especially, of wealth (rich against poor, *plousios* against *penês*) frequently frustrated the translation of formal equality of citizen status into universal equality of outcome.

Second, there was equality of generalised *eudaimonia*, or 'well-being', 'well-faring'. Strict economic equality 'was not a serious issue and belonged in the sphere of comic surrealism or abstract theoretical schemes' (Raaflaub 1996: 155), but the good life, in a sense that was not narrowly materialistic nor mathematically calculated, was theoretically a possible and viable individual option or social goal. Ancient Greece was no exception to the rule, cross-culturally valid, that equality is urged as an idea or ideal against some perceived inequality, particularly in moments of revolutionary upheaval. In 427, for instance, the democratic partisans of Corcyra were loud in their demand for what they styled *isonomia politikê* (Thucydides 3.82.8). Thucydides regarded this as merely a sloganising cloak for the selfish ambitions of a power-mad clique, however, and certainly a phrase amounting to something like 'constitutional government with the equal sharing of power by all people' was vague to the point of vapidity – for what in practice was to count as an 'equal' sharing of power, and who were the 'people' entitled to share it? *Isonomia* indeed might be appropriated just as easily by Greek oligarchs (Thucydides 3.62.3) as by Greek democrats, and Aristotle was not the only oligarch to propound a theory (or ideology) of 'geometric' equality according to which some citizens were literally 'more equal' than others (Harvey 1965). Even democrats, who more honestly espoused the opposite 'arithmetical' conception (every citizen must count strictly for one, and no one for more than one), were prepared to concede that, in practice, equality was not everything (Cartledge and Edge 2009).

The Greeks had a notably rich and flexible appraisive vocabulary of equality. Besides *isotês* and *to ison* ('the exactly, mathematically equal thing'), they deployed a wide range of compound nouns prefixed by *iso-*. *Iso-nomia* stood for the most general and unspecific principle of political equality; *iso-kratia* and *is-êgoria* connoted, respectively, its oligarchic and democratic constructions. *Iso-timia*, not certainly attested before the third century BCE, captured the social notion of equality of consideration or respect, parity of esteem; and, finally, *iso-moiria* did the same for the economic idea of the equal distribution of some communal goods.

This verbal flexibility in itself improves markedly on our own restricted and ambiguous vocabulary. The Greeks went further still, however. They recognised that equality by itself was not in all circumstances fair or just. So *isotês* was complemented pragmatically by *homoiotês*, especially in prepositional phrases meaning 'on an equal and fair basis', acknowledging that the operative criterion governing equality's implementation is not sameness or identity but similitude or likeness. For Aristotle, a *polis* had to consist of similars (*homoioi*); indeed, according to one of his definitions, the *polis* is 'a kind of association of similars' (*Politics* 1328a35–6). A properly Aristotelian golden mean is struck in his formulation that 'the *polis* aims at being composed, as much as possible, of similars and equals' (*homoioi kai isoi*, 1295b25–6).

One of the strongest theoretical charges pressed against ancient democracy by its diehard opponents was that it treated unequals equally, a procedure that was manifestly absurd and unjust. At any rate, in democratic Athens from about 460 BCE onwards, all Athenians were indeed considered to be officially equal on principle *qua* citizens. That strong principle of citizen equality was grounded in the claim that the essence of democracy was freedom, so that all Athenian citizens were *ex hypothesi* free – both by birth and by political empowerment, since they were 'kings over themselves' (to borrow Shelley's oxymoronic phrase) and masters of each other's collective destiny. On the grounds that they were all equally free in this civic sense, they were all equal. In hard material fact, though, Athenian citizens never were, nor were they always treated as if they were, all exactly equal, identical and the same, in all relevant respects. For example, the Athenians resorted pragmatically to the use of election to fill the highest public offices, which favoured the privileged elite few, the seriously rich, rather than employing dogmatically the peculiarly 'democratic' mode of sortition (use of the lottery).

Athens was only one of about 1,000 (at any one time) separate, usually radically self-differentiated Greek communities (Hansen 2006). Most of them in Aristotle's day could be classified straightforwardly as governed by variants of either democratic or oligarchic regimes. The classification of classical Sparta proved problematic, however, as indeed it still does for modern students of the ancient Greek world. The Spartans identified themselves as citizens under several titles, the most relevant of which to the present discussion is *homoioi,* meaning 'similars' or 'peers', not (as it is too often translated) 'equals'. Despite their universal and communally enforced educational system, and their membership of communal dining messes (both, we learn from Aristotle, considered by outsiders to be 'democratic' features), Spartans did not recognise or seek to implement *isotês* in any sense other than the ideal enjoyment of an exactly equal lifestyle (*isodiaitoi*: Thucydides 1.6.5) – a peculiar local variant of the *eudaimonia* sense of equality (above). Towards all outsiders, Greek and non-Greek, Sparta turned a homogeneous and exclusive face, but, internally, Spartan citizens were self-differentiated according to multiple hierarchies of birth, wealth, age and 'manly virtue' (*andragathia*). In political decision-making, too, the Spartan method of open voting by shouting in the formally sovereign Assembly (Thucydides 1.87) implicitly denied the egalitarian one man, one vote principle.

Probably the major cause of these sharp differences between democratic Athens and (on the whole) oligarchic Sparta was the Spartans' servile underclass of helots ('captives'), native Greeks enslaved upon and tied to the territory their free ancestors had once owned, who were politically motivated and far more numerous than their masters (Cartledge 2003). There was no place for genuine equality in the state of 'order' (*kosmos*) that Sparta ideally represented itself to embody. Spartans could not afford to practise genuine egalitarianism, only the pseudo-egalitarian 'geometric' variety favoured by Athenian oligarchs. This key difference between the *politeiai* – 'ways of life' as well as 'constitutions', as we shall see – of Sparta and Athens is a suitable point with which to end this opening chapter.

# CHAPTER 2

# The Greek invention of the polis, of politics and of the political

[P]*olis andra didaskei* ('a *polis* teaches a man' [to be a citizen]).
(Simonides, quoted by Plutarch, *Mor.* 784b [*Should Old Men Govern* 1] = eleg. 15, David Campbell 1991: 517)

**Politics**, n. A strife of interests masquerading as a contest of principles. The conduct of public affairs for private advantage.
(Ambrose Bierce, *A Devil's Dictionary*, 1911)

## THE PRIMACY OF POLITICS?

In my own relatively short lifetime at least two so-called 'Ends' have been widely canvassed – the End of Politics (in the 1950s) and the End of History (in the late 1980s) – not to mention several 'post's (postmodernism, -structuralism, etc.). Is politics really ending, though – or is it rather evolving, possibly out of all recognition? Does the fact (if it is a fact) that hierarchy, certainty, bureaucracy, homogeneity, class affiliation, centralisation and the State are giving way, to some degree, in developed Western polities to market egalitarianism (so-called), uncertainty, diversity, heterogeneity, multiple identity, decentralisation and globalised confusion mean or imply a terminus of politics? Or, rather, does it mean the opposite – that is, more individualism, more democracy (however defined precisely), in the service of a genuinely consensual and free-willed politics? Advances in an undoubtedly democratic sense can most obviously be detected in the politics of, say, Germany, Japan and Italy, especially as compared to their dictatorships or authoritarian regimes of the 1930s. On the other hand, the attempt, however possibly well intentioned, to blitz Iraq into 'democracy' by extra-political means in 2003 has been an unequivocal setback for the 'progress' of democracy on the global scale.

At the other extreme of reception, the capacity of 'politics' to embrace every important issue of collective social life has been questioned by many, and not only by conservative proponents of elitist theories of democracy. There is a suspicion, on this view, that politics, both as theory and as practice, is a contingent, peculiar and perhaps quite eccentric way of dealing with human predicaments. What the comparative political or social historian can at least try to do (see Golden 1992), however, is compile and evaluate an inventory of major or basic differences. This, it is hoped, will help us to understand a little better both the politics of ancient Greece and our own (modern Western) political institutions, constitutions and culture, and also to grapple intelligently with the politics (in yet another, metaphorical sense) of trying to bring the two into a fruitfully significant relationship.

There has been a debate within ancient history over the 'primacy of politics' (Rahe) – over whether or not the political aspect of Greek culture and civilisation is the fundamental, dominant and directional one. According to one modern but Greek-inspired definition of politics and 'the political' (Meier), as the public sphere or space of collective debate and decision-taking, it surely was. For the Greeks, the civic space of the political was located centrally and actively (note the directional accusative case) *es meson*, both literally and metaphorically at the heart of the community, which was itself construed as a strong political community of actively participating citizens. The civic *agora* or 'place of gathering' and the *akropolis* or 'high city' were the twin, symbiotic nodes of ancient Greek political networking.

This has to be qualified in several ways, however, for two main reasons. First, in light of the intrusion of economic, class interests, which may have a political application or expression but yet go deeper than that. Second, because politics does not only take place or is not only about the public sphere: the private sphere can also be a political space, as, for example, when public laws governing legal marriage impact on the ownership and transmission of property and so on the economic basis of society.

It is unquestionably right, however, to emphasise the primacy of politics in an intellectual sense: just as Greek politics presupposed the existence of the peculiar state form known as the *polis*, so the invention of political theory (abstract, theoretical reflection) presupposed practical politics, and, arguably, specifically democratic politics (chapter 6). The *polis* was never the universal Greek state form – many Greeks lived within a political framework known as the *ethnos* (chapter 8); and both before and, especially, after the conquests of Alexander the Great the *polis* was to be variously transcended, transgressed and superseded. All the same, the *polis* was the core Greek political institution and the source of Greece's most original contribution to Western political theory: its invention.

'So a *polis* was part city, part state' (Hansen 2006: 58). That is to say, it was both a physical, geographical entity – if not necessarily all that urban, by modern standards – and a metaphysical abstraction. It is important to be clear at the outset, however, what sort of a state it was – or, rather, was not. To quote again Mogens Hansen (2006: 149 n. 3; emphasis in original), the nonpareil director of the incomparable Copenhagen Polis Project over a remarkably fruitful decade, 'A much narrower concept of state is commonly found in jurisprudence and political science: the state is not only a government empowered to enforce a legal system within a territory over a population; it is also an *abstraction*, i.e. a continuous public power over both ruler and ruled, and a community must have a *sovereign* government and must be in possession of *full external sovereignty* in order to be a state.' There was no such narrower-sense state – or State – in ancient Greece. The *polis* was, rather, a stateless (not acephalous) community of politically empowered and actively participating citizens (Berent 2004), a citizen state (although admittedly both these English words are latinate, not hellenic, in their etymology . . .).

Therefore, there were no legally entrenched 'rights' (even of the citizen, let alone of man in the abstract), as opposed to the reciprocal powers and duties of citizens as they ruled and were ruled in turn; and especially there were no rights of 'the individual' to be entrenched against a mighty, impersonal and potentially intrusive State. Actually, even 'government' may be a misleading phrase, if it conjures up a notion of an elected government with a specific mandate to rule. Greek citizen bodies selected officials in various ways, but these officials were not 'magistrates' in the strong Roman sense, let alone members of a party with shared ideology and platforms. Rather, Greek citizen bodies ruled themselves turn and turn about, and did so through the vehicle of *nomos*, an ambiguous term that could mean both positive law – i.e. the enactments of duly appointed and empowered organs of government – and custom, including both habitual modes of doing things and self-consciously chosen and valued mores and traditional practices. Politics in an ancient Greek *polis* was thus both institutional (what we call constitutional) and cultural (a question of civic norms, both public and private, subject to constant negotiation).

Our political terminology is mostly Greek in its etymology: 'monarchy', 'aristocracy', 'oligarchy', 'democracy', to begin with just the most obvious examples, besides 'politics' itself and its derivatives. Only 'republic', 'citizen' and 'state' have an alternative, Latin derivation – and a strictly limited application, at best, to ancient Greece. This is not a purely formal, linguistic observation. Politics in one of its many guises is an argument, and arguments about words and their meanings are precisely political arguments, whether we are talking of such academic exercises as *Begriffsgeschichte* (the history of concepts) or the negotiation of terms such as 'democracy' or 'good citizen' in everyday political practice.

Ideologically, mythically and symbolically, too, it is the Greeks who function as 'our' ancestors in this field, and it is they who are credited by sober critics with having discovered or invented politics in the strong sense – that is, communal decision-making in the public sphere on the basis of substantive discussion about issues of principle as well as purely operational matters (Finley 1983; Farrar 1988; Meier 1990). Whether it was in fact the Greeks – rather than the Phoenicians of the Levant, say, or the Etruscans of central Italy – who should be so credited has been questioned. What is unquestionable is that the Greeks' politics was not ours, theoretically or practically. This is not only or primarily because they operated within a radically different institutional framework, but chiefly because, for both practical and theoretical reasons, they enriched or supplemented politics with – as we would see it – ethics. Their ethics, moreover, comprised radical stipulations, including appeals to notions of nature that are not ours.

For Aristotle, for example, *ta politika* did not mean 'politics' in any universally applicable sense, but specifically matters concerning the *polis*; and the *polis* as he construed it was a natural organism within which alone could generic man attain his intrinsic natural end of living the good life. That life was defined as one of political but above all of moral and philosophical activity, an ideal combination of *praxis* and *theôria*. Aristotle's construction of politics includes a measure of teleology that was peculiar to his system of thought, but it remains recognisably and distinctively ancient Greek, in that it comports a great deal more than merely a theory of government.

Normally and normatively, the politics studied by modern Western political theory and 'science' is an utterly different animal. Today politics tends
to be reduced to a question of power, or, more precisely, force, exercised
on a national scale, and modern political science is a technical, notionally value-free analysis of the workings of the state in the narrow sense.
Greek political thought, by contrast, 'spen[t] most time trying to make
citizens good' (Aristotle, *Nicomachean Ethics* 1099b13). This difference of
scope and aim is underlined in the introduction to Aristotle's *Nicomachean
Ethics* (Part I of the bipartite project completed by the *Politics*): 'A young
man is not a fit person to attend lectures on political theory, because he
is not versed in the practical business of life from which politics draws its
premises and subject matter' (1095a).

'Politics' today seems to be an artificial and formal affair, not a natural
activity, and a lower-order phenomenon to be judged in terms of more fundamental ideas and values. The ancient Greeks' view could not have been
more different, indeed opposite (even if their practice did not always live up
to their ideas). Scholars differ considerably, though, over how precisely to
characterise 'the political' in ancient Greece. One school of thought, exemplified variously by Hannah Arendt (1958) and Sheldon Wolin (2004), seeks
to extrude from it every hint or taint of sordid materialism. The political,
on this almost Platonically formalist view, was precisely the non-utilitarian.
Others, more realistically and accurately, deny any absolute separation of
politics and economics. The Thessalians were explicitly praised by Aristotle (*Politics* 1331a30–31b3) for instituting a formal, physical separation
between their commercial agora and what they called the 'free' – meaning
political – agora, but their practice was (regrettably, in his view) exceptional
among Greeks.

Another salient distinction between their thought and ours is that,
whereas modern political theory uses the imagery of machinery or building construction, ancient political theory spoke in organic terms of share-
holding (*methexis*) and rule (*arkhê*) rather than sovereignty or power (*bia,
kratos, anankê*). A further issue is the place of religion. The Greek city was
a city of gods as well as – indeed, before it was – a city of humankind;
everything for an ancient Greek, as the early intellectual Thales is said to
have remarked, was 'full of gods'. Greek religion, moreover, like Roman,
was a system ideologically committed to the public, not the private, sphere.
The relationship of men and gods was never purely and solely unidirec-
tional, however. Protagoras's famous dictum, that man was the measure
of all things that are *that* they are (or are not), embraced a sophisticated

philosophical restatement of the generally accepted fact that the gods owed their status and prestige to mankind almost as much as men and the city owed their (continued) existence and prosperity to the gods. It was the human city that laid down the limits to be observed in the due recognition of the gods, most obviously through the medium of public sacrifice and communal banqueting, but also through enforcement of its laws on impiety (see especially chapter 7). In the Greek civic context, therefore, to prescribe an ideal utopia in the form of a perfect theocracy, as Plato did in the *Laws*, was a profoundly unconventional move.

REPUBLICAN POLITICS ANCIENT AND MODERN

Republicanism almost by definition believes in the public good, but that means very different things in different republican systems. United States republicanism, for instance, according to which universal rights are attached to a particular regime and republican government is accorded a universal basis, differs crucially from, say, the Italian version, though less so from the French. On the other hand, the seemingly paradoxical claim that '[m]ost governments try to suppress politics' (Crick 1992: 168) is applicable to all modern varieties of republican states, as it is also to difficult-to-classify hybrids such as the constitutional monarchy of the United Kingdom. For modern governments are part and parcel of the State (capital 'S'), an entity of which the ancient Greek world was happily, even blissfully, innocent and ignorant, and that difference is a key element of the explanation of the differences between the politics (including political culture no less than formal political institutions) of the *polis* and that of modern State-centred polities.

Positively, two differences obtrude. Political action in Greece was direct, unmediated, participatory. On the other hand, the category of those entitled to participate was by modern standards very restricted. Neither difference was purely the function of unavoidable material or technological factors; they were the outcome, rather, of deliberate political choice. Hence the emphasis in ancient Greek political theory on self-control, and on the desirability as well as necessity of self-help – as opposed to State intervention – in everyday Greek political practice. Provided that they could control themselves, the citizens can and are entitled to rule others – their own wives and children and other disfranchised residents, no less than outsiders in a physical sense. Failure to control oneself would lead to transgression of the communally defined limits of appropriate behaviour. When accompanied by violence, such trangression was both informally castigated and formally punished as *hubris* – the ultimate civic crime (Fisher 1992).

Thus the famous texts inscribed on the Temple of Apollo at Delphi – 'Know yourself' and 'Nothing to excess' – were political precepts in the strongest sense, inscribed at the symbolic centre of Hellenism. They were the community's metaphors for necessarily decentralised and personal self-policing. More literal self-policing in the form of self-help was a function of the total or partial absence of institutionalised public organs of law enforcement (Nippel 1995). Athens, for example, not only lacked an office of Director of Public Prosecutions (DPP), but possessed only the most rudimentary of law enforcement agencies to see to the practical execution of any judgement handed down in the People's Court. This institutional weakness was complemented, and to some extent compensated for ideologically, by a stress on the intrinsic value of personal as well as civic autonomy.

Negatively speaking, the statelessness of the *polis* reveals itself by a series of comparable and directly consequential absences, striking by comparison with the modern liberal State community. There was no civil society distinct from a government and its agents; no concept of official public toleration of civil dissent, and so no conscientious objectors to appeal to such a concept (as the trial of Socrates most famously demonstrates: chapter 7); above all, as noted above, no rights. There are, of course, relative exceptions to the absolute statelessness of the ancient *polis* – there are always exceptions. Its validity as a (Weberian) ideal type, however, is confirmed on the one hand by Sparta, the partial exception in practice, and on the other by Plato's *Republic* and *Laws*, the total(ising) exceptions in ideal(ising) theory.

Conversely, the peculiarly modern ideals of liberalism, usually represented now under the guise of liberal democracy, and pluralism *are* peculiarly modern because they presuppose or require the existence of the strong, centralising and structurally differentiated State. Liberalism has the older pedigree. It is at least in part, often its most crucial part, the product of an attempt to disengage the State from the enforcement of virtue; as such, its roots can be traced back to humanist struggles with absolutist doctrine and monarchy (Dunn 1993: 29–56). Pluralism holds, roughly, that political freedom depends on a rich mixture of competing, autonomous groups, and on the flourishing of associations relatively independent both of each other and of the State. It was invented early in the last century as a response to claims for the exclusive sovereignty of the increasingly potent State. Competing schools of throught trace different genealogies from antiquity to the political thought of early modernity, and from there to today, but as usual the confrontation of ancient and more or less modern thinking within the general framework of republicanism has the merit of highlighting and focusing attention on differences (see Nippel 1994a). Two of those are now considered in more detail.

PUBLIC AND PRIVATE

Compare and contrast, first, Greece with Rome. The Romans opposed *res publica*, literally 'the people's thing', to *res privata*, but the Greek equivalent of *res publica* was not *to dêmosion*, the public or people's sphere, or *to koinon* (the commonwealth), but *ta pragmata* (political) affairs or transactions. Would-be revolutionaries in ancient Greece struggled for control of *ta pragmata*, and the Greek equivalent of revolution was *neôtera pragmata*, 'newer [that is, too new ] affairs'. The Greeks' equivalent of *res privata* was *to idion*, the opposite of which might be either *to koinon* or *to dêmosion*. The private/public distinction, in other words, occupied overlapping but different semantic spaces in Greece and Rome, and in Greece there was no straightforward opposition of the public = the political to the private = the personal or domestic.

To pursue cross-cultural semantics a little further, we may note that in contemporary Anglo-American culture 'The personal is the political' can be a counter-cultural, radical, even revolutionary slogan. For the Greeks, however, it would merely have been a banal statement of the obvious. For example, the Athenian volunteer (*ho boulomenos*) prosecutor claimed to be bringing his public lawsuit on behalf of the *koinon*, yet simultaneously claimed to be acting from private and personal motives. To our way of thinking this is a contradiction, but Athenians, lacking the State, lacked also our notions of bureaucratic impersonality and facelessness, and therefore required individual citizens to place their persons on the line in public causes. For them, moreover, there existed no realm of private morality that was on principle not the law's business. Society, not the individual, was their primary point of collective reference, and individualism did not constitute a rival pole of attraction; indeed, there was no ancient Greek word for 'individual' in our (anti-)social sense. Thus the semantic passage from Greek *idiôtês*, a citizen viewed in a private – unofficial or lay – capacity, to English 'idiot' starts ultimately from the Greeks' blurring of the boundary between public and private, and their privileging of public, political, collective space.

## GENDER

In no Greek city were citizen women – that is, the mothers, wives and daughters of citizens – accorded full public political status, and the (hundreds of) societies of classical Greece were both largely sex-segregated and fundamentally gendered. War, for instance, was considered a uniquely masculine prerogative, and the peculiar virtue of pugnacious courage that it demanded was labelled *andreia* (literally 'manliness'). For mainly economic and cultural reasons, the private domain of the *oikos* (household) could easily be represented as more of a feminine than a masculine space, and the *oikos* understood as being opposed to – rather than simply the basic component of – the *polis*. On the other hand, it would be wrong for us to draw the boundary between the two domains too sharply: for most important political purposes, *oikos* and *polis* are better viewed as inextricably interwoven, as the following illustrations, all involving religion, demonstrate.

The Greek city, as already noted, was a city of gods as well as humans. More accurately, it was a city of goddesses as well as male divinities, and maintaining the right relationships with the divine was thought to require the public collective religious participation of women no less than that of the male citizens; indeed, on occasion it required their exclusive participation in women-only festivals (such as the Thesmophoria).

Second, there was the institution of marriage. In itself this was a purely private arrangement between two *oikoi*, or, rather, their male heads, and the marriage rituals and ceremonies, however publicly visible, were nevertheless legally speaking quite unofficial. On the issue of marriages between citizen households depended the perpetuation and continuity of the citizen body, however. The law therefore stepped in to prescribe and police the boundaries of legitimacy of both offspring and inheritance, positively as well as negatively.

My final illustration is distinctively Athenian. When boys who had been orphaned by the death of their father in battle and raised at public expense came of age, they were paraded in full armour as part of the opening ceremonies of the annual Great or City Dionysia play-festival. Athenian tragic drama was set in mythical time and often in a place other than the city of Athens, but it was enacted in Athenian public political space and time, within the context of a state-sponsored religious festival. One of the central functions of Attic tragedy was to scrutinise critically the community's most fundamental values, and both the prominence of particular women and the dominant role played by issues of gender, household and kinship in this quintessentially political form of dramatic contest neatly demonstrate the inseparability of *oikos* and *polis*, at least in democratic Athens (Cartledge 1997b).

Freedom, together with equality, constituted the prime political sentiments or slogans of the ancient Greeks, as they are our own. What exactly did political freedom mean for the Greeks, though (see Raaflaub 1985)? Not, remotely, what it means to us. It was, rather, a value of a very different kind, precisely because it was so differently institutionalised, being embedded in societies whose political, social and economic arrangements were irreducibly alien to modern Western ones. A strong hint, at least, of this core value difference comes from a key feature of Aristotle's political philosophising. Slaves, especially those wholly owned human chattels who were accounted as subhuman items of property, were the physically living but socially dead embodiments of the denial of human freedom. Nonetheless, not only did Aristotle advocate a doctrine of natural slavery but he made it central to his entire sociopolitical project of description, analysis and amelioration. In other words, Aristotle, whose thought we otherwise tend to admire extravagantly, was prepared – or, rather, required by his political-philosophical system – to defend a doctrine of 'natural' slavery (Garnsey 1996; Cartledge 2002: ch. 6).

That in itself is one good reason for arguing that Greek civilisation and culture – as a whole, not just those of particular Greek societies – may properly be regarded as based on, shaped by and determined by slavery. What was it about slaves, though, that made them seem to Aristotle utterly indispensable? It was not their strictly economic function, for, in Aristotle's terms, slaves were necessary not for *poiêsis*, economic production, but for *praxis*, living the life of the citizen. To Aristotle, slaves were the basis of the good life in the *polis*, indispensable for enabling free Greek citizens to achieve their full humanity, above all because they provided their masters with the requisite leisure for practising politics and philosophy.

In fact, though, there was more to it even than that: it was not solely a question of slaves' instrumental value. Rather, consideration of a wide range of texts, literary, historical and medical as well as philosophical, indicates that the Greeks' very notion of freedom depended on the antinomy of slavery: being free for a Greek was precisely *not* being, and not behaving in the allegedly stereotypical manner of, a slave (Cartledge 1993).

The modern political theorist, preoccupied with the distribution and exercise of power, could not have delayed for so long the discussion of strictly constitutional questions. Greek political theory was not by any means solely about power, however, and *politeia*, the Greek word that we translate as 'constitution', both was used (and maybe coined) to denote citizenship and had a wider frame of reference than either our 'constitution' or 'citizenship'. This reflected the fact that the *polis* was imagined as a moral community of active participatory citizens, not as a mere political abstraction. 'You left me friendless, solitary, without a city (*apolis*), a corpse among the living;' so the eponymous hero of Sophocles' *Philoctetes* (line 1018) bewails his isolated fate, in terms instantly familiar to a Greek audience.

*Politeia* thus came to denote both actively participatory citizenship (quite different from the passive possession of the formal privileges of a citizen) and the *polis*'s very life and soul (Bordes 1982). Greek constitutional political theory is first unambiguously visible in Herodotus's 'Persian debate' (chapter 6). Already in Herodotus, indeed, we find the germ of Plato's fully developed sixfold classification of 'rule', whereby each genus has both a 'good' specification and its corresponding deviation or corruption (a reminder, if we needed it, that for the Greeks constitutions were moral entities and not merely technocratic devices). Thus rule by one might be the legitimate, hereditary constitutional monarchy of a wise pastor – or the illegitimate despotism of a wicked tyrant; and so forth.

Plato, however, had relatively little interest in practical terrestrial politics, let alone in the comparative sociological taxonomy of political formations. For his star pupil Aristotle, by contrast, the natural scientist with a teleological bent, these were precisely the major preoccupations of his *Politics*, a study based on research into more than 150 separate Greek and non-Greek polities. He was careful, though, to preface the *Politics* with the *Nicomachean Ethics*, less of a moral treatise than the title might lead us to expect, but not altogether dissimilar in general orientation from, say, John Rawls' influential *A Theory of Justice* (Rawls 1999). In direct and no doubt deliberate opposition to his master, Aristotle liked to begin from and return to what he called the *phainomena* and the *endoxa* – that is, the received and reputable opinions and perceptions entertained by the men of political prudence, the *phronimoi*, whose ability to translate their beliefs into effective political action depended importantly on the accuracy of their empirically derived knowledge and understanding of 'affairs' (*pragmata*). For that method to work, Aristotle had to have been able to convince not only himself but also his readers that his own perceptions and opinions were no less empirically accurate than those of the *phronimoi*.

In his account of actually existing constitutions he was not content, therefore, merely to distinguish Platonically between the 'good' versions of rule by some and rule by all, namely aristocracy and polity (a rather confusing application of *politeia* in a specialised constitutional sense), and their respective deviations, oligarchy and democracy. He further distinguished with some pride four subspecies each of both oligarchy and democracy. Similarly, after a partly theoretical discussion of the definitional question 'Who is a citizen?', Aristotle conceded somewhat ruefully but with laudable honesty that his preferred definition is more aptly suited to the citizen of a democracy than of an oligarchy. Finally, in place of the idealist *tabula rasa* approach of his mentor, Aristotle preferred to suggest practical ways in which defective arrangements might be brought into closer harmony with his theoretical aims. That explains why the central section of the *Politics* is devoted to the prevention (rather than the cure) of the Greek city's endemic disease of *stasis*.

### FACTIONS

Already in the 'Persian debate' Herodotus's 'Darius' had warned of the fierce and bloody *staseis* that were apt to erupt in oligarchies, and Herodotus in his own voice had lamented the awfulness of 'intestine war', so much worse than war against an external foe (8.3). Thucydides (3.82–3) famously devoted perhaps his most brilliant pages to a single-minded analysis of the phenomenon of *stasis*, which he claimed, with pardonable exaggeration, came during the course of the Atheno-Peloponnesian War to engulf the entire Hellenic world. Aristotle, as we have just seen, took *stasis* seriously enough to make it one of the pivots of his practical political theory of the city. Nor was this merely a preoccupation of historians and philosophers: there is no question but that *stasis* was a widespread, frequent and grave phenomenon in Greece.

Its prevalence can be accounted for positively as well as negatively. Positively, a major source of faction was the contradiction between the notional egalitarianism of the citizen estate, expressed by the term *isonomia* (chapter 1), and the existence of sometimes extreme socio-economic stratification, which expressed itself politically as 'class struggle on the political plane' (de Ste. Croix 1983: 278–326). The poor were always with the Greeks, who operated with a very broad definition of poverty: everyone was deemed to be 'poor' except the very rich, at one end of the scale, and the destitute, at the other; political thinkers did, however, occasionally allow for the existence of a few relatively well-off *mesoi*, who fell 'in between' the rich and the poor. The criterion of distinction was leisure: what mattered was whether or not one was sufficiently 'rich' not to have to work at all for one's living. Typically, indeed almost automatically, the relationship of rich and poor citizens was conceived as one of permanent antagonism, which too often took an actively political form.

A further inflaming or exciting factor was the existence of exceptionally charismatic individuals, such as Alcibiades, who considered that they were being denied their due measure of honour and status (*timê*). Politics in the narrow sense of political infighting was construed by the Greeks as a zero-sum game of agonistic competition, and honour, according to Aristotle, was the goal of politics in this sense (de Ste. Croix 1983: 80, 531 n. 30). Athens under the democracy was exceptional in being *stasis*-free for long periods because the *dêmos* did not feel – and, indeed, had no good reason to feel – that it was being deprived by the elite of its fair share of honour. It was the elite rather than the mass which felt its honour to be unduly compromised – hence, in part, the two successful Athenian oligarchic counter-revolutions of 411 and 404 BCE.

From the negative point of view, the Greeks had no formally instituted separation of powers. Whoever ruled – one, some or all – did so legislatively and judicially as well as executively. Sovereignty, insofar as it was an issue or, indeed, a concept, remained blurred, despite modern legalistic attempts to identify a notion of the 'sovereignty' of law (or of the laws) that would supply the motive force for civil obedience. Moreover, since there were no political parties in the modern sense, there could be no concept of a loyal opposition – indeed, no legitimacy of opposition for its own sake. Finally, the already noted absence of State forces of law and order played its contributory role here too.

Various solutions to the problem of *stasis* were proposed. Intellectually the most satisfying was the notion of the *miktê* (sc. *politeia*) or 'mixed constitution', the aim of which was to mediate and mitigate the political class struggle between 'rich' and 'poor' citizens. In its earliest known form, the notion proposed a mixture of persons and powers, a 'pudding' theory. This is alluded to by Thucydides (8.97.2) in the context of his account of the oligarchic counter-revolutions at Athens of 411: he praised the moderately oligarchic 'constitution of the 5,000' for its 'moderate blending in the interests of both the few [sc. rich] and the many [sc. poor citizens]'. Predictably, however, the fullest exponent of a mixed constitution theory on record was Aristotle, again resorting to the standard dichotomous model of a citizen body divided structurally between the few 'rich' and the mass of the 'poor' (*Pol.* 1308b29–30). Later, in the Hellenistic era, a theoretical system of constitutional checks and balances – a 'seesaw' theory – was first adumbrated by the Greek politician-historian Polybius in his sympathetic analysis of the constitution of Republican Rome, and this was to be developed enthusiastically by Niccolò Machiavelli and Charles Montesquieu among many others (see Nippel 1980).

Not all Greeks, however, were always absolutely against all forms of *stasis*: Solon, the Athenian lawgiver of the early sixth century BCE (chapter 4), was even supposed to have promulgated a law to the effect that every Athenian had to take sides in a time of *stasis* – that is, had to take a stand (one of the several meanings of the term *stasis*). There was a sense, too, in which *stasis* was but the logically extreme form of the division that bound together any Greek citizen body when it made a decision *es meson*; here lay the paradox of *stasis*, as a phenomenon both execrable and yet somehow inevitable, given the framework of the Greek city (Loraux 2002). On the other hand, precisely because of the dangers of a peaceable division turning into an outright civil war, the governing ideal remained *homonoia*: not merely consensus or passive acquiescence in the will or power of the majority, but literally and full-bloodedly 'same-mindedness', absolute and total unanimity.

The contrast between ancient Greek and early-modern European political thinking on faction is as sharp as could be. From Thomas Hobbes to James Madison, faction was construed wholly negatively, in line with the general abhorrence of direct popular participation, as a horrible antique bogey to be exorcised utterly from modern political life. That reactionary tradition was honed and polished with the rise to political prominence in industrialised countries during the nineteenth century of an organised working class. It was not until the conservative virtues of representative democracy had been fully perceived and exploited, and faction institutionalised in the relatively harmless form of political parties, that democracy could be held up once again as a shining ideal. Today, as noted above, we are all notionally democrats of one stripe or another. Nothing could illustrate better the gulf between the political culture of ancient Greece and the modern Western world.

# Narrative I: The prehistoric and protohistoric Greek world, c. 1300–750 BCE

Between the world of the prehistoric Mycenaean Greek palace and the world of the historical Greek *polis* there was a gulf fixed. That makes a convenient aphorism, no doubt, but nevertheless it is a tellingly accurate distinction too. Strictly, the world of Mycenaean or Late Bronze Age Greece (*c.* 1600–1100 BCE) was protohistoric rather than prehistoric, in that it was an age that possessed a form of literacy dedicated to the keeping of records. That literacy was of a special or restricted kind, however, practised only by skilled record-keeping scribes who were familiar with the 200 or so signs and pictograms devised to transcribe an early form of the Greek language. What the scribes recorded were interminable lists of people and things on a short-term basis; it was only an accident of destruction by (presumably hostile) fire that transformed the temporary clay tablets on which the 'Linear B' script was deployed into permanently legible baked artefacts.

The masters whom the scribes and their script served were sole rulers who called themselves high kings and lorded it over kingdoms of varying size, shape and power – from Thessaly in the north of mainland Greece to the island of Crete in the south-eastern Mediterranean, midway between Europe and Africa. We call the culture and period 'Mycenaean' because Mycenae in north-east Peloponnese was archaeologically the richest and most powerfully defended of these central sites, and because in the West's earliest literary fiction, the *Iliad*, it takes pride of place as the seat of great King Agamemnon, the overall leader of a united Hellenic expedition against Troy. Homer's Troy, archaeology suggests, lay at Hissarlik, a major thirteenth-century centre in touch both with the major Hittite Empire of the Anatolian plateau to its east and with the Greek world only a few days' sail away to the west. Whether there ever really was such a united Greek coalition, however, let alone an expedition to Troy lasting – whatever its motivation – as long as ten years, is more than doubtful.

Towards the end of the thirteenth century some major catastrophe over-took both the Greek and the non-Greek eastern Mediterranean world.

Indeed, the Hittite Empire too collapsed around the same time, leaving a vacuum into which the Peoples of the Sea mentioned in contemporary Egyptian records somehow insinuated themselves. Several of the Mycenaean palatial centres show signs of destruction (hence the firing of the Linear B tablets), and the pattern of a small number of prosperous and regionally unified centres was decisively abandoned. With the palaces disappeared the accoutrements of palatial society and politics, including all forms of writing. The exception was the survival of a syllabic script on the island of Cyprus, to which a number of mainland Greek refugees migrated during the twelfth and eleventh centuries. This migration was just one in an age of *Völkerwanderungen* that saw Greek-speakers eventually established firmly all along the western coastline of Anatolia. Athens later claimed the credit for this 'Ionian migration' (as it is compendiously if inaccurately labelled), but at most the site of Athens offered the last port of call in mainland Greece for many of the migrants. At all events, Athens was one of the very few mainland settlements to show something like a continuity of occupation from the thirteenth century into the eleventh century and beyond.

Elsewhere, there began a period suitably labelled a 'Dark Age', even if the darkness was not by any means uniformly distributed throughout the enlarged if fragile Greek world. The most recent authoritative account of the centuries from the twelfth to the eighth BCE has rightly concluded that 'what has been called the "Dark Age" was, like the Collapse that brought about the conditions for its onset, a real phenomenon' (Dickinson 2006: 239). Oliver Dickinson is inclined to link the collapse with the increasing turmoil detectable simultaneously in the Near East and to identify instability of all kinds as 'a major if not the primary factor in causing the relative depression and backwardness of the "Dark Age"' (242).

Two areas that showed early signs of increased light apart from Athens were the islands of Euboea and Crete. A large building of the later tenth century on Euboea has been credited to some sort of minor princeling, who was buried in some state and style alongside his consort and burial offerings that included foreign exotica. Elsewhere, most glaringly in the area of southern Peloponnese that Sparta would later make its own, the gloom persisted until well into the eighth century. By the middle of that century, however, the signs of renewed prosperity are so many and so distinctive that scholars reach hopefully for the word 'renaissance'. One of the most obvious is that a combination of relative overpopulation and the enhanced technology associated with the regular use of iron for edged implements in both peace and war had produced an equivalent of the voyages of discovery associated with the European Renaissance.

Amongst the earliest long-distance sea traders, who were also the first to found permanent settlements abroad, were men from Euboea. To begin with, in their search for metals, slaves and other necessities, they headed east – to the Levant by way of Egypt and Cyprus. Soon afterwards, tipped off no doubt by the ubiquitous Phoenicians (of modern Lebanon), they headed west also, and, via the Straits of Messina between Sicily and the toe of Italy, they had by 775 fetched up in the Bay of Naples – just south of the questing Etruscans' southernmost point of expansion from their native Tuscany. Here the Euboeans founded settlements, first on the island of Ischia (anciently Pithecoussae) and then at Cumae on the Italian mainland. Later, Cumae at any rate developed into a fully-fledged polis, but Pithecoussae, which anyway had not been an exclusively Greek settlement, revealingly was abandoned within a century or so of its foundation. The world of the *polis* was an invention of the period after rather than before 750.

Within the later horizon at Ischia one artefact from a burial assemblage speaks loudly of the nature of the advance for Greek culture that this western outreach represented. It is a fairly standard kind of wine-drinking vessel, made on the far side of the Aegean on the island of Rhodes. What makes it distinct – indeed, distinctive, and even distinguished – are the three lines of verse incised upon its outer surface in a local Euboean alphabet:

> Nestor had a drinkworthy cup –
> Whoever drinks from *this* cup
> [Him] straightaway will lust for golden Aphrodite seize!

The use of a fully phonetic alphabetic script, the Greeks' radical improve-ment on an original Phoenician non-vocalic model, is itself revelatory. The Greeks had learned to write again – and in a script far better suited to their language than the clumsy, bureaucratic Linear B syllabary *plus* pictograms. In principle, now, even a small child could learn to be fully literate, and quickly too, once he or she had mastered the mere twenty-four to twenty-eight signs required (depending on the epichoric – that is, local – variants). The cause or causes of this far-reaching Greek reinvention are uncertain, but they will have included commercial motives. Culturally no less inter-esting, however, is the fact that from early on the alphabet was used to write down verse, and metrical verse at that. The suggestion has even been made that the alphabet was devised precisely for that purpose, and, even more specifically, to write down one particular kind of verse, namely the heroic epic hexameters that went under the collective name of 'Homer'.

Far-fetched though that suggestion may seem, it does derive some support from our humble Ischian pot. The Nestor referred to cannot be any other than Homer's garrulous king of Messenian Pylos (south-west Peloponnese), who did indeed possess a highly desirable pot, or, rather, a mighty goblet made of costly metal and elaborately adorned into the bargain. So, through his three lines of verse, two in epic hexameters, our writer in the far, far west of the then Greek world has betrayed knowledge of a poem that was created and circulated originally in the far Greek east. Moreover, so culturally at ease with Homer did our writer feel that he – surely 'he' – didn't scruple to have a joke at Homer's (and Nestor's) expense. No doubt, he was writing not only on a cup, but also in his cups – that is, at a *symposion* or all-male drinking party. In this upper-class milieu, aristocrats – 'those who shared a cultural pattern of life and values consciously conceived and upheld from generation to generation' (Starr 1992: 4) – or would-be aristocrats sedulously cultivated such knowing literary sophistication as a mark of social distinction as well as superior wealth and leisure. Our interest in the world or worlds of Homer is more prosaic, though, and less . . . well, sexy: was it one that knew the *polis*? Was there indeed ever a – real – world of Homer?

# CHAPTER 3

# Rule by one: the politics of Homer,
## c. 750 BCE

> The best reason why Monarchy is a strong government is that it is intelligible government. The mass of mankind understand it, and they hardly anywhere in the world understand any other.
>
> (Walter Bagehot, *The English Constitution*, 1867)

Monarchy runs like a red thread through Greek political history and thought (see also chapter 8). It was never normal or normative, though. Herodotus indeed (2.147) throws scorn on the Egyptians for their seemingly congenital incapacity to live without kings. There again, though, the same might be said of the – wholly Greek – Spartans, whose odd double kingship reminded Herodotus precisely of non-Greek royalty (Egyptian, Persian, Scythian) (see further chapter 10). The fact that there were always two Spartan kings, however, reigning jointly, from two different royal houses is, in a way, exactly the exception that proves the rule. The concentration of power that full-blooded monarchy represented was always at bottom felt to be incompatible with the fundamental *polis* principles of freedom and equality.

If the *wanax* of Mycenaean times is put on one side, the continuous story of Greek kingship begins in Homer; but the Homeric epics are as slippery as a historical source as they are outstandingly brilliant as literature. Was there a single 'Homeric society', locatable in a specific time and place, and, if so, when and where? If there was, what were its politics? Where, to put it more bluntly, is the *polis* in Homer? Alternatively, and perhaps more accurately, how was the political dimension expressed therein?

'Homer' means the *Iliad* and the *Odyssey*, two hugely long epic poems, each focused on the heroic feats of one man (though, interestingly, only the *Odyssey* is heroically eponymous). Both are traditional oral poetic epics, combining scope and economy in their heavily formulaic hexameter lines. They are based on a myriad of individual poems in multiple recensions, performed over some five centuries and shaped into their existing, monumental form by (two probably different) monumental composers, round about 700–650 BCE. That would have been up to six centuries after the actual time in which the supposed events would have happened (the Late Bronze Age or Mycenaean era of the thirteenth century BCE) – if, indeed, they ever did happen, or in anything like the ways the poets describe...

The *Iliad* is from its very first word about the anger of Achilles. To do his theme justice, the brilliantly original monumental composer has selected from the mass of myth and legend surrounding the fall of Troy (which is not actually described in the *Iliad*, and which is reported in the *Odyssey* only in flashback) in order to focus intensively on just one great doomed Greek hero: Achilles from Thessaly, son of a mortal father and a divine mother (Thetis). His anger is directed at Agamemnon, the overall Greek leader of a multi-Greek expedition to Troy on the Dardanelles (Hellespont) designed to recover his brother Menelaus's adulterous wife, the über-gorgeous Helen. What occasioned Achilles' wrath is that Agamemnon, invoking a spurious entitlement to compensation, had robbed him of his favourite female captive (Briseis) and thereby insulted him, causing him to lose out in the crucial heroic dimension of face. Agamemnon could claim that he had not started the quarrel, however. It was a just return for his having been compelled, by divine agency, to give back his own favourite female captive (Chryseis). The whole epic, therefore, is to do with heroic men's responses to the loss of the females by whose ownership their own public status is critically measured. Closure, so far as the poem's selective treatment of the legend allows, is achieved finally by a moving reconciliation between Achilles and the father of Troy's hero Hector, whom Achilles has slain in single combat and whose corpse he has then rather gruesomely dishonoured. Troy has yet to fall, though, and Helen has yet to be recovered... Politically, all is still left to play for by the poet, who cares for other things.

Instrumental in that final political closure is the eponymous hero of the comparably monumental (and presumably slightly later) *Odyssey*, which has given its name to a genre of writing – and cinematography. The eponymous epic recounts the travels and travails of a king from the far west of mainland Greece, which took him ten long years to return from Troy to his little rocky island kingdom of Ithaca and faithful wife Penelope. Odysseus is formulaically styled 'of the many wiles', not least of which is the Trojan horse. He also rates as 'much enduring', however, having a terrific amount to contend with, above all from the mighty god Poseidon (whose monstrous son, Polyphemus the one-eyed Cyclops, he memorably blinds in Book 9). On the other hand, Odysseus has a major divine supporter in Athena, thanks to whom he does eventually get back home – alone.

The historicity of the epics may be tested both by mute archaeological evidence from between – at the outer limits – the thirteenth and the eighth centuries, and by the written evidence of the so-called Linear B tablets. Archaeology has revealed the existence of a number of palatial economies and societies in mainland Greece from Thessaly to the very south of the Peloponnese and across the water on Crete. Of these, Mycenae in the north-east Peloponnese was the richest and biggest – in conformity with the poem's presentation of Agamemnon as overall leader of the Greeks at Troy, despite the fact that he was not the greatest hero nor in charge because he was personally the mightiest warrior or ruler. Just what sort of a king any real-life Agamemnon would have been is a separate question, to which we shall return, as is the issue of whether there was in any sense a politically united 'Greece' for him to lead.

The Linear B tablets, accidentally preserved by conflagrations, have been recovered from a number of major Mycenaean centres, most recently Thebes. The syllabic – not alphabetic – script was deciphered finally in the 1950s, as an early form of Greek. This clumsy creation was solely a scribal, bureaucratic script, however, designed and used only for keeping palace accounts. There was never any literature, history and so forth written down in Linear B. What the tablets do massively confirm, however, is that there were indeed palaces and kingdoms in historical reality, as in the epics. Unfortunately for literalists, though, they also prove that Homer's kings were no Mycenaean-style rulers, since their fictional kingdoms were infinitely less large and complex than any Bronze Age originals.

A famous third-century BCE Greek intellectual, Eratosthenes of Cyrene, posed the problem of Homeric historicity most pointedly. He would believe the *Odyssey* to be historically authentic, he said, when he was presented with the cobbler who sewed the leather bag into which Aeolus stuffed all the winds of the world. In other words, the *Odyssey*, like the *Iliad* only more so, is riddled with elements of folk tale, fiction and saga that at least obscure any history that might be lurking beneath. Besides, such history as there is is not an 'authentic' recreation of a definite past. 'Even where apparently concerned with mundane matters, an epic cannot be a trustworthy guide to reality' (Dickinson 2006: 240). *A fortiori*, it is not a trustworthy guide to the supramundane 'reality' of divine intervention that shapes and directs the action, either.

When Heinrich Schliemann set off to 'excavate' Troy, and later Mycenae and other contemporary sites, he did so in the conviction that Homer was a historian. The dominant modern view is not entirely at odds with Schliemann's, except that it locates the history at the other end of the five- to six-century span the process of Homeric production embraced – in the eighth century, in other words. My own view, however, coincides with that of John Myres (1958), on the one hand, and that of Anthony Snodgrass (1974), on the other. Myres finds the world of Homer to be immortal precisely because it never really existed outside the poet's (we should say, rather, poets') fertile imagination. Snodgrass demonstrates in a potent article – recently reprinted, rightly – that Homer's inextricably confused combination of mechanical and social technologies (bronze with iron, bride price with dowry, and so forth) was one that could hardly have occurred in any single, real time in real-life society.

Thus, as Moses Finley (1978) observed (though he in my view was no less wrong in his specific location of a Homeric society in the tenth and ninth centuries), Homer's kings and palaces are but poetically enlarged and 'heroised' versions of the really rather petty local chieftains who in fact ruled a poverty-stricken and disunited Greece in the 'Dark Age' (eleventh to ninth centuries) that followed the great Late Bronze Age and preceded the 'Renaissance' of the eighth. The creation of epic saga presupposes ruins, and a poignant memory of a bygone and distant age of glorious deeds (in which men could lift boulders such as not two men could lift today, etc.). The Homeric epics themselves are undoubtedly products of the upswing of Greek civilisation from 800 and especially 750 BCE on, however, a period during which Greek traders started to go east to Syria for trade in metals and slaves (a role attributed solely to Phoenicians in Homer) and to 'colonise' (i.e. settle permanently) in first the west (south Italy, Sicily, later north Africa, southern France, eastern Spain) and then the north-east (round the Black Sea). Though they reflect the eighth and seventh centuries in many of their social and economic details, politically they at best merely hint at the most momentous single development of the period, the rise of the *polis* or citizen state.

The word *polis* (or *ptolis*) and kindred words (*ptoliethron*, etc.) certainly do occur in Homer – indeed, quite frequently. There are no *politai* – citizens – at Troy, however, nor on Ithaca. Not only does the word *politēs* not occur in Homer but the nearest we get (not very near) to descriptions of real-life citizen politics occur in wholly fictional passages. That is, in the description in *Iliad* Book 18 of human communal activities both peaceable and warlike on the shield fashioned for Achilles by the lame Olympian craftsman-god Hephaestus (below), and in the neverland fantasy world of the island of Phaeacia, Odysseus's last port of call in the tenth year of his post-Trojan-War wanderings before he finally returns to his native island of Ithaca (*Odyssey*, Books 9–12).

On Ithaca itself not a single Assembly has been held for twenty years – since Odysseus left, in fact; and, when one is at last called right at the beginning of the *Odyssey*, this is only because of the exceptional crisis caused by the king's absence: his son Telemachus is under-age, and siege is being laid to his palace and to his wife, Penelope, by precisely 108 young noble suitors. Moreover, when that Assembly is called, the people have literally no say. Johannes Haubold, a very good scholar, has recently (2000) tried to excavate a significant role for the *laos* or masses of common folk in Homer, but, unless one redefines *laos* in such a way that it refers as much if not more to the elite as to the mass, the genuine humble and meek masses tend to appear on the whole only in the political background. Likewise, Dean Hammer's valiant attempt (2002) to read the *Iliad* as in and of itself a 'performance of political thought' seems to me to be clutching at straws in the wind. Authority and obedience, issues of importance to the community that are somehow settled in the public arena, are indeed correctly to be labelled as political. Institutionally speaking, though, as even Hammer is forced to concede, the world of the *Iliad* is pre-political, or, more specifically, pre-*polis*.

In the epics altogether a score or so of assemblies of various sorts are mentioned or described, but not one is truly a decision-making assembly. For in Troy as on Ithaca it is the 'kings' and their representatives, above all Agamemnon of Mycenae and the other 'best' men, who call all the political shots. It is entirely up to Agamemnon, for example, whether or not he consults the army as a whole, and when he does decide to he does it to test its feelings, not because it has a right to be consulted, let alone to decide any issue. It is therefore an abuse of language to classify as a 'decision' the way the Greeks at Troy in Book 2 of the *Iliad* react to an assembly called by Agamemnon after nine long years of unsuccessful siege, by drifting or, rather, running back to their ships, in the hope that the expedition will at last be called off. By thus voting with their feet, however (not – be it noted – in any formal way; the counting of votes was even further off: see chapter 4), these Homeric Greeks do arguably give a strong hint of a real eighth-century situation, in which the masses of ordinary Greeks were beginning to make themselves and their opinions felt.

It is in the context of the break-up of that deliberately testing assembly that a key confrontation is staged (lines 155–283): between Odysseus, a hero with a great future as well as a distinguished past, and Thersites, a nobody from nowhere who after this one emblematic appearance disappears without trace from the epic (though his remembrance was ensured much later, by references in Xenophon and elsewhere). Odysseus, as representative of the established monarchic-aristocratic order, is pitted against Thersites, as an admittedly quite exceptionally uppity and self-appointed 'representative' of the *dêmos* (the ordinary soldiers, whose military role, though crucial, is systematically under-described by the oral epic poets, for social as well as expository reasons).

The assembly is likened to a ship 'shaken as on the sea' (lines 144ff.), and the soldiers start to go back to the ships with a view to returning to their Greek homelands. 'Then for the Argives [Greeks] a homecoming beyond fate might have been accomplished...', had not Hera (wife of Zeus, enemy of Troy) spoken a word to Athena (likewise enemy of Troy, and special protector of Odysseus), who in turn roused Odysseus, 'the equal of Zeus in counsel' (line 169 – no mean praise!). The divine intervention is a crucial element in the poet's causal representation, but for us what counts is how precisely Odysseus is divinely inspired to act. As a first step, he seizes hold of the sceptre of great lord Agamemnon himself – the staff and symbol of not only office but power, and, as we shall see, a weapon in the literal as well as figurative sense.

Armed with the sceptre, Odysseus manfully stems the flood tide of retreat, adopting a radically binary approach to the two hierarchically differentiated categories into which the poet – knowing his audience – divides the Greeks at Troy. On the one hand, first, to 'some king, or man of influence' (line 188), he says – softly, persuasively – 'Are you not ashamed to fall below your proper standard of behaviour? Don't play the coward' (a socially as well as morally loaded term, later an explicit equivalent of 'low-class') but 'hold fast' – that is, first get control of yourself and stick to your post – and then, from your position of both natural and culturally assumed superior authority, 'check the rest of the people' (line 191), the *dêmos* in the sense of the (unwashed) masses. On the other hand, though, 'when he saw some man of the people shouting' (line 198) – that is, some vulgarian Greek nonentity – then – before and in preference to using words – 'he would strike at him with his staff' (line 199) – Agamemnon's sceptre, rather – and only after that would he address him in words. Not with soft, winning words, moreover, but words of harsh reproof, violent scorn and withering sarcasm (lines 200–6):

> Excellency! Sit still and hearken to what others tell you,
> those who are better men than you are, you skulker and coward
> and thing of no account whatever in either battle or council.

> For sure, not all of us Achaeans [Greeks] can be as kings here.
> Manifold lordship is not a good thing. Let there be one ruler,
> one king, to whom the son of crooked-counselling Cronus
> gives the sceptre and the right of judgement, to watch over his
> people.

Odysseus's ideal is conservative, even reactionary. It is kingship – though he does not use any abstract term such as *monarkhia* or *basileia* – of a traditional kind, supported by a council of aristocratic advisers but sharing its divinely authorised power with no other person or persons.

At which point, something quite extraordinary happens. Reality breaks in – but not the supposed reality of the Heroic Age in which the *Iliad* was notionally set, but the historical reality of the period and world in which the *Iliad* became the *Iliad*, between *c.* 750 and 650 BCE. 'Now the rest [of the *dêmos*] had sat down', as ordered by Odysseus, and were once more 'orderly' (line 211 – another key value term), both taking and knowing their proper place; 'the rest' – apart, that is, from one troublemaker, Thersites 'of the endless speech' (line 212). He (lines 212–19)

> knew within his head many words, but disorderly;
> he was vain, without decency, apt to quarrel with the lords
> with any word he thought might amuse the Argives.
> This was the ugliest man who came beneath Ilium [Troy]. He
> was bandy-legged and lame in one foot, he had shoulders
> stooped and hunched together over his chest; and above
> his skull rose to a point, with the wool sparsely grown upon it.

His outward appearance, in other words, precisely reflected his inward moral turpitude and social malformation. This is the exact inverse of the qualities arrogated to themselves and ultimately abstracted by the elite as *kalokagathia*, 'beauty-and-goodness'. All the same, the poet gives Thersites a set speech to deliver (lines 225–42), its venom mainly directed against Agamemnon personally but also seeking to rouse up the masses to take decisive action *against* the lords. After a while, Odysseus again takes the floor, partly to defend Agamemnon but chiefly to abuse and humiliate Thersites: his words are ill-considered, he is morally the worst of all the Greeks at Troy, he is a mere troublemaker and rabble-rouser, not really worth arguing with, but fit only to be violently beaten in a demonstration of public shaming. Odysseus straightaway matches deeds to words and so whacks Thersites as to cause him to cry.

At which the assembled Greeks react with what I take to be, from the poet's point of view, an exemplary show of complicity: though somewhat sorry for Thersites' pain, they laugh out loud and declare, somewhat hyper-bolically (but what else can you expect of a mob?), that what Odysseus has just done 'is by far the best thing he has ever accomplished' (line 274)! It is a telling commentary on the cast of post-antique political thinking that, if you look up the epithet 'Thersitical' in the *Oxford English Dictionary*, you will not, curiously enough, find it defined as 'visionary', 'progressive' or 'egalitarian', but as 'abusive and foul-mouthed'. The aristocratic Homer, by way of Xenophon's Socrates and the – until very recently – dominant 'anti-democratic tradition in western thought' (Roberts 1994) triumphs still, theoretically or ideologically speaking.

The speech of Odysseus that I have quoted from above is arguably the single most crucial passage in the entire *Iliad* so far as our theme of pol-itics in action is concerned. One notes especially – or, rather, is struck by – the polysyllabic abstract noun *polukoirania*, translated here as 'mani-fold lordship'. This is the earliest hint of that abstraction of thought and vocabulary that has been rightly identified as one of the preconditions for the invention of political theory in Greece, namely the mental and symbolic transformation so well described and analysed by Jean-Pierre Vernant (1957) and others. This complex transformation of consciousness comprised the search for a new secularising rationality, the allegorical inter-pretation of myth, the birth of historical reflection; in short, the crisis of the traditional forms of communication and of the values that accom-panied them. All contributed in their different ways to delineate a series of profound changes in the theory and practice of politics (in the broad-est sense) in later archaic Greece: from myth to *logos*, from gift exchange to instituted political exchange, from divine to human understanding, from concrete to abstract reasoning, from unwritten to written law; in sum, from a city of gods to the city of reason. That is another story, though.

To stay for the moment with the *Iliad*: in Books 3 to 12 the fighting continues, but it goes very badly for the Greeks: so much so, indeed, that a formal embassy is sent to the skulking Achilles (Book 9) to implore him to resume fighting. To be noted is the assumption that only a great warrior can conduct a successful fight, that the masses have only supporting roles. In this context the famous and much-quoted exchange between Sarpedon (a son of Zeus) and Glaucus, both of Lycia and Trojan allies, is paradigmatic (12.310ff.): Sarpedon's 'explanation' or justification of aristocratic rule is given in terms of the fulfilment of the duty to be in the forefront of 'the fighting where men win glory' (line 325) – and as a result get to eat the flesh of fat sheep and quaff sweet wine. Achilles, however, always less than stereotypical, refuses all entreaties, and the fight goes on, getting worse and worse for the Greeks – until the Trojans are actually among the Greeks' ships and setting fire to them (Book 16.123).

As usual, the Trojans are here led by mighty Hector, oldest son of aged Priam, king of Troy, and a leader favoured by the two main pro-Trojan deities, Zeus (12.437) and Apollo (15.254ff.). He is really the hero of the central part of the *Iliad*, characterised as an unstoppable force (12.465–6), a 'rolling stone' (13.137). Individual Greek heroes – Diomedes, Ajax – do great things; but the Greeks are still getting worsted. Book 14 is inserted as light relief from the travails of the battlefield: a seduction scene of Hera, the long-suffering and politically opposed sister-wife of Zeus, distracting her husband with amorous play. We are quickly brought back to the deadly serious business of war, however, between men inspired as ever by gods and goddesses.

Thus Apollo inspires Hector, which in turn inspires Achilles' best mate Patroclus (15.390ff.) to try to stir Achilles to re-enter the fray (15.402). Even he has no success, though, and Achilles continues to complain that he has been 'fouled' by Agamemnon (16.53). On the other hand, he is sufficiently moved by the Greeks' plight to permit Patroclus to fight on his behalf and, as it were, in his name, most obviously by wearing his – Achilles' – armour. The main subplot of the last third of the *Iliad* is therefore the glorious deeds and death of Patroclus (Book 16.130 ff.), especially the killing of Sarpedon (line 490), and his death at the hands of Hector, aided crucially again by Apollo, followed by a whole book (23) devoted to the magnificent funeral games staged for him by an inconsolably grief-stricken Achilles. The Patroclus subplot subtends the main plot of the *Iliad*'s last third: Achilles, goaded at last into fighting by Patroclus's death, as champion of the Greeks engages Troy's champion Hector in a deathly decisive individual combat. Hector's death (Book 22) and the eventual return of Hector's body to Priam by Achilles (Book 24) are the sandwich around Patroclus's funeral games.

Politically speaking, the latter part of the *Iliad* raises two major issues. The first is that of patriotism, the second the status of the two 'cities', cunningly worked into the decoration of the replacement shield of Achilles fashioned by the lame Olympian craftsman-god Hephaestus at the request of Achilles' divine water nymph mother Thetis. There are, as I have said, no citizens in Homer, and there is therefore directly attested no *polis* in Homer. There is a notion of patriotism, however, and there is described in Book 18 a legal process that at least parallels contemporary eighth/seventh-century real-world litigation.

Patriotism, the sentiment that one has a 'country' for which one must fight, is most famously placed in the mouth of Hector, Troy's rock and chief defender. 'One bird sign is best,' he declares (12.243), namely to fight back in defence of one's *patra* ('country', 'fatherland'). As expressed in the *Iliad*, however, this is a Trojan not a Greek notion. Is this a part of Homer's relatively even-handed, non-ethnocentric treatment of Trojans and Greeks, or, had the boot been on the other foot, with the Trojans camped outside Mycenae, might its source have been reversed? A passage of the *Odyssey* suggests the latter: when Odysseus in disguise at the court of King Alcinous on the island of the Phaeacians hears the court bard Demodocus sing of the Trojan horse ruse (Odysseus's own, of course), he wept 'like a woman who throws her arms around the corpse of her dear husband who has fallen in battle before his city and people, fighting to defend his city and children from the day of death' (*Odyssey* 8.523–5). Precisely as Hector had: a hero who had been driven to his ultimate fate by a sense of 'the patriotic obligation to the community that must take precedence over the drive to personal and familial glory' (Greenhalgh 1972: 534).

The (new) shield of Achilles (Book 18.478–607) lovingly crafted by Hephaestus is equally lavishly described by the poet. Upon it Hephaestus somehow contrives to depict – hardly realistically or practically, despite modern 'reconstructions' – 'two cities of mortal men' (lines 490–1). Typically Greek, Hephaestus operated with binary polarisation, for one of the cities was at peace, the other at war. Even within the city at peace, however, there is killing. It is killing that is handled peaceably, though, by due process of litigation. Two men are at odds 'over the blood price for a man who has been killed' (lines 498–9). Since the aggrieved relative would not accept what price the offender offered, resort was had to an act of public arbitration, to be performed by a group of seated 'elders' assisted by heralds keeping order among the heated crowd of onlookers in the public agora. The two men pleaded their case in turn, 'and between them lay on the ground two talents of gold, to be given to that judge [among the elders] who in this case spoke the straightest opinion' (lines 507–8). Much discussion has surrounded this enormous sum. One might have expected it to be used as compensation to the victim's family, or even possibly considered as the equivalent of a monetary fine, a strikingly progressive alternative to the 'eye for an eye' *lex talionis* that was no true 'law' at all. Instead, it is on offer in the middle, as a prize for one of the judges – a clear sign that we are still dealing here with a radically inegalitarian system of justice, if 'system of justice' is what it really is. Why, too, does Homer leave no indication about the conflict's resolution (see Farenga 2006: 128)? This is a sign, I should say, that real-world justice systems were then still distinctly inchoate.

To sum up so far: is there a *polis* in Homer? Well, there are hints of its existence elsewhere, outside the epic frame, in the organised mode of fighting by the non-heroic massed soldiers, in the declarations of a form of 'patriotism' attributed, significantly, to the Trojan Hector, not to any Greek leader, and in the City at Peace, where due process of legal judgement is cunningly depicted on the shield of Achilles. Is there politics in Homer? Not in any strong sense of that term, as defined by us in chapter 2. Is there evidence of political thought in Homer? Yes, indeed, and most strikingly in the defence by Odysseus of legitimate hereditary *monarkhia* (not so-called) against Thersites' alleged threat of the abstraction *polukoirania*. Does that amount to establishing the existence of political theory in Homer, though? Very far from it. For that, we must look to the career and surviving writings of the Athenian Solon – though even there, I argue (chapter 4), we shall not actually find it. Before we leave early Greek epic, however, we must turn to our first direct and unambiguous literary evidence for the emergence of the *polis* – in Hesiod's *Works and Days*.

The main body of this curious poem, which probably owes its survival to its author's much more famous and authoritative *Theogony*, consists of a farmer's almanack, interspersed with richly loamed moral homily – the sort of thing Thomas Tusser was to do for Elizabethan England over two millennia later. What interests me, though, is the framing of the poem, its ostensible motivation. For by giving a personal quarrel a universal significance Hesiod both gives birth to the author (see Thomas 2005) and provides us with our first – if negative – instance of practical Greek politics within a properly *polis* context.

Hesiod, apparently a real individual of that name and the first to speak in his own poetic voice, hailed from Ascra, a smallish village within the territory of the *polis* of Thespiae in Boeotia, and he was a local before he became a national poet. He flourished about 700 BCE. The cause or occasion of *Works and Days* was the public political decision given – or, as Hesiod would have it, procured – in favour of Hesiod's brother Perses in their bitter dispute over their paternal inheritance. Their father, an immigrant from Asia Minor, had clearly done well enough to make it worth the two of them fighting over his landed legacy. According to Greek norms, inheritance was partible – that is, to be equally divided among surviving legitimate sons. Yet somehow, Hesiod claims, Perses had wrested the unequally larger portion – and convinced the powers that be to recognise his illicit claim.

Hesiod memorably lambasts the petty 'kings' or lords of Ascra, the ruling elite who gave the decision, as 'gift-devouring' or 'bribe-swallowing' (Greek tellingly uses the same word *dôron* for 'bribe' as for 'gift'), and he directs at them the monitory myth of the hawk and the nightingale, implying that unjust rulers in the end bring disaster on their communities, as well as upon themselves. All the same, Hesiod remains an impotent voice crying in the wilderness. He could rant and rave all he liked, but the titular 'kings' of Ascra were under no obligation even to listen to him, let alone revisit or reverse their prior decision. The true political significance of Hesiod's testimony, therefore, is that genuine amelioration – 'justice', as Hesiod understood and advocated it – would require major political, economic, social and not least military changes of the sort to be described in the following narrative.

# Narrative II: The archaic Greek world,
## c. 750–500 BCE

May god be kind [?]. This has been decided by the *polis*: when a man has been Kosmos, for ten years that same man shall not be Kosmos. If he should become Kosmos, whatever judgements he passes, he himself shall owe double, and he shall be disempowered as long as he lives, and what he does as Kosmos shall be as nothing. The oath-swearers [shall be] the Kosmos, the Damioi and the Twenty of the *polis*.

The foregoing text was inscribed on a humble block of schist limestone some time in the second half of the seventh century BCE. It was laid out in boustrophedon ('as the ox ploughs') style, back and forth across the stone. It has a good claim to constituting the oldest extant inscribed law from Greece, as old almost as the laws ascribed to the earliest lawgivers that are attested by (usually much later) literary sources. One of those lawgivers reputedly came from Crete: an entirely plausible claim, insofar as a large number of the earliest physically attested laws do also. The text we have quoted is from Drerus in eastern Crete.

Drerus was never any great shakes in the larger picture of ancient Greek history, never a major player on any big or bigger stage. The presence in this early text, therefore, of three words (*kosmos, polis*; the third is Damioi, from *damos* = 'people') with deep significance for the development of Greek political thinking and practice tells its own story. It is a powerful testimony to the extent to which that development had both spread and become embedded in Greek consciousness. *Kosmos* was a word the Greeks applied ultimately to the entire world or universe. Its root meaning is 'order', and because orderliness was found attractive it came secondarily to mean 'adornment' – whence our word 'cosmetics'. When used of the highest executive and judicial office at Drerus in seventh-century BCE Crete, however, *kosmos* retained the full force of its primary signification. The highest executive official named Kosmos was there to establish and maintain order.

Specifically, his publicly appointed role was to establish and maintain political order. For Drerus, as the text informs or reminds its addressees twice in the space of a few lines, was a *polis* or citizen state. We cannot put a precise date on when 'the *polis*' rose; in any case, it will have emerged at different times and different speeds in different parts of Hellas. It had not yet emerged very definitely, as we have seen in the last chapter, so far as the poets of the *Iliad* and *Odyssey* were concerned. One historical phenomenon that is certainly alluded to in the *Odyssey*, however, will have done nothing to slow the process down, and probably did a great deal to speed it up. This is the phenomenon known by scholars, alas inaccurately and potentially misleadingly, as colonisation.

Actually, very few of the 230 or so new settlements (Tsetskhladze 2006: lxiii) established around much of the Mediterranean and Black Seas between about 750 and 500 were colonies in any modern sense. They were overwhelmingly, from the first, more or less autonomous political entities, and soon enough – by 700 at the latest – communities of the *polis* genus. Cumae, founded on the Bay of Naples *c.* 750 by settlers from the Aegean island of Euboea, may already have been such; Taras, also in southern Italy, founded in about 700 certainly was. Nonetheless, the troubled foundation stories or myths surrounding Taras's foundation bear witness to the political confusion and instability in old Greece that either caused or promoted the movement in the first place. The settlers had a designated oikist or founder, Phalanthus, and they were backed up by an oracle delivered allegedly from the seat of all wisdom in early Greece, the oracular shrine of Apollo at Delphi. The oracle did not mention Taras, however, but Satyrion, a place a little way down the coast; the founder was on one account murdered, and by all accounts the men of Taras coexisted very unhappily ever after with their Italic neighbours the Iapygians. Moreover, the settlement seems not to have been authorised from the start by the *polis* that later came to be regarded as Taras's *mētropolis* or mother city, namely Sparta. Rather, the settlers were a group of disaffected half- or sub-Spartans denied what they considered their due political and social status and recognition at home.

Another factor hastening the emergence and development of the *polis* was warfare, which during the century between 750 and 650 became both regularised and significantly uniform in style. Indeed, the settlement of Taras was a consequence of what later tradition regarded as one of the most major of all historical wars in post-Mycenaean, pre-classical Greece, the so-called First Messenian War. The Spartan elegiac poet Tyrtaeus, who flourished around the middle of the seventh century, referred back to a war fought by his countrymen a couple of generations previously against the neighbouring Messenians – a war that had allegedly lasted as many as twenty years (or twice the length of the Trojan War!). Implausible as that duration undoubtedly was, it yet signified a contest of immense scale and significance. It marked the beginning of the rise of the *polis* of the Spartans to the position of a Greek superpower by the second half of the sixth century.

Within that period Sparta achieved a kind of constitutional concordat that may represent the earliest formalised political arrangement of its kind in all Greece. Mythically, the reform was associated with one wondrously omniprovident lawgiver, Lycurgus, to whom was ascribed one 'Great' *rhêtra* (Plutarch, *Lycurgus* 6) and several lesser ones. *Rhêtra* means a 'pronounce-ment' or 'ordinance' (see appendix I.1, a text from Olympia, inscribed *c.* 500), in this case one divinely sanctioned by the oracular authority of Apollo at Delphi. On the one hand, the Great Rhetra enshrined and entrenched the overriding aristocratic power of Sparta's two hereditary kings and other Heracles-descended aristocrats, embodied in the elective thirty-member Gerousia (Senate) of which the kings were members ex officio regardless of their actual age. On the other, it formally recognised the Spartan *damos* (people), the citizen body of hoplite warriors, as a political power, one that had the final right of sign-off on matters of peace and war, for crucial instance. This peculiar compromise survived the vicissi-tudes of external and internal Spartan politics for over 300 years, until the revolution of the third century BCE (chapter 9).

The seamless combination of religion and politics in the Great Rhetra was thoroughly Greek and typically Spartan. Sparta could hardly be described as a typical, or even a normal, Greek *polis*, however. In size its territory was more than double that of its nearest competitor, Syracuse. Within its 8,000 or so square kilometres (some two-fifths of the whole Pelo-ponnese) were embraced two further distinct sets of population besides the Spartans themselves: the Perioeci or 'circumdwellers', who were free but possessed of less than full civic rights in Sparta itself (where lay the seat of civic power and decision-making); and, second, the Helots, who, though Greek, were an unfree class of quasi-serfs. In status the Helots were not quite unique – parallels could justifiably be identified both among other Greek peoples (the Penestae of Thessaly, for example) and among non-Greeks (the Mariandyni or Bithyni, for instance, who lived at the western end of the Black Sea, or the Cyllyrioi of Sicily). In political effect, though, they were unique, being the economic base of a state that partly chose, partly was forced, to turn itself into a military machine – with all sorts of odd political consequences, such as, most notably, the maintenance or establishment of a unique joint, hereditary kingship.

One effect of Sparta's unique political situation and complexion was that it avoided one of the characteristic phenomena of the immediate pre-classical epoch: the emergence of tyranny. The word itself, *turannis*, was probably non-Greek in origin. Its earliest application in a Greek text was to a Lydian ruler, who – as we know from contemporary Assyrian texts – flourished in his capital of Sardis during the first half of the seventh century. The poet-adventurer Archilochus, himself a 'colonist' from Paros to Thasos, boldly, perhaps controversially, stated that he did not care personally to hold a *turannis* such as Gyges'. From the middle of the seventh century on, however, a succession of Greeks throughout the mainland and the Aegean did just that, and their form of extra-constitutional one-man dictatorships may be said to have been one of the most powerful engines of political change between about 650 and 500 BCE.

On the one hand, they served to split and dethrone the power of the old aristocratic ruling classes – the Homeric and Hesiodic 'kings' (*basileis*) – irreversibly. Only a very few *poleis* thereafter were strictly aristocracies, governments of the 'best' men who defined their claim to exclusive rule in terms of noble descent ultimately from a hero or a god. Rather, as the elegiac poet Theognis of Megara lamented (probably in the mid-sixth century), wealth – based still in most cases on the ownership of farmland, but also in some cases significantly also on spectacular commercial profit – had come first to confuse and then to outrank the pure claims of birth as a political criterion. On the other hand, tyrants were bound to look for support outside the old ruling elites, downwards towards the 'mass' that was coming to identify itself as a *dêmos*. Some scholars have identified a current of 'middling' ideology associated with such extra-elite outreach – in the middle, that is, between the upper echelons of the elite and the mass of the lower orders. How general such a current was is, however, disputable, but it can at least be given one very specific and concrete illustration, which will both conclude this chapter and lead us into the next.

The other major Greek state of this period besides Sparta that did not – to begin with – enjoy or suffer a period of tyranny was Athens. It could have done so, in the sense that by 600 conditions were in place there – including severe economic and political distress – that elsewhere had enabled or fostered tyranny. One of Athens' most charismatic early political figures deemed otherwise, however, and the reforms he proposed were put forward, enacted and, for a time, implemented precisely as an alternative to tyranny. That heroically memorable reformer was Solon, who went down in Athenian history – or, strictly, myth-history – as a founding father of democracy.

# CHAPTER 4

# Rule by some: the politics of Solon,
## c. 600 BCE

**Aristocracy**, n. Government by the best men. (In this sense the word is obsolete; so is that kind of government.)

(Ambrose Bierce, *A Devil's Dictionary*, 1911)

Nothing appears more surprising to those who consider human affairs with a philosophical eye than the easiness with which the many are governed by the few.

(David Hume, 'First principles of government', *Essays*, 1742)

Democracy, ancient-Greek-style, is probably the most key theme of my 'key theme'. It could hardly be more acutely topical. In Myanmar today, for instance, ordinary people are literally dying for democracy, or what is counted as democracy nowadays. At all events, they want something the opposite of what they have, a military junta, which is what the Greeks would have called a *dunasteia* or non-responsible collective tyranny. In the longer-established of the modern democracies, however, the very fact of democracy is somewhat old hat or *vieux jeu*. Perhaps indeed it is only at its instauration that democracy really tastes 'sweet', to use a political metaphor current among the ancient Greeks themselves (Herodotus 7.135.3). When exactly should we date its instauration, though?

I realise that from another – globally comparative – point of view (Detienne 2007) the date at which democracy was first invented in the world may seem relatively unimportant. From my point of view, however, concerned as I am with the relationship between ideas and practice in ancient Greece, where as a matter of fact democracy was first invented, it is of the greatest moment to try to find out when that happened. There is no issue about *where*: it happened in the *polis* of the Athenians. Just to complicate the chronological issue, however, the Athenians themselves at different times and in different contexts subscribed to two different views. According to conservative fourth-century BCE Athenians (and most fourth-century Athenians were conservative), democracy was their 'ancestral constitution' (Finley 1971), and its founder was undoubtedly Solon. According to Herodotus, however, and the Athenian source or sources he followed, the founder of 'the democracy and the tribes for the Athenians' (6.131) was equally indubitably Cleisthenes.

We may, of course, choose to regard both views as merely typical instances of the Greeks' personalisation of historical process, and of their invincible devotion to the mythology or myth-history of the *prôtos heuretês* ('first discoverer'). The two alleged founders hold an interest and importance well above and beyond mere ideology, however. In this chapter we canvass the claim of Solon, in the following that of Cleisthenes.

The seventeenth-century radical John Milton, it has been well said, was more profoundly involved in public affairs than any other major English poet. Even he, however, was not as profoundly, directly and centrally involved as was Solon at Athens (b. *c.* 640, fl. *c.* 600), who sought to justify his politics in competent elegiac verse. Retrospective appropriations of his achievement have, however, done their worst, and the original motives and intentions, and indeed the precise verbal details of Solon's laws, are now for the most part unrecoverable – although it seems that as late as the time of Aristotle (d. 322) full texts not only of his legislation but also of his poems were available to those with the curiosity and assiduity to seek them out. Thus we do at least have some of Solon's *ipsissima verba*, including some self-justificatory verses that take us to the heart of his preferred understanding of the socio-economic and political crisis at Athens in 594/3 BCE that he was called upon to resolve both as arbitrator (*diaitêtês*) for the present and as lawgiver (*nomothetês*) for the future.

Solon seems to have thought it his proper and most immediately crucial task to strike an appropriate balance of political power and privilege between two contending socio-economic groups or classes:

> I gave the common people (*dêmos*) as much privilege as they needed,
> neither taking honour from them nor reaching out for more.
> But as for those who had power and were admired for their wealth,
> I arranged for them to have nothing unseemly.

In another poem he resumes his fundamentally dichotomous representation of the citizenry for whom he was writing laws, using the characteristic archaic (but not solely archaic) mixture of moral and social terminology:

> I wrote laws (*thesmoi*) equally for bad [that is, poor, lower-class] and good [rich, upper-class, elite].

It is to be noted that for 'laws' Solon uses the word *thesmoi*, not what later became the standard word, *nomoi*. This was not merely for technical, metrical reasons, but because *thesmoi* both was the current term in his day (it survived in the collective name of the six Thesmothetai who formed the majority of Athens' nine annually selected chief executive officers, the Archons) and carried the august overtone of regulations that were divinely inspired and authorised. That overtone, too, was preserved in current usage even after *nomoi* had become available to mean both secular and divine 'laws'.

What little reliable evidence we have suggests that the political essence of Solon's reforms consisted in a twofold movement. On the one hand, he aimed to deprive the self-styled 'best' (*aristoi*), the ruling hereditary aristocracy of Athens known collectively as Eupatridai or 'descendants of good fathers', of their monopoly of political power and to throw open the major offices of government to the wealthiest Athenian citizens. On the other hand, he aimed to give a voice – including the formal registering of decisive votes – on some major public issues to ordinary, poor citizens. The latter move certainly marked a major advance in status and privilege for the majority of Athenians, but – as shall be made clear – it did not amount to anything like granting majority citizen rule.

Almost three centuries later the author of an extant *Athenian Constitution* (*Athenaiôn Politeia*, or *Ath. Pol.*) surveyed what he saw as the progressive political development of Athens from the time of Theseus to the end of the fifth century. This work, attributed to Aristotle but very likely by a pupil, was composed in the unimaginably different conditions of the latter part of the fourth century, by when Athens had been a democracy for well over a century. Since Solon was also by then credited with being a founding father of that democracy, a large degree of anachronism is to be expected, and indeed occurs. For conspicuous example, the author (*Ath. Pol.* 9.1, as translated by Rhodes 1984, modified) attributes to Solon's legislation a *politeia* of which the 'three most demotic [see below] features' were:

first and most important, the ban on loans on the security of the person; next, permission for anyone who wished to seek retribution for those who were wronged; and the one which is said particularly to have contributed to the power of the masses, the right of appeal to the jury-court – for when the people are masters of the vote they are masters of the constitution.

(i) It is interesting, to say the least, that the author puts economic reform first. Athens had clearly been suffering for some time an economic crisis, at the heart of which lay rural, agrarian debt; and one of the consequences of debt for ordinary Athenians was a form of bondage, the loss of personal freedom. Solon's 'shaking-off of burdens' (*Seisachtheia*), as he called it, consisted centrally of a universal cancellation of existing debts – coupled with a legal prohibition for the future on giving one's own body as security for a loan. Thereafter, so long as the letter of the law was observed, no Athenian could be enslaved legally within the *polis* of Athens, and, conversely, the possession and exercise of citizenship necessarily entailed personal freedom.

Already in Solon's own poems we find the notion of freedom used as a metaphor: he says he 'freed' the black earth (from stone markers, which somehow indicated that the land was not the former owner's to use and dispose of freely as he wished). But the literal, legal sense of freedom for Athenian citizens was much the more important, substantively as well as symbolically. For it had a key socio-economic consequence too. The Athenian elite who hitherto had been able to reduce Athenian citizens to quasi- or actual slave status now had to find other human beings to perform those necessary economic tasks for them; in other words, genuine slaves in the full sense – natally alienated outsiders compelled to labour by brute force backed up by the force of the law. Typically, in order to acquire such slaves, the Athenians – like other Greeks – now began decisively to turn to non-Greek barbarians. These slaves were later labelled *argurônêtoi,* literally 'bought by silver' (sc. money) in the rapidly growing slave markets of the Aegean, notably the offshore island of Chios. And they were, moreover, chattel slaves, wholly owned and depersonalised commodities treated as mere items of property.

(ii) Under the developed Athenian democracy of the later fifth and (as restored in 403) the fourth century, the volunteer principle was firmly and explicitly established. Any citizen 'who wished' was invited to address the Assembly. Any citizen 'who wished' was invited to read the decrees and other decisions of the Assembly publicly inscribed and displayed on stone or bronze tablets. Most relevantly here, any citizen 'who wished' was invited to bring a lawsuit on matters of importance to the Athenian community as a whole, regardless of whether the matter in question directly affected that citizen or not; and such a lawsuit was formally labelled a *graphê* ('writ') to distinguish it from a *dikê* that only parties directly affected by the matter (e.g. a homicide) could bring. But in Solon's day *dikê* had meant either justice as a general concept or any sort of litigation or lawsuit, not yet a particular defined class of lawsuits. There is therefore at the very least some anachronism at work here in *Ath. Pol.*'s (mis)representation of the second 'most demotic' feature of Solon's reform package.

(iii) *A fortiori*, the implication of the third 'most demotic' feature is wildly anachronistic. The Athenian *dêmos* could not be accurately said to have become 'masters of the state' (*politeia*) until well after Solon. All the same, the establishment by Solon of a court of appeal known probably as the Heliaia ('assembly', literally, though to be distinguished from the political assembly, called Ekklêsia) was indeed the forerunner of a system of properly democratic courts and litigation, and it was here if anywhere that the fundamental, egalitarian democratic principle of 'one citizen – one vote' was very likely first instantiated (Larsen 1949). That is, not only were the appeal-court members to decide the appeals by formal vote, but their votes were to be delivered individually and counted individually – and equally.

It remains, though, very unclear just exactly which (class of) citizens were to be entitled to membership of this new court. The likeliest hypothesis, in my judgement, is that entitlement would have extended no lower in the social scale than to members of the hoplite class, that is, to those who could afford to equip themselves as heavy-armed infantrymen fighting in a more or less well-ordered phalanx formation (Hanson 1995) – and that would have accounted for only about a third of all citizens at most. Nevertheless, such a body could justifiably be considered as representative of the *dêmos*, in the sense of the sub-elite masses, and as set in judgement over the elite: that is, the well-born and now also, thanks to Solon, the (not so well-born) rich, who jointly were granted exclusive access to executive and legislative power.

I have reproduced above the excellent translation of Peter Rhodes, but changed his 'most democratic' to 'most demotic'. Greek *dêmotikôtata* can indeed be used to mean 'most democratic', and very possibly that is how the author writing in the third quarter of the fourth century BCE meant the superlative adjective to be taken. As my first Cambridge doctoral student (Stephen Todd) insistently pointed out to me, however, before Rhodes' translation appeared, it literally means 'most in favour of (*or* in the interests of) the *dêmos*', and that is indeed how Martin Dreher's equally excellent German translation (1993) renders it: 'volksfreundlichsten'. That falls well short of entailing full or even partial democracy on the ancient Greek understanding, and corresponds perfectly to Solon's own retrospective construction of what he thought or claimed he had done – namely, as we have seen: 'I gave the common people (*dêmos*) as much privilege as they needed.' That is to say, more, much more, than the old ruling aristocratic elite reckoned their sordid inferiors deserved, but significantly less than at least some of the more articulate and politically conscious among these hitherto subordinated citizens were vociferously demanding.

The fact that Solon's laws were not just written down but displayed publicly and centrally is another feature of them that anticipates an essential feature of Athenian democratic ideology, instantiated with conspicuous regularity. It would be strictly anachronistic, however, to describe Solon as in any sense a democrat – though that is precisely what, much later, the Athenians did in mythologising vein. At most, if we are to speak historically, certain of Solon's measures might be allowed to acquire retrospectively a proto-democratic connotation.

Let me conclude this chapter by trying to place what Solon did actually achieve in the widest possible Greek context. First, he set his face against, and through his reforms put an end to, old-style non-responsible government by an elite of birth. Of course, mere birth without accompanying wealth would have been pretty impotent, and Aristotle's definition of aristocracy (*Pol.* 1301b) as birth *plus* ancient wealth gives away that it was not just *Blut* (blood) but *Boden* (earth – landed property) and its accompaniments as well, such as the breeding and rearing of horses in a country with extremely restricted pasture land, that had been the basis of Athenian aristocratic status and power. The wider the circle of those outside the old aristocracy whose wealth equalled or exceeded that of the aristocrats became, however, the more vocally and visually aristocrats liked to insist on the unique and indefeasible claims of noble birth (*eugeneia*) and bloodlines – genes, as we would say today. For example, they went to enormous trouble and expense to project an ideal image of themselves, especially through the setting up of marble statues of the *kouros* (naked youth, often over-life-size) type, which proliferated from about 600 (precisely Solon's time) onwards. Solon, though himself an aristocrat, to his great credit rose above all that ideological clamour.

Archaic Greek aristocrats and aristocracy nevertheless did not lack for supporters elsewhere than in Athens well into the fifth century (the poets Alcaeus, Ibycus, Stesichorus, Simonides and Pindar were all full of praise for *eugeneia*). Indeed, they have even had their modern defenders, such as Chester Starr (1992: 15), who insisted that the aristocrats' constitutional guarantees of justice were nothing less than 'the spiritual base of the *polis*'. Such insistence does ring rather hollow, however, when set against the fact that well before Solon's time, at Corinth, anti-aristocratic political propaganda had taken precisely the form of a claim to set Corinth to rights – that is, institute a regime of justice conspicuously absent under the hereditary regime of the Bacchiads. The successful issuer of that claim was Cypselus, himself an aristocrat, but one who by overthrowing the ruling Bacchiad aristocracy of his native city in about 650 had become the earliest known sole ruler of the type called 'tyrant' (*turannos*): an extra-constitutional sole ruler, dependent for his authority ultimately on force (provided by the hoplites), but not necessarily ruling despotically – indeed, Greek tyrants of the so-called 'age of tyrants' (roughly 650–480) might actually proclaim themselves champions of the people and even behave as if they really were (Morgan 2003).

For Solon, however, that proclamation was not enough. It was precisely because tyranny was not legally grounded that he explicitly abjured such a form of power for himself, even though he had supporters calling upon him to seize it, and he warned his fellow citizens of the dangers of tyranny, which were, as he rightly foresaw, impending. Tyranny is indeed what Athens got, a generation or so after the passage of his reforms into law, in the shape of the dynasty of Peisistratus and his son Hippias, who ruled Athens from about 545 (after a couple of false starts) until 510. It was a peculiarity of Athens, however – and one that does much to explain the peculiarity of Athens' transition to democracy more or less directly from a regime of tyranny (see chapter 5) – that the Peisistratids largely upheld, at least in principle, the system of government introduced by Solon. They tampered with elections to the archonship, but otherwise did not formally undermine the new Solonian political structure. Besides, they enacted further necessary reforms that had the effect of solidifying the relatively large, disparate and far-flung *polis* territory of Attica into a consciously unified and centralised entity.

Solon had thus sought to shield his *polis* from the forms of one-man rule, *mon-arkhia*, that had hitherto affected or afflicted much of the Greek world. Against them he proposed what would later become known as *olig-arkhia*, the rule of a few (Ostwald 2000). He did so in a very particular form, though as a pioneer of a 'middle way'. Very interestingly, Solon described himself as standing 'in the middle' between the two main contending political forces, the elite rich and well-born, on the one hand, and the mass of the poor, on the other. Later, anachronistically, he was himself also regarded as having been 'middling' in his socio-economic status, and standing publicly for the interests of such 'middling' citizens by introducing a 'middling' constitution. In fact, the main thrust of the contemporary discourse of 'middleness' – quite widely dispersed in Greece – was quite narrowly anti-aristocratic, privileging the interests and demands of well-to-do citizens who were not by birth *aristoi*, and who believed there was a need for a widening of the effective power-holding franchise beyond the old elite aristocracy – such as Solon himself did effect at Athens.

Phocylides of Miletus in Ionia was probably endorsing such an approach when he wrote (around the mid-sixth century): 'Many things are best for those in the middle; it is in the middle that I want to be in the *polis*' (fr. 12). A neat concrete instance of such 'middling ideology', also from the sixth century and also from Miletus, is preserved through oral tradition by Herodotus (5.28–9). Internal political dissension in this leading Asiatic Greek city had reportedly reached such a pitch that there was felt – as at Athens in *c.* 600 – an imperative need for independent arbitration. Whereas the Athenians had managed to find an internal arbitrator in Solon, however, the Milesians felt obliged to look outside, and selected for the purpose some no doubt distinguished and wealthy men from the Cycladic island of Paros. After conducting an on-the-spot inspection – not just of the central place but, rather, of the farmland surrounding the town centre – these arbitrators awarded the controlling share of government to those whose fields seemed best managed and tilled – that is, to the most prosperous of the middling agrarian hoplites (Hanson 1995). That story may well be *ben trovato* rather than strictly *vero*, but something like that situation was the outcome of a process affecting much of Hellas during the sixth century, of which Solon was an early intellectual harbinger.

At any rate, it seems that, apart from the reactionary island state of Aegina (a sort of anti-*polis* to its near-neighbour Athens), there was no ruling aristocracy functioning anywhere in the Greek world after 500. Instead, the norm by then – as heralded by Solon's reforms at Athens – was rule by moderate oligarchies of wealth. It took some while, though, both for the word 'oligarchy' to be coined and for it to be (variously) theorised (from Herodotus 3.81 on) or, eventually, caricatured (see the 'Character' of the 'Oligarchic man' as limned by Aristotle's star pupil Theophrastus of Lesbos). At the opposite, visceral, gut-conviction, end of the spectrum, however, from the moderate, speculative, ideal or fictional, there was no shortage of ideological oligarchs on the ground. Indeed, some, as democracy became more widespread and the political struggle between democrats and oligarchs intensified, were prepared actually to swear a religiously binding oath to plot as much harm as possible against the hated Demos (Aristotle, *Pol.* 1310a8–12, with de Ste. Croix 1983: 73).

A collective form of such visceral anti-democratic oligarchy might well attract the label of *dunasteia* (collective tyranny), as for example in the case of the 'Thirty Tyrants' at Athens in 404/3. This vicious junta was led both theoretically and practically by the pro-Spartan Critias, whose sculpted tombstone apparently showed a woman representing Oligarchy literally torching a female figure representing Democracy. In the long run, as Critias would have noted with grim satisfaction, oligarchy won out over democracy by a considerable distance. Nevertheless, even the oligarchs who dominated the Greek cities from Alexander's time onwards (narrative V) were well reminded by Plutarch's 'Advice on public life' pamphlet of the Roman proconsular jackboot that loomed menacingly over their heads (chapter 10).

The order of the chapters in this book broadly follows the historical movement of *polis* governance. We began with monarchy and aristocracy as attested in fiction (Homer) and in fact (Hesiod's Boeotian *basileis*, literally 'kings', and the nobles of pre-Solonian Athens). From there we have moved on to oligarchy, not yet so called, in Solon's 'constitution' as drawn up for, accepted by and published in the midst of the Athenians in 594/3. Hereafter, in entering the classical phase of Greek political history, we shall progress (certainly) to democracy properly so called, before regressing (perhaps) to the recrudescence of monarchy in the Greek world, thanks especially to Alexander the Great of Macedon. He, moreover, originated from an *ethnos-* not *polis*-type state, and inaugurated an era dominated by territorial monarchies, although there persisted still in the post-Alexander period some residue of *polis* autonomy, and even some democracy, if in a much-reduced sense of that term.

# CHAPTER 5

# Rule by all: the Athenian revolution,
## C. 500 BCE

You can never have a revolution to establish a democracy. You must
have a democracy in order to have a revolution.
(G. K. Chesterton, *Tremendous Trifles*, 1909)

To one who advised him to set up a democracy in Sparta, 'Pray,' said Lycurgus, 'do
you first set up a democracy in your own house.' (Plutarch, 'Sayings of Spartans',
*Moral Essays* 228cd)

### INTRODUCTION

In 1993, or thereabouts, the notional 2,500th anniversary of the reforms
at Athens credited (or debited) to Cleisthenes in 508/7 BCE was widely
commemorated in the academies of the Western world. This was largely
on the grounds that the introduction of these reforms was at least a strong
candidate for marking the origin of democracy in the world *tout court*,
not only at Athens. More recently, however, there have been powerful
voices – both from within ancient history (Detienne 2007) and from
without (Goody 2006) – arguing against what they see as inappropriate
Hellenocentrism. The Greeks, they urge, are not our – or at any rate not
our unique – ancestors in the political sphere, and exaggerated as well as
falsely based homage to the ancient Greeks has, they believe, distracted
attention from the no less, or even more, important fact that many other
peoples in history have made breakthroughs, even revolutions, into forms
of democracy. Without wishing to diminish let alone disparage these other
alleged democratic or (often) 'democratic' advances, I submit that on sound
comparative grounds the palm must still be awarded to the Greeks, and
in terms of absolute priority to the Athenians specifically. Comparison
should serve to highlight differences as well as noting relevant similari-
ties, and the Hellenic institutional and ideological complex – of the *polis*
together with the citizen *plus* politics in the strong sense *plus* the institu-
tionalising of the direct, unmediated, decisive power of the non-aristocratic

ordinary citizen people – seems to me one not found anywhere else in the world before the late sixth century BCE in Athens, and not one that has appeared with any frequency or strength anywhere else in the world, for that matter.

The near-coincidence of 1993 with the ending of the Soviet empire of 'people's democracies' lent the commemorations extra force. A decade and a half further on, following the flawed US presidential election of 2000 and the no less flawed war against the Saddam Hussein regime in Iraq in 2003, there are no signs of interest withering any time soon. The democracy we have lost is an ever-recurring and ever-present lament (Barber 1984; Keane 2003; Skocpol 2003). Of the many recent contributions to democracy debates ancient and modern, surely one of the most intriguing is Brook Manville's and Josiah Ober's *A Company of Citizens* – subtitled immodestly, but not immoderately, *What the World's First Democracy Teaches Leaders about Creating Great Organizations* (Manville and Ober 2003). Two other recent and complementary projects catch the attention in this same context: the suitably millennial publication, in 2000, of *The Cambridge History of Greek and Roman Political Thought*, edited by Christopher Rowe and Malcolm Schofield, which naturally privileges ancient democracy's ideological and conceptual dimensions; and the recently completed 'Copenhagen Polis Project', issuing from the Copenhagen Polis Centre directed inimitably by Mogens Hansen, which emphasises instead the practical and empirical dimensions of Greek *polis* life, including the workings of ancient democracy (Hansen 2006).

I began the previous chapter with two possible 'founders' of Athenian democracy, Solon and Cleisthenes. The fate of Cleisthenes' reputation as an Athenian political innovator has, however, been almost the exact opposite of Solon's. In antiquity he sank virtually without trace, while moderns have usually either denied him anything more than a figurehead role in the reform bill associated with his name, debited him with a proto-Machiavellian ambition for disguised personal power or – ultimate degradation and deprivation – sought to transfer the credit for introducing true, or full, democracy at Athens from him to Ephialtes and his junior coadjutant Pericles in the late 460s. In other words, they have done almost anything but endorse the ringing declaration by our nearest contemporary source, Herodotus, who wrote (6.131.1) that Cleisthenes 'introduced the tribes and the democracy for the Athenians'. I shall beg to dissent from the common herd and make a case for the plain Herodotean view – although that view must itself be deconstructed and contextualised, for it is within a much wider framework than the political history of just Athens that the origins and development of democracy in ancient Greece ought now to be contemplated (Robinson 1997; cf. Robinson 2003).

Two other preliminary points follow from and recapitulate the discussion in the first two chapters of this book. First, ancient Greek democracy, like any other *politeia*, was a total social phenomenon, a culture and not merely an institutionalised political system (as we would understand that). Second, all ancient democracies, including therefore that of Athens, differed radically from all modern ones in the following six, often basic, ways: (i) theirs were direct, ours are representative; (ii) in an ancient democracy the *dêmos* (the mass, the majority, the poor) had their grip on power (*kratos*); (iii) there was no separation of powers in any ancient democracy, either in theory (constitutional or philosophical) or in actual political practice; (iv) in ancient democracies, as in indeed in all Greek *poleis* of whatever constitutional or ideological hue, citizenship was construed and constructed actively, as a participatory sharing; (v) the ancient Greeks, including – and perhaps especially – the democratic Athenians, did indeed distinguish a public from a private realm, but the 'rights' they were concerned to protect or encourage were civic/citizen rights, not human rights or minority rights; and (vi) there was no concern, finally, to protect 'the individual' from the State (which in a post-Hobbesian sense did not exist).

## THE INVENTION OF *DÊMOKRATIA*: THE THING

Different, often irreconcilable claims have been made for identifying the 'beginning' of democracy in Greece (let alone the world). One reason for disagreement is that Greek democracy was not a single immutable animal. There were four main species of the genus, according to Aristotle's bio-political classification, and each species could undergo internally generated evolution and even mutation, as well as change resulting from external pressures. What sort, or what stage, of democracy we have in view, therefore, is a very material consideration. Another part of the disagreement is due to the different criteria scholars apply for establishing the existence of 'real' or 'true' or 'full' democracy at Athens or elsewhere. Not least, there are inevitably substantive disagreements, too, over how to interpret the evidence that is deemed usable and relevant. I begin with the last issue.

The earliest ancient source to offer a precise moment for democracy's invention is Herodotus, who (as noted) states categorically that it was the aristocrat Cleisthenes who 'invented the tribes and the democracy for the Athenians' (6.131.1). Later sources occasionally corroborate that statement, but more often they either fail to do so, because they have so little to say about Cleisthenes in general, or positively credit not Cleisthenes but Solon – or even Theseus! – with the invention. Modern scholars have only rarely argued in support of the Solon thesis – and I have argued in the previous chapter that they would be wrong to do so. It seems to me revealing that not even Aristotle, whose ideal democracy was very much less radical and demotic than that which the Athenians of his day (the third quarter of the fourth century) actually enjoyed, would have been able in conscience to classify the post-Solonian Athenian *politeia* as a *dêmokratia*. The most we can, I think, profitably do is identify certain features of Solon's reliably attributed reforms as *proto*-democratic, in the sense that they were found much later on to be integral components of or at least compatible with a genuinely democratic structure of governance. They would not have been even to that degree proto-democratic, however, had not Peisistratus, a tyrant or absolute ruler, chosen to coexist with them, to allow them to operate more or less without interference over a long and internally stable period (*c.* 545–528), such that not even the nearly twenty-year period of much more unstable tyranny that succeeded his reign (528–510) could entirely dislodge them from the general Athenian consciousness.

The other major candidate for the invention of Greek democracy, still at Athens, is the reform bill associated with Ephialtes supported by Pericles in 462/1. A strong case can be made for this Ephialtes–Pericles view. The reform package that the Assembly passed in 462/1 removed the last formal aristocratic piece from the board, the ultimate legal veto of the Areopagus Council of ex-archons (chosen by lot since 487), and replaced it with the full empowerment of the People's Court (the Heliaia, as instantiated by particular jury-courts or *dikastêria*) as a court of first instance, at the same time as the effective power of the people in assembly was reinforced through further administrative strengthening of the Council of 500 that had been introduced by Cleisthenes. A daily 'wage' for People's Court jurymen was added on in the 450s to the use of sortition – the quintessentially democratic mode (see Herodotus 3.80.6) – for selecting archons and most of the other (700 or so?) domestic officials. These measures together helped to ensure the practical realisation of a truly democratic idea of equality of opportunity and participation. All that is true (in my opinion); but it does not amount to saying that democracy per se was invented in 462/1 and, therefore, to denying the truth of Herodotus's categorical statement. The onus of proof (insofar as proof is available) rests on those who would so deny.

For me, in short, the post-462/1 democracy is a different, more evolved democracy, but not Athens' first. I would be the last to deny that the task of defending Herodotus's statement is far from transparently straightforward, however, for two main reasons. First, Herodotus was never at his best (as we historians of political institutions tend to put it) when dealing with the details of political institutions. There is even room for legitimate argument over just how 'political' a historian Herodotus was, though I myself find him perfectly adequately politicised in all sorts of interesting ways, not least in his general contrasting of the political Greeks with the pre-political, non-Greek peoples by whom they were surrounded (Cartledge 1990, 2002), and in his preserving the earliest developed example of political theory properly so called (see chapter 6). Others, such as Norma Thompson (1996), would go further than I believe is justifiable in claiming Herodotus for political thought. The second problem with Herodotus's witness is that it comes riddled with bias, derived from his tainted, anti-democratic sources.

At 5.66.2 Herodotus is describing the means whereby Cleisthenes came to be in a position to introduce what he (Herodotus) later in his own person calls a *dêmokratia* (6.131.1). What exactly does he mean, though, by saying that Cleisthenes *proshetairizetai* the *dêmos*? Here it is most important to consider the point of view from which such terminology would seem natural or usable. For, formally speaking, 'adding (for his own benefit) the people/masses to his *hetair(e)ia*' or 'making (for his own benefit) the people/masses his *hetairoi*' is either an impossibility, a contradiction or, at best, an oxymoron. A *hetair(e)ia* was by definition a small band of *hetairoi* (intimate comrades), and in 507 – or even 407, for that matter – the word *hetairos* retained a good deal of the force of aristocratic peer-group solidarity and comradeship that it had had in Homer. *Proshetairizetai* must, therefore, be being used here in some metaphorical sense, and such a metaphor would, I suggest, come most easily to an aristocratic informant of Herodotus who by no means necessarily endorsed or approved either the means that Cleisthenes so successfully employed or the goal, *dêmokratia*, that he thereby (in Herodotus's view) achieved. On the most economical hypothesis, such an informant would be a fellow aristocrat of Cleisthenes, even a fellow member of the leading political family of the Alcmeonids (since it is tolerably certain that Herodotus counted Alcmeonids among his direct informants), and one who both thoroughly disapproved of Cleisthenes' reforms and regarded their author or sponsor as a traitor to his family and class. Precisely the same attitude would be taken towards the later democratic reformer Pericles, also an Alcmeonid, and for similar reasons (see by implication the Pseudo-Xenophontic *Politeia of the Athenians*, the 'Old Oligarch' [appendix II], 2.20).

In short, Herodotus's use of the formally inaccurate or misleading verb *proshetairizetai* is due, in my view, to his reproduction of an aristocratic, possibly Alcmeonid source, one who was keen to 'spin' Cleisthenes' in fact revolutionary transformation of the terms of the political game as a case of aristocratic 'business as usual'. It is not at all surprising, either, that Herodotus should have been willing to employ such a metaphor, for he himself was by no means a wholehearted advocate of the system the Cleisthenic reforms ushered in. He may have approved of *isêgoria*, equality of free public speech, which he uses as a kind of synecdoche for *dêmokratia* (5.78), because of its transformative impact on Athenian military prowess. Against that, though, he also rather contemptuously reports (5.97) that it was easier in 500/499 to fool 30,000 Athenians than one Spartan (a king). (Actually, never did anything like as many as 30,000 Athenian citizens all gather together in an assembly on the Pnyx hill at the same time; the gross exaggeration is itself revealing of Herodotus's negative attitude.)

Cleisthenes, in other words, did not, in reality, either 'add the people/ masses to his *hetair(e)ia*' or 'make the masses/people his *hetairoi*'. Rather, he transformed the whole nature of Athenian politics, precisely by finessing or overriding the previously taken-for-granted, aristocratic factionalism model of political infighting. This is also what Ober – correctly, in my, view – argues, though on different grounds (below). By appealing to the people as a whole, or, more narrowly, to the effective sub-aristocratic majority of them, and by offering them what he was able to persuade them they wanted from political participation – namely some sort of decisive say – he won them round to his way of thinking and for the first time incorporated them centrally in the political process (see 5.69.2, though that is also biased in its expression). This appeal might be interpreted cynically, at one level, as merely a self-serving and vote-catching political manoeuvre (though I would take a rather more elevated view of it), but it was not at all the same thing as doing what Herodotus's anachronistic phraseology at 5.66.2 misleadingly implies – namely winning them over, as a whole new faction, within the conventional rules of the traditional political game.

Ober would go even further than I. He has put forward a strong, and strongly populist, version of the Cleisthenes view, according to which it was not so much a Cleisthenes acting independently from above, but a Cleisthenes impelled or even compelled by popular pressure from below, who refashioned the Athenian *politeia* into a *dêmokratia*. Nonetheless, the extent to which a genuinely popular or populist self-consciousness can be said really to have existed by 508, and the extent to which such a self-consciousness was the principal driver of the Cleisthenic reform bill, seem to me, among others, highly dubious or problematic. On the other hand,

I do agree with him that some theoretical or proto-theoretical notion of what a *dêmokratia* (not yet so named, of course) might entail was indeed a prerequisite of the success of the sort of mass action that occurred in and after 508. As Aristotle rightly said, one of the conditions for a *politeia* to work is that the relevant people in relevant numbers should actively want it to.

Even more to the immediate point at issue, I also agree with Ober – and Herodotus – that what Cleisthenes introduced for the Athenians was a form, however inchoate, of 'democracy'. My reason for believing that has two dimensions, an internal and an external. Internally, the cardinal fact – which no one, I think, denies – was the invention of the deme. It is common ground, among ancients and moderns alike, that the deme (local village, ward or parish) was crucial to the Cleisthenic reforms, even if the interpretation of its rationale and more especially its motivation has been hotly disputed, and that the deme remained throughout its history the basis of the Athenian democracy. It was through the deme that an Athenian became a citizen – that is, achieved his status as an adult citizen of Athens, by being entered as a member on the written register of one of the 139 or 140 demes. The relevance of that to Herodotus's statement is that the demes were the foundation of the (ten new) tribes that he credits Cleisthenes with creating – and the tribes, in turn, were the basis both of the new central administrative Council of 500 and of the reformed organisation of the state's hoplite army. The further significance of that for our problematic of the mutual relationship of political theory and practice is that the deme thus formed part – indeed, the ultimate building block – of a political system that was both complex and theoretically informed.

So much for the internal dimension. Externally speaking, one critical test of an ancient democracy – that is, of whether a polity was in any useful sense democratic – is how it goes about determining foreign policy, the taking of decisions regarding 'peace and war' in ancient Greek parlance. Immediately in 508/7, then again in 500/499 and most famously in 490, the Athenians in their Assembly took properly democratic decisions: respectively, to seek aid from Persia against Sparta, to aid the Ionians in their revolt from Persia and to resist the Persians in pitched hoplite battle. The actively participating *dêmos* of these years was in socio-economic terms no doubt mainly a hoplite (and above) *dêmos*, very different from the active post-Salamis *dêmos*, in which the poor who rowed the fleet came to preponderate. No doubt, too, the newly introduced Council of 500 was inevitably at first filled by at least reasonably well-off farm-owning demesmen; the archons who were to compose the Areopagus were still elected rather than selected by lot; and the Areopagus they were to compose still held a 'guardianship of the laws' or ultimate veto.

Against all that, however, citizenship and so potential membership of the Assembly were now determined at the level of the local deme, a face-to-face institution if ever there was – as was membership of the Council, which acquired a new, more independent identity vis-à-vis the Areopagus; the new office of the Generalship, filled by open voting within the Assembly, overrode the old post of War Archon (Polemarchos, which was remodelled to serve different, peaceable functions); and the newly galvanised *dêmos* was both politically self-confident and, at least on home soil, militarily effective. It is illegitimate, no doubt, to argue from observed consequences directly back to inferred intentions, but the success of the new regime and its sophisticated articulation would seem at least to imply the existence of some sort of organising intelligence or guiding spirit. More to the point, this new post-Cleisthenic *dêmos* can surely be legitimately held to have been wielding some form of *kratos,* and for that reason this 'Cleisthenes view' is the view of the origins of democracy at Athens that I myself espouse.

In an ancient Greek democratic political community 'the political' (*das Politische*) – that is, the political space or political sphere – was located *es meson* or *en mesôi*, transparently available 'in the middle' to all citizens who wished fully to participate there (Vernant 1965). The famous Periclean Funeral Speech in Thucydides (2.35–46) is in fact not a simple hymn to democracy, by any means, but ideologically slanted and rhetorically overdetermined in all sorts of confusing ways (Yunis 1997; Hesk 2000). Nevertheless, when Thucydides' Pericles is made to say there that Athens's *politeia* was called a *dêmokratia* because governance was effected in the interests of the many (citizens) rather than the few (2.37.1), he was stating a fact; likewise, all allowance made for the exaggeration of the 'we alone', there is a key truth in the claim that 'we alone judge the person who has no share in those [*ta politika*, active political life] to be not (merely) a quietist but useless' (2.40.2).

### THE INVENTION OF THE WORD *DÊMOKRATIA*

Our 'democracy' is derived from Greek *dêmokratia*, literally people-power, but democracy today has little or nothing to do with power or the people, let alone the power of (all) the people. In Athens they did – and said – things very differently. *Dêmokratia*, at first the name for a system of governance, ultimately became sacralised, presumably in response to secular opposition both at home and abroad, as the name of a goddess. We do not know, and probably never will know, who coined the term *dêmokratia*, or how and when precisely it became accepted, but it is worth dwelling a little on the implications of the naming process.

The speech attributed to 'Otanes' in Herodotus's Persian Debate (3.80; see appendix I.2) is a case of the dog that did not bark in the night. For the reasons discussed in chapter 6, he does not label democracy *dêmokratia* but *isonomia*. The earliest attested usages of the term *dêmokratia* as applied to Athens are therefore either Herodotus 6.131.1 (cited above) or those in the so-called 'Old Oligarch' (appendix II), the Pseudo-Xenophontic *Politeia of the Athenians*, which may have been composed as early as the 430s or as late as the 410s, but in my view falls most probably in the 420s, after – I believe – the 'publication' of Herodotus's *Histories*. Hansen once put forward an ingenious argument that to name an Athenian Demokrates, as was done possibly in the 470s but certainly no later than the 460s, implied the existence of the abstract noun by that date, but that is by no means probative. I should myself place greater weight on the phrase *dêmou kratousa kheir* (the 'controlling hand of the *dêmos*') in line 604 of Aeschylus's *Suppliant Women*, a tragedy most plausibly to be dated to 463, where in obedience to the rule of avoiding the most blatant terminological anachronism the playwright seems to use a punningly concrete poetic synecdoche implying the abstract term's prior existence. Regarding both those examples, I would add that the second quarter of the fifth century seems to me the 'right' sort of time for the word to have been coined, for several reasons.

The earliest 'buzzword' used to evoke the post-Cleisthenic political order or system was apparently *isonomia*, precisely the word employed by Herodotus's Otanes. By that seems to have been meant something along the lines of the equality of active citizen privileges under the laws, combined with equality of interpersonal respect. If Herodotus was right, as I am sure he was, in seeing a direct connection between military prowess and political order or perception (5.78), then the Battles of Marathon and Salamis in particular, together with the ostracisms of the 480s (see narrative III) that were respectively their consequences and facilitators, provided the impetus for both institutional and linguistic change. *Dêmokratia* could be no simple replacement or modernising of *isonomia*, however: it could too easily be construed negatively – and that may indeed have been how it was originally meant to be construed, if its inventor was a, literally, anti-democratic individual or group. If that were so, however, why and how did *dêmokratia* become not just current but officially accepted parlance? How, in other words, are we to explain its upward mobility?

The answer, I suggest, is that it occurred as and when members of the Athenian elite (*aristoi*) opted to join rather than try to beat the ever more dominant *dêmos*, by becoming its self-proclaimed 'champions' (*prostatai*). In such a scenario the word *dêmos* would denote primarily the people as a whole, but 'progressive' members of the elite would also have been endorsing an institutional system whereby the poor and humble masses of the people enjoyed preponderant political weight, literally as well as figuratively, and, crucially, seeing them no longer as the despised *kakoi* ('bad') of Solon's time and later, but as equal citizens or sharers in the democratic *politeia*. The absence from all Greece of very much in the way of democratic theory properly so called, even in the fourth century, has often been noted; but the coinage – or maybe the reminting – of *dêmokratia* must have involved at the very least some articulate speculation as to its differences from, and alleged superiorities to, any previous system of governance (see Nippel 1994a, 1994b).

# Narrative III: The classical Greek world I,
## c. 500–400 BCE

Athens was the first Greek, and the world's first, *dêmokratia*. Most of the rest of the Greek world was at first very slow to catch on to democracy's supposed benefits, however. Indeed, in the eastern Mediterranean at any rate, there was something of a revival of tyranny in the first quarter of the fifth century, inspired by the looming menace of an autocratic Persian empire that preferred to deal, as most empires in history always have, with one or a few loyal supporters in its subject communities rather than with a potentially volatile, even disloyal, crowd. In the far west of Hellas, too, in Sicily, the early fifth century was a great age of family-based dynastic tyranny centred on the two major cities of Gela and Syracuse. There personal tyranny could be backed by a triumphant political argument from military success, since under Gelon of Syracuse the Sicilian Greeks repulsed an attempt by the Phoenicians, colonisers of Carthage and western Sicily, to 'barbarise' the entire island.

That success coincided precisely (480–479) with the successful resistance of a handful of loyalist Greek cities to an attempted conquest of mainland Greece by Persia under Great King Xerxes. The leaders of that resistance were, by land and by sea respectively, Sparta and Athens. For Athens, the Graeco-Persian Wars gave a huge boost to the lower orders of ordinary citizens, who (together with some slaves, perhaps) had supplied the muscle power to propel the triple-banked trireme warships (170 rowers in each one) at the victorious naval Battles of Salamis (480) and Mycale (479). An extensified and intensified democratic regime at Athens, building on the foundations laid between 508 and 483, seemed only the natural consequence, though this came at the cost of considerable further internal upheaval involving either the exiling or the murder of the most prominent modernisers.

Themistocles, champion of the navy, was forced out by 470, thanks to the peculiarly democratic process of ostracism: a sort of reverse election, whereby the Athenian *dêmos* collectively selected out the man they most wished to see exiled for ten years. Aeschylus's *Persians* tragedy of 472, sponsored financially by a very young Pericles, had made the strongest possible case for Themistocles as an Athenian hero – though observing the dramatic proprieties by stopping short of actually citing him by name. The Athenians voted otherwise a year or so later, however, and Themistocles was compelled to leave Athens. For most politicians exiled in this way, ostracism spelled the effective end of their careers; only for Themistocles did it mark the beginning of a new one – ironically enough as a pensioner of the very king, Xerxes of Persia, whom he had played such a crucial role in defeating.

Further democratic tweaking – for example, the chief annual executive office below that of the generals was thrown open to the vagaries of the lot in 487 – presaged wholesale democratic reform in the late 460s, associated with the names of Ephialtes and (very much the junior partner at this stage, since he was only about thirty) Pericles. For his pains, Ephialtes was assassinated, but his reforms remained in force, and were consolidated in the 450s under Pericles' leadership. The passage of a revised citizenship law in 451, which narrowed on grounds of legitimate marriage and birth entitlement to the enormously enhanced slew of political privileges open to the mass of ordinary Athenian citizens, set the seal on Athens' enhanced democratisation.

For Sparta, however, the result of the Graeco-Persian Wars had apparently merely confirmed the wisdom of its peculiar political status quo. Even in conservative or reactionary Sparta, though, a regent (Pausanias, victor of Plataea) could be accused of insubordination and, worse, tampering with the helots, for which alleged crimes he suffered a virtual judicial murder. Moreover, within a decade of Plataea a couple of Sparta's allies in the military league that had formed the backbone of the Greeks' resistance to Persia by land were showing suspiciously demotic – if not quite outright democratic – tendencies. They were joined on the populist road by Argos, always Sparta's enemy and rival for hegemony of the Peloponnese. If Sparta favoured oligarchy and oligarchs abroad, that in itself gave a terrific fillip to the democratic cause at Argos. In about 460 democratic Athens and democratic Argos became allies – an alliance to which Aeschylus made a warmly approving reference in his *Oresteia* trilogy of 458 (replacing Homer's authentic Mycenae with an anachronistic 'Argos').

Another of Aeschylus's extant plays of the period was set in Thebes, the city that was often cast as a sort of anti-Athens, an Athens turned upside down. Thebes in Boeotia had long been resolutely oligarchic; indeed, Thebans later shamefacedly explained away their city's pro-Persian leanings at the time of the Persian invasion precisely on the ground that it had then been ruled by a narrow oligarchy, a *dunasteia*, implying that in 480 the majority of Thebans would have taken a more robustly loyalist pro-Hellenic stance if they had been offered the chance. Democratic Athenian expansionism in the 450s brought changes even to stolid Boeotia, however, and in 447 under the joint leadership of Thebes and Orchomenus the Boeotians formed themselves into a progressive kind of unitary federal state on moderately oligarchic lines. Not all Boeotians, however, joined the party even so. Plataea, conspicuously, preferred to remain an ally of Athens and refused to join the federal state altogether – a stance for which in 427 it paid the ultimate price of annihilation as a physical as well as political entity. Within other Boeotian cities there were more or less democratic and/or more or less pro-Athenian factions, which periodically surfaced, only to be slapped down by an ever more dominant Thebes.

Between 460 and 445 there was fought, mainly between the allies of Athens and Sparta, respectively, what has come to be known in retrospect as the First Peloponnesian War. It was early in that conflict that Aeschylus produced his *Oresteia* trilogy, a celebration among much else of Athenian law and – by implication, democratic – order. Seven years later Pericles sealed his predominance by promoting the new citizenship law. Pericles it was too who – as elected general for the umpteenth year in succession – took Athens into 'the' Peloponnesian War fought (with intermissions) from 431 to 404. Thucydides, a combatant and victim as well as the war's most acute observer, noted the increased spread and ferocity of the *polis*'s besetting vice of *stasis* – civil strife, or outright civil war, as was most unhappily exemplified on the island of Corcyra (Corfu) in 427. His older contemporary Herodotus, initially of Halicarnassus and then – thanks also to *stasis* at home – of the new foundation of Thuria (or Thurii) in south Italy, set that observation in context: civil-war *stasis* was, he said, as much worse morally than a united war against an external enemy as war was worse than peace.

He could have been – and probably was – foreshadowing the course and outcome of the savage Peloponnesian war, which had remarkably contradictory implications and consequences for Greek politics, not least democratic politics. On the one hand, it pitted Athens for the first time in war against another seriously large and successful democratic *polis*, Syracuse in Sicily, where democracy had followed upon the overthrow of the tyrant house and was to flourish for half a century until, in its turn, it was overthrown in 405 by yet another tyrant, Dionysius I (ruled 405–367). It was precisely because it was then a democracy that Syracuse was able to respond so flexibly and successfully to a massive assault by Athens between 415 and 413. On the other hand, the Peloponnesian war can be held significantly responsible for one of the ancient Greek world's most controversial political decisions: the trial and excution of Socrates at Athens in 399. A case can be made – and I shall make it (chapter 7) – that according to its own lights the democracy behaved quite properly in condemning Socrates for impiety and political subversion; but that is a deeply controversial view.

The Peloponnesian War, as Thucydides portrayed it, was massively destructive and politically destabilising. Nonetheless, warfare in general, as the enigmatic Ephesian sage Heraclitus had gnomically put it at the very beginning of the fifth century, could also be massively creative, the progenitor of far-reaching changes in thought as well as praxis. Indeed, it was precisely within this turbulent century of intra-Greek internecine civil strife and war that the Greeks – some Greeks, that is, somewhere – invented full-blown political theory, thereby realising the potential unleashed by the explosive creation of the *polis* as a framework both for the political as a general space and for the practice of politics, in a strong sense of that much-misused term.

# CHAPTER 6

# The human measure: the Greek invention of political theory, c. 500–400 BCE

> They that are discontented under a monarchy call it tyranny, and they that are displeased with aristocracy call it oligarchy; so also, they which find themselves grieved under a democracy call it anarchy.
>
> (Thomas Hobbes, *Leviathan*, 1651)

Debates about government and the state go back to the very beginnings of extant Greek literature in *c.* 700. What concerns me here, though, is a narrower and sharper definition of political theories properly so called, according to which they 'are, by and large, articulate, systematic, and explicit versions of the unarticulated, more or less systematic and implicit interpretations, through which plain men and women understand this experience of the actions of others in a way that enables them to respond to it in their own actions' (MacIntyre 1983).

The moment dividing such articulate, theoretical systematisation from implicit practical interpretation is hard to pin down precisely, but its *terminus post quem* (earliest possible date of invention) was the pioneering intellectual activity, from the first half of the sixth century on, of the Milesian School of *historia* ('enquiry'; *historiê* in Ionic Greek dialect), represented above all by Thales, Anaximenes and Anaximander, all of Miletus. In Homer we found political thought, of a sort, but no *polis* to provide its context. In Hesiod we found both the *polis* and a more developed form – and in a more precise sense – of political thought. The beginnings of the transition from political thought to theory may perhaps be traced as early as the Athenian Solon in *c.* 600 BCE (see Vlastos 1946, Irwin 2005 and Lewis 2006), though he looks backwards rather than forwards, partly for intellectual, and partly for political, reasons. The decisive breakthrough came, however, with the mental and symbolic transformation associated with the so-called Ionian Enlightenment of the sixth century BCE.

What these novel Ionian thinkers 'enquired' into was the non-human, 'natural' cosmos, asking especially what the ultimate constituent of all observable matter was. It was, not coincidentally, another Ionian from Miletus, Hecataeus, who in about 500 took the key next step of applying Milesian-style intellectual thought and method to a new subject matter: humankind and the stories told about the human past or pasts. The complex transformation of consciousness that their enquiries collectively implied gave rise to a new non-mythical rationality, and to the birth of historical reflection. In short, a crisis occurred, affecting both the traditional forms of communication and the traditional values that accompanied them. All these factors contributed in their different ways to delineate a series of profound changes in the theory and practice of politics (in the broadest sense) in late archaic Greece: from myth to *logos*, from gift exchange to instituted political exchange, from divine to human understanding, from concrete to abstract reasoning and from unwritten to written law. In sum: from a city of gods to the city of reason (Vernant 1957; cf. Lloyd 1979: ch. 4).

By 500, it might fairly be claimed, the old paradigms for understanding the world of the gods and the – ever more distinct – world of men no longer held good; 'normal science', as it were, would no longer work. There therefore occurred, and had to occur, an intellectual revolution, which not only preceded but also precipitated a political revolution: the revolution of democracy, or, as that term had not yet been invented (chapter 5), *isonomia*. The first detectable sign of the mutual crossover of political revolution and intellectual revolution is to be found in Alcmaeon of Croton's politically derived metaphor of *isonomia* (Rahe 1992: 208–9; see also Vlastos 1953, 1964); the fact that Alcmaeon came from Croton in the very south of Italy indicates further that the intellectual movement he speaks to had spread from the Greek east to the Greek west.

Central to this revolutionary process was what Vernant (in Vernant and Vidal-Naquet 1988) has called the 'tragic moment' at Athens: the old divine and heroic myths were subjected to a democratically inspired rereading within the framework of a revolutionary genre, tragic drama. Tragedy as a religiously inflected art form at Athens goes back to the third quarter of the sixth century, when Athens was ruled by a tyrant dynasty, but a strong case can be mounted that the annual Great or City Dionysia religious festival was reinvented as a democratic tragedy-festival in about 500; that is, soon after – or, rather, as an integral part of – the Cleisthenic intellectual-political revolution. Salient details of Cleisthenes' reforms have been canvassed in chapter 5. Further democratisation of Athenian political institutions occurred in the 480s and the late 460s, the latter promoted by Pericles in association with his senior partner Ephialtes (who was murdered by diehard anti-democrats). A close correlation can be traced, through the career of Aeschylus above all, between the development of Athens as a democracy and the development of political thinking on the tragic stage.

Aeschylus's *Persians* was performed in early spring 472 under the financial sponsorship, as noted, of a very young, pre-political Pericles. It is our earliest extant tragic drama. Among much else, it contains a long and subtle reflection on the salient differences between autocracy and the kind of republican self-government the Athenians were growing familiar with. The Persian great king is painted garishly as a tyrannical figure in the precise democratic sense that he is not responsible, either formally or informally, to those over whom he rules autocratically. A decade later, in *Suppliant Women* (463), Aeschylus offers a reflection on kingship from within a Hellenic perspective. His mythical-era Pelasgus, king of Argos in the Peloponnese, becomes magically transformed into a citizen king, one who before taking a major political decision declares he must await the prior decision of the Assembly of Argos to be taken by the counting of votes. Aeschylus's phrase 'the decisive hand' (*dêmou kratousa kheir*, l. 604) stops this side of gross anachronism, but only just. Since it was by raising their right hands in Assembly that the ordinary citizens of democratic Athens in 463 took all their decisions of public policy, the phrase *dêmou kratousa kheir* comes as close to the (then neologistic) word 'democracy' as the genre would permit (Meier 1993). Five years on, in 458, Aeschylus's great *Oresteia* trilogy problematised human as opposed to divine, temporal as opposed to eternal, justice, by dramatising the inauguration of the court of Areopagus as a court for trying cases of intentional homicide and thereby transferring responsibility for avenging familial blood guilt from the family to the political community as such. In Athens from *c.* 450 on can thus be documented 'a conscious political analysis and reflection . . . continuous, intense and public' (Finley 1983: 123).

Aeschylus remained a dramatist, not a political theorist. Even less of a theorist was his contemporary Pindar, the Theban praise-poet (d. 447). It is a poem of Pindar, however, speaking poetically of the tripartition of governmental authority, that indicates how the politicisation of early Greek philosophy and poetry was on the brink of giving rise to political theory as a separate sub-branch of *historia*. That final crucial step was taken some time during the lifetime of Herodotus, who probably 'published' his *Histories* around 425. The *terminus ante quem* for the emergence of Greek political theory in this strong sense would seem to me to be Herodotus's 'Persian Debate' (3.80–2; appendix I.2), on the meanings and implications of which the rest of this chapter will mainly be focused.

His older contemporary Hippodamus, again not coincidentally from Miletus, had practised literally on the ground the theory of equality he preached. He is the earliest known author of an ideal political utopia (see chapter 9), but he was also commissioned mundanely to remodel Athens' port city of Peiraieus around 450. Another thinker attracted to Athens – clear testimony to its centripetal force as the hub of a growing empire, in a cultural as well as military, political and economic sense – was Protagoras, an almost exact contemporary of Herodotus, who, like Democritus, came from Abdera in northern Greece. He was commissioned to draft laws for the new south Italian foundation of Thuria (or Thurii) sponsored by Athens in *c*. 444/3, and, more to the point, as we shall see, through those laws he bestowed on Thuria a democratic constitution.

Protagoras was a leading figure among the so-called 'ancient' Sophists. These Sophists (capital 'S'), almost all non-Athenians like Protagoras, were a movement, not a school, of thought. Some were generalists, some specialised in one particular area of learning or thought. All, however, were – or claimed to be – experts in and teachers of *sophia* in some sense: wisdom, most generally, or a specific skill or technique or knack (Stüwe and Weber 2004: text 2). *Sophistês* (the agent noun of *sophizomai*, masculine in gender) seems originally to have meant simply a 'wise man'; Solon of Athens is so labelled by Herodotus (1.30), for instance. By the time of Plato (*c*. 428–347), however, the term was just as often used to mean a purveyor of false or fake wisdom, someone who claimed to be able to teach true wisdom but who, actually, was a charlatan, an intellectual con man. Indeed, it was thanks chiefly to Plato, as the famous sixty-seventh chapter of George Grote's *History of Greece* (1846–1856) demonstrates, that the negative sense of *sophistês* won out, and not only in ancient Greek but also in the European languages variously descended from or borrowing from ancient Greek. Hence, for instance, English's unambiguously negative 'sophistry' and 'sophistical', and its ambivalent 'sophisticated'.

Nonetheless, not all Athenians by any means had always shared and endorsed Plato's negative view of all Sophists. Athens, the 'city of words' (in the apt phrase of Simon Goldhill 1988: ch. 3), was full of officially authorised forums for agonistic public debate. The Theatre of Dionysus graced by Aeschylus, Sophocles and Euripides (capacity around 15,000) served this purpose as well as the Assembly (usually 6,000 or so attendees) and the Lawcourts (staffed by large juries of ordinary citizens selected by lot). If we may believe Thucydides' Cleon in the Mytilene debate of 427 (3.37), among other sources, ordinary Athenians also loved listening to informal public debates between Sophists, where the outcome would be purely personal enjoyment or instruction, not decisive public action. Among these debates, formal or informal, public or private, there is one kind that is of direct and central interest to our discussion here: the debate over what was the best form of state, what laws were best and who were best fitted to rule.

The earliest version of such debates on record is preserved in Herodotus, and there are reasons both formal and substantive for supposing that behind at least part of that 'Persian Debate' (3.80–2) lay the thought – however expressed, precisely – of Protagoras of Abdera. Protagoras is known to have written *antilogiai*, two-sided theoretical debates, of which a debased, anonymous example known as the *Dissoi Logoi* ('Twofold Arguments') survives. Herodotus's debate in its preserved literary form is a three-cornered fight, not a *dissoi logoi,* although each individual speech takes the form of a Protagorean antilogy, directed predominantly against one of the other two speeches, not against both equally.

Herodotus asks his hearers and readers to believe that this is a version of a genuine historical debate that originally took place in Susa between three noble Persians in about 522 BCE. That is surely an incredible ask. Wherever one locates, and whenever one dates, the supposed original of Herodotus's version, however, if indeed there was a really existent textual or oral original, it does seem in its extant form to presuppose the emergence of democracy as the 'third term' following rule by one and rule by some. The *terminus post quem* would therefore have to be *c.* 500 or not much before, which is entirely compatible with the shared usage of the key conceptual term *isonomia* both in the literary debate and in post-Cleisthenic Athenian actuality (see below).

Behind the Persian debate lies a stunningly but deceptively simple intuition: that all constitutionally ordered polities must form species subsumable in principle under one of just three genera: rule by one, rule by some or rule by all. That is a beautiful and fruitful hypothesis, marked by the combination of scope and economy that distinguishes all the best Greek theoretical thought. It is this that marks the 'moment' of the first emergence of Greek – indeed, all – political theory properly so called. Fifth-century tragedy, epinician poetry, epideictic oratory, and history all in some sense 'do' political thought, just as the epic and lyric genres of the Archaic period had done before them. The Persian Debate, though, informed as it is by Sophistic discourse, moves qualitatively onto a different and higher plane of political thinking from anything visible previously, in terms both of abstraction and of sophistication: onto the plane of theory proper.

Even so, the nature of the change is in danger of being misrepresented. All Greek political language always remained consciously and deliberately value-laden; there was not even a gesture made towards the – probably in fact unrealisable – ideal of Weberian *wertfrei* ('value-free') political 'science', here or elsewhere. I restrict myself to just one, telling, illustration. The first speaker in the debate is Otanes (see appendix I.2 for a full translation). Although clearly advocating *dêmokratia* – indeed, in a pretty radical or extreme form – he does not actually use the term *dêmokratia*, even though Herodotus in his own voice does employ it elsewhere (see chapter 5 for 6.131.1), including in what he believed to be a Persian connection (6.43). Why does Otanes not? The clue is given by Herodotus himself, when he makes Otanes advocate *isonomiê* and assert that it – not *dêmokratia* – has 'the fairest of names'. For, regardless of whoever precisely first coined *dêmokratia*, and why, and whenever it first became common currency at Athens, the word *dêmokratia* always contained and actively retained the etymological potential for negative interpretation.

That is to say, the word *dêmos*, in the eyes of a member of the socially and economically elite few opinion-makers, did not mean only or merely 'people' (all the people, the citizen body as a whole) but also – and rather – the masses, the poor, the lower-class, often underprivileged, majority of the citizens. Coupled with *kratos*, which had an underlying physically active sense of a 'grip' on power (or on those who were disempowered), *dêmokratia* could therefore be interpreted negatively (by a reactionary Greek anti-democrat) to convey something of the flavour of the Leninist phrase 'the dictatorship of the proletariat'. It was better therefore by far for Otanes to avoid giving a potential linguistic hostage to fortune, and to advocate – as he in fact does – a programme summed up in a single word bearing an intrinsically positive connotation. For all right-minded Greeks of goodwill would surely have agreed that *isonomiê* – equality under or before the laws – was in itself a choiceworthy ideal; any disagreement would concern rather who precisely were to count as relevantly 'equal', and how. It was in this positive sense, it seems, that *isonomia* had been the slogan publicly associated with the democratic political revolution at Athens in 508/7 (chapter 5).

Thus, in short, Otanes' non-use of *dêmokratia* says nothing about whether or not the word was already coined, either at the dramatic date of the debate (it could not have been, since that was *c.* 522) or at the time Herodotus's version of the debate was composed (it almost certainly was, even if the prototype of Otanes' speech goes back to 450 or somewhat earlier). It says everything, on the other hand, about the context-specific resonances of key, value-laden and essentially contested political terminology.

One other feature of the Persian Debate as represented by Herodotus is worth dwelling on: the sophistication of its twofold argumentation (again, see appendix I.2 for the detail). Arguably, it was not until the writings of Plato that philosophy, including political philosophy, developed as a full-blown genre-specific *technê* or skill, though there was still plenty of room for aggressively agonistic claim and counterclaim as to what truly counted as *sophia*. (This indeed was how *sophistês* came to acquire its pejorative overtones.) The Persian Debate nevertheless contrives to anticipate Plato's apparently more comprehensive sixfold analysis of constitutional development, and degeneration, by making each speaker argue *for* what he considers the best and most persuasive version of his preferred constitutional form and *against* what he takes to be the worst and least persuasive.

Thus Otanes argues against autocracy (non-responsible tyranny, the worst form of rule by one) and for 'isonomy' (the best, most egalitarian and fair form of rule by all). Both Megabyzus and Darius argue against mob rule (the worst form of rule by all, since the masses are the 'worst' people, and make the 'worst' decisions); but, whereas Megabyzus advocates aristocracy (the best form of rule by some – the 'best' people will, naturally, make the 'best' decisions), Darius argues against that form as well and in favour of legally sanctioned monarchy (the best form of rule by one – that is, the one obviously 'best' man). Darius, of course, not only gets the last word and in that sense 'wins' the debate, but *has* to win it, since – historically – he did in fact become great king of Persia in *c.* 522, thereby both putting an end to a period of chaotic confusion in large parts of the Persian Empire and becoming in effect its second founder (after Cyrus the Great).

# CHAPTER 7

# The trial of Socrates, 399 BCE

It has been well said that we tend to forget the value of freedom – until we have lost it. Freedom itself is an essentially contested concept (there is no universal agreement on one single core meaning), but there would, I imagine, be widespread assent to the proposition that for the West one particular freedom, freedom of speech, is the most fundamental civil liberty. Without it, there can be no others – or at any rate only in a distinctly weakened sense. There is a high price to be paid for free speech, however: the price of offence, even though feelings of being offended can arguably never by themselves justify any kind of official, state-imposed or state-directed censorship. The trial of Socrates, it has been often thought, constitutes a standing insult to that democratic civil liberty principle. One modern interpreter indeed (I. F. Stone [1988]) has gone so far as to claim that in trying and then condemning Socrates, a man of politically directed speech rather than political action, the democratic Athenians sinned against their own free-speech credo.

Stone was himself a major supporter of the Athenian style of democracy in general, but most intellectuals from Socrates' own day onwards have not been; indeed, they have pretty often been the reverse of supportive (Roberts 1994). One thinks, at once and above all, of Plato and his pupils, not excluding Aristotle, though the Stagirite was far more tolerant than his mentor had been of the majoritarian principle of decision-making as such. Thus the trial and death sentence of Plato's own mentor Socrates have regularly been seen and portrayed as the supremely awful act of censorship by an intolerant, unenlightened, mob-ruled democracy. Even John Stuart Mill, who was in general a defender of the Athenian many against its right-wing oligarchic critics (see Irwin 1998), saw the trial of Socrates as exemplifying what in his tract *On Liberty* (1859) he most feared, namely the tyranny of the majority.

Are Stone and Mill quite correct in their objections, criticisms and fears, though? This is not an easy matter to decide, not only because it is never easy to revisit and reimagine the hothouse atmosphere of a court of law operating under quite different norms and codes from those with which we today might be familiar, but also because the evidence for making a retrospective re-judgement in this particular case is systematically skewed. On the one hand, Socrates is, quite probably, the most famous philosopher ever to have lived, at least within the Western tradition – quite an achievement for a man about whose life (469–399) we know very little for certain, and who apparently never wrote down a word of his philosophy or teachings. On the other hand, as a result we have first-order problems of deciding what were 'his' views, let alone correctly interpreting them. Moreover, as regards his trial for impiety, we hear only the case for the defence; and that case is, besides, conveyed to us only indirectly, with doubly or trebly forked tongue. Not surprisingly, 'the trial of Socrates is a subject that arouses a high degree of moral involvement in many scholars, sometimes at the expense of maintaining an appropriate distance from the historical object' (Giordano-Zecharya 2005: 350).

All the same, with hand on heart and heart in mouth, I shall venture to argue the position that the Athenian jury of 399 BCE, consisting of 501 citizens in good standing duly entered upon the annual album from which jurors for particular cases were randomly drawn by lot on the day of the trial itself, were indeed right to convict Socrates. More especially, I shall argue that they did so on the basis of the main charge, that of impiety. It may perhaps seem odd that it is felt necessary to argue this at all, since the action brought against Socrates was formally a *graphê asebeias*, a writ of (sc. alleging) impiety heard within the court presided over by the basileus ('king'), the archon responsible for the oversight and enforcement of major religious law. Socrates' own defenders at the time, however, and probably the majority of interpreters since then, have thought or claimed that the real charge against him, the one that effectually sent him down to his death, concerned relations not between men and gods but between men and men. For them, the real reason for Socrates' arraignment and condemnation was politics in the narrower sense of that word, a continuation by other, legal means of the ugly and often violent political infighting that had disfigured the streets as well as the formal political arenas of Athens for over a decade. I argue against that view; but I would also preface my rebuttal by reiterating (chapter 1) that, in ancient Athens, religion was itself not just politicised but political – part of the essence of 'the political', indeed. It would therefore be anachronistic and misleading to distinguish a 'political' from a 'religious' charge.

I start my attempted defence of the Athenian *dêmos* by setting out a series of four 'articles' concerning religion in the ancient Greek city in general, not only or specifically in the democratic city of Athens in 399. I then present a further series of four 'propositions' regarding the specific circumstances of the city of Athens at that time. The heuristic point of the distinction is this: whereas, according to the four 'articles', classical Athens was a normal Greek city, according to the four 'propositions' not only was Athens a highly abnormal Greek city, but the circumstances of 399 were also highly abnormal when seen within the history of classical, democratic Athens as a whole.

### ARTICLE I

The Greek *polis* was a city of gods as well as of men – or, rather, of gods before men. Being properly Greek was, crucially, knowing your place in the world economy, knowing that you were by unalterable nature not divine and inferior to the divine universe. The Greek city was a concrete, living entity placed under the sure protection of the gods, who would not abandon it as long as it did not abandon them. Religion therefore was implicated with everything, and everything was imbricated with religion – even though the Greeks did not happen to 'have a word for' religion and often used some such periphrasis as 'the things of the gods' (*ta tôn theôn*). Religion thus either determined (or occasioned) human behaviour, above all of a ritual character, or gave to behaviour that was not primarily or exclusively religious a religious dimension, association or at least flavour. For example, a meeting of the Athenian Assembly began with the ritual slaughter of piglets, with whose blood the meeting place on the Pnyx hill was ceremonially purified.

### ARTICLE 2

Greek *polis* religion was not a religion much like those in which (I assume) the vast majority of my readers were brought up, or with which they are at any rate more than vaguely familiar: one or other version of Judaism, Christianity or Islam. Ancient Greek religion, that is, was not a purely spiritual monotheism, revealed and dogmatic, nor essentially a matter of personal faith, or of sacred books interpreted and administered by a professional, vocational, hierarchical priesthood. The distinction and opposition may be summed up as follows: according to the unquestionable dogmas of Judaism, followed by Christianity and Islam, God (singular) created the world; according to the mythology of the pre-Christian Greeks, however, the world pre-existed the gods (and goddesses), whom it in some sense created.

ARTICLE 3

Greek religion was not separable from politics in the broadest sense of communal self-determination and government. In the narrow sense of politicking or political infighting, Greek politics may be separated analytically from religion, though by most modern liberal-democratic standards the link between them was pretty tight even here. For relevant example, a regular Greek term for a revolutionary political conspiracy was *sunômosia*, which means literally a joint oath-fellowship, and oaths were by definition religious, being sworn in the name of the gods (as witnesses and guarantors). Technically speaking, Meletus's indictment of Socrates was an *antômosia*, a counter-oath-swearing: Meletus swore against Socrates in the sight of the gods as his witnesses that what he alleged against him was true. Our naturalised English term 'affidavit', borrowed from Latin, is the equivalent of *antômosia*, but – tellingly – it has lost the powerful original spirit and essence of the Greek term.

ARTICLE 4

Greek *polis* religion down to and beyond Socrates' time was essentially, of its nature, a public matter, expressed primarily by collective ritual action undertaken under communal civic direction. The typical expression of *polis* religion, its beating heart, were its feasts or festivals (*heortai*), which were observed systematically in accordance with an ultimately meteorologically based calendar, the regulation of which was an important part of the *polis*'s business. Hence our modern conceptual dichotomies or polarities, such as action as opposed to belief, or ritual as opposed to faith, were not operative in the classical Greek city. Greek religious ritual itself implied, took for granted, faith, which in its turn was not some more or less explicit intellectual or emotional attribute but something experienced and affirmed implicitly in and through action (including words as well as non-verbal behaviour: for example, the phrase *nomizein tous theous* used in the indictment of Socrates involved questions of belief as well as participation in cult acts).

In terms of those four 'articles', classical democratic Athens was thoroughly normal and typical, only even more so, in that Athens managed to celebrate annually more festivals than any other Greek city. It was very much otherwise with the following four 'propositions', the combined effect of which is to reveal Athens as both an abnormal Greek city in key ways and undergoing in 399 a time of such abnormality within the framework of its own history as to justify use of the often overworked term 'crisis'.

PROPOSITION 1

Athens in 399 was a democracy ('people-power'), as most Greek cities then were not. (That situation was to change within the next quarter-century or so, such that the period from *c.* 380 to 350, which saw for instance the refoundation of the Boeotian federal state on a moderately democratic basis, was the great era of democracy.) It was, moreover, a radical or thoroughgoing democracy, as most Greek democracies were not (either then or later). Only five years earlier, however, Athens had ceased to be a democracy at all, for the second time within a decade. This was thanks to a Sparta-backed coup that brought to power a small cabal or junta of extreme anti-democrats who thoroughly earned their hateful nickname of the Thirty Tyrants. The lessons to be drawn from this experience are twofold. First, Athens more than any other Greek city gave genuine power to the mass of the ordinary, poor citizens; and that *kratos* included religious power, the power to determine what was, and what was not, right and proper behaviour vis-à-vis the gods whom the city recognised. Second, however long established (and Athens had had versions of democracy since 508/7: see chapter 5), democracy was vulnerable and fragile (see narrative III), so that the price of continuing democratic self-government was eternal vigilance. In 399 that need for democratic vigilance was perceived, rightly, to be paramount.

PROPOSITION 2

Democracy was exercised by the people in courts of law no less than in the Assembly. Indeed, according to one definition – Aristotle's (*Politics* Book II, 1274b31–78b5, esp. 1275b19–20) – being a Greek citizen, whatever the city's constitutional complexion, meant 'sharing in office (*arkhê*) and in judicial judgement (*krisis*)'. Though not himself a citizen of Athens, Aristotle was an acute observer of the Athenian scene, and it was probably with Athens in mind that he added that his general definition applied more especially to being the citizen of a democracy. Certainly, the democratic Athenians took the notion of popular jurisdiction in their People's Court as far as it could reasonably go; and they knew nothing – and would have wanted to know less – about the early-modern and still accepted liberal doctrine of the separation of the powers of government (legislative, executive and judicial).

Athenian-style democracy was direct, participatory democracy in more than one sense. The citizen volunteer (*ho boulomenos*, 'he who is willing') who, as Meletus did in 399, brought a public legal action against another citizen did so overtly, ideally, indeed ideologically on behalf of the city as such, thereby fulfilling the role played by the Director of Public Prosecutions in states where government is not so conceived and conducted. Athens, of course, had no DPP, because it chose not to need one. Prosecutors such as Meletus were therefore bound (in more than one sense) to invoke on their side what they represented to be the communal interest: not only what was allegedly in the community's best interests at the time, but what they claimed to be traditionally and conventionally understood as the community's best interests.

In other words, they claimed to have *nomos* (custom and convention) behind them, as well as to be publicly defending *nomos* in the sense of statute, or law and legality more generally. This was in full accord with the dominant ideological conception of what litigation was, and was for, in democratic Athens. In practice, often enough, it was not so much – and sometimes it was not at all – about finding out the truth of what had actually happened in regard to the breach or otherwise of the city's laws. It was, rather, a matter of dispute settlement, involving individuals – of course, the prosecutor and defendant at the least – but also the good of the community as a whole, in the interests of citizen harmony and solidarity. Such dispute settlement could acquire strong religious overtones, like those of a ritual cleansing and purification of the city's Augean stables polluted by alleged criminality, even when the overt content of the court case was not religious – as it was in the trial of Socrates.

### PROPOSITION 3

This generally recognised and accepted social function of litigation at Athens made particularly good sense in the specific context of 399. For Athens was then in crisis – in the modern sense of that Greek-derived term: economic, social, political and, not least, ideological (including religious) crisis. Athens had recently lost a uniquely long, costly and debilitating war, the Atheno-Peloponnesian War of 431–404. Athens had then immediately suffered the second of two exceptionally nasty and brutal bouts of *stasis* – that is, civil discord boiling over into outright civil war and political revolution. On top of Athens' purely military disasters – such as those in Sicily (413) and at Aegospotami in the Hellespont (405) – the city had suffered also what we call a major 'natural' disaster, the Great Plague of 430 and later (this took off perhaps as much as one-third of the citizen population). We sometimes call such disasters 'acts of god', figuratively speaking; for the ancient Athenians, though, they were literally that. Even Pericles the supreme rationalist (who himself died in 429 from the plague's effects) is made by Thucydides (2.64.3) to refer to it as *daimonion*, 'heaven-sent' or supernatural. Ordinary, non-intellectual, believing Athenians would have had no difficulty, or hesitation, in regarding so huge, unexpected, uncanny and untreatable an accident (*sumphora*, which also meant 'disaster') as the work in some sense of a *daimôn* or *daimones* (plural), a supernatural, superhuman power or powers.

On top of that *daimonion* disaster, the Athenians had also been made to suffer during the Atheno-Peloponnesian War two man-made disasters involving relations with the gods. First, in 415, there occurred a widespread mutilation of the herms (stone figures of the god Hermes, sporting an erect phallus) that adorned both private houses and civic shrines. This deed was a darkly ill-omened manoeuvre, as it coincided, no doubt deliberately, with the despatch of the Athenian and allied naval expedition to Sicily, the mightiest armada yet to emerge from a single Greek city, and Hermes among his other divine attributes was the god of travellers. Around the same time the leading promoter of the Sicilian expedition, Alcibiades, a former ward of Pericles, was arraigned for profaning the sacred Eleusinian Mysteries: not exactly parodying them (as is often misleadingly said), but holding unauthorised celebrations of the secret rites within private houses, outside the immediate control of the hereditary Eleusinian priesthood, not to mention the ultimate control of the Athenian people as such – who legislated regularly, most recently in about 422, to try to ensure that the benefits of this near-panhellenic shrine located on Attic soil should accrue differentially to the Athenians. Most Athenians were initiates (*mystai*) in the mystery-cult of Eleusis – hence Aristophanes' use of a chorus made up of initiates for his main chorus in his highly successful *Frogs* comedy of 405. Hence too the arraignment of Alcibiades by his enemies on that particular charge in 415; this was a kind of anticipation of the charging of Socrates, Alcibiades' teacher, with religious crimes that almost all Athenians would unhesitatingly and unthinkingly deem to be heinous and capital.

In the extraordinarily awe-ful circumstances of 399, ordinary pious Athenians were practically bound to ask themselves the following questions:

since the gods (or 'the god', 'the divine') were manifestly angry with the Athenians, causing them to lose the Atheno-Peloponnesian War and experience civil war, suffering so acutely in the process, was this because the Athenians had omitted to honour duly (some of) the established gods, or because there were unestablished gods whom they ought to have been propitiating and honouring but for some reason were not? Put another way, had the gods deserted the Athenians – or had the Athenians deserted the gods? Or both? This is the proper framework within which to consider my final proposition.

### PROPOSITION 4

The Athenians provided a public, political context within which open speculation, not excluding questioning the very existence of the gods, could be taken to the limits – though not beyond them. There were limits – and the limits of official toleration of such intellectual speculation were quite clearly set by public ordinances, which indeed were drawn more tightly as the fifth century proceeded. We do not know when the crime and procedure of the *graphê asebeias* (writ of impiety) under which Socrates was prosecuted were first introduced, nor what exactly the Athenians understood the charge to cover. The Athenian democratic justice system eschewed expert jurisconsults or professional lawyers, so that legal definition or specification of crimes was deliberately left constructively vague. We do know, however (at least, we do if we believe that the sources of Plutarch's *Life of Pericles* chapter 32 were accurate and accurately reported), that at some time during Socrates' adult lifetime a seer (*mantis*) called Diopeithes, a self-styled religious expert, successfully proposed a decree before the Assembly 'relating to the impeachment of those who do not duly recognise the divine matters (*nomizein ta theia*) or who teach doctrines relating to the heavens' – meaning incorrect and untraditional doctrines, especially, perhaps, atheistical ones.

There are problems concerning the historicity of all but one of the trials allegedly held under the auspices or within the ambit of this decree, for example that of Pericles' non-Athenian associate Anaxagoras of Clazomenae. The one certain exception is, of course, the unambiguously historical trial of Socrates. What explains the force, significance and applicability of Diopeithes' decree is that its main target was the thinkers and teachers lumped together, by no means justly, under the opprobrious title of Sophists (*sophistai* – charlatans, quacks: see chapter 6). Plato, however, not Diopeithes, is chiefly responsible for giving the Sophists an enduringly bad name, desperately keen as he was to refute the contemporary Athenian perception that his revered mentor Socrates was nothing but a Sophist. That was how, for prominent example, Aristophanes had portrayed him in his *Clouds* of 423 BCE, significantly privileging (as we shall soon see) the religious dimensions of his alleged sophistry. Against that slur, as he saw it, Plato emphasised above all that Socrates – unlike the purely or largely mercenary Sophists – did not practise his art for sordidly materialistic reasons, and that his pursuit of genuine wisdom was a disinterested quest for the truth, or at least self-enlightenment, even or especially if that came at the cost of creating greater perplexity or bafflement (*aporia*) in his auditors. Socrates, Plato's Socrates, was thus keen to deny that he *knew* anything, in any strong epistemological sense: if he was indeed the wisest man on earth, as the Delphic Oracle (fount of all religious wisdom) was said to have announced, that was (only) because he knew he knew nothing. An overstatement, no doubt, or perhaps, strictly, a logical contradiction, but one that was entirely consistent with the famous Delphic injunction 'Know yourself' (*Gnôthi seauton*) – as indeed was the burden of Socrates' philosophising as a whole, as that is represented by Plato.

Plato's defence of Socrates in particular was far less successful than his attack on the Sophists in general. During a famous show trial over half a century after Socrates' death, the leading politician Aeschines referred back to him and his condemnation as follows (Aeschines 1, *Against Timarchus*, 173): 'Athenians, you had Socrates the Sophist put to death because it appeared that he was the teacher of Critias, [the leading] one of the Thirty who destroyed the democracy.' Actually, during most of Socrates' own lifetime not all Athenians by any means had always shared Plato's negative view of all Sophists, and merely being thought to be a Sophist would not necessarily have been a disaster for Socrates – in ordinary, happy circumstances for the city. In 399, however, Athens was no longer a happy place of free and open speculation and uninhibited debate. It had by then become, thanks to the rigours of the failed Peloponnesian War, precisely the sort of place that Pericles in the version of his funeral speech of 430 attributed to him by Thucydides (2.37) had proudly proclaimed Athens was *not*: 'We do not get into a state with our next-door neighbour if he enjoys himself in his own way, and we do not give him the kind of black looks which, though they do no real harm, do hurt people's feelings. We are free and tolerant in our private lives.' In fact, 'we' (the Athenians) were by 399 acting uncomfortably like the stereotypical traditional Mediterranean villagers – suspicious, conservative, superstitious, irrational. Indeed, even more so than that stereotype suggests, for in 399 the Athenians no longer contented themselves with merely shooting black looks but took their fellow citizens to court and prosecuted them on major capital charges, such as impiety. In 400/399, in fact, there were to our knowledge no fewer than six major public trials, all relating in some way to the disastrous events of the last years of the war and its aftermath.

Two of these six trials – those of Socrates and of the tricksy politician Andocides (charged for his role in the Eleusinian Mysteries and herms scandals of 415) – explicitly involved religion. Insofar as the defendants could be portrayed as irreligious free thinkers, the trials also constituted a popular, anti-Sophistical reaction, literally with a vengeance. For they were seeking to exact revenge for the religious pollution that the Athenians felt they had or might have incurred by harbouring in their midst men who either by word or by deed had allegedly violated the city's most basic religious norms and code. In spirit, therefore, if not also in the letter, these trials breached the oath of amnesty (*amnêstia* – not-remembering) sworn in 403. This, possibly the first general amnesty in all recorded history, was a publicly enacted, ritualistic declaration of official forgetfulness of the 'bad' – that is, anti-democratic – deeds of the years prior to 403, an oath sworn by all Athenians on the restoration of democracy after the tyranny of the Thirty.

The chief prosecutor of Socrates was the little-known Meletus. The charge sheet is preserved, surely accurately, by the third-century CE doxo-graphic biographer Diogenes Laertius (in his *Lives of the Philosophers* 2.40). The accusation, which also took the form of a religious oath or affidavit, comprises a twofold charge, with the first and possibly also the second main charge being further subdivided into two sub-charges. (There is other evidence that Socrates was formally charged with 'making the worse seem the better argument', a standard Sophistic debating trick. That could have been the other half of the 'corrupting the young' charge.)

Meletus, son of Meletus of the deme Pitthus, has brought this charge and lodged this writ against Socrates son of Sophroniscus of the deme Alopêcê. Socrates has broken the law by [Ia] not duly acknowledging the gods whom the *polis* acknowledges and by [Ib] introducing other new divinities. He has also broken the law by (II) corrupting the young. The Penalty proposed is Death.

Charge Ia is negative, an accusation of omission expressed in language very similar to that of Diopeithes' decree: Socrates has not duly recognised the gods that the city recognises. The clue to what Meletus was getting at is provided for us by the far less sophisticated – but, for that very reason, far more instantly comprehensible – of the two *Apologies* (Defence

Speeches) of Socrates that are extant: that composed by another of Socrates' upper-class Athenian disciples, Xenophon. In fact, Socrates seems not to have delivered any sort of coherent *apologia* at his trial but, rather, to have employed, unconventionally, his usual technique of question-and-answer and directed it at the chief prosecutor, Meletus; a fictionalised sample of it is preserved in Plato's version. Xenophon, however, by far the more conventional thinker, predictably offers a standard set-speech defence, integral to which is Socrates' claim that he has indeed duly acknowledged the gods by performing regularly all the sacrifices (*hiera*) that the city requires and enjoins.

Sacrifice, especially in the context of major public festivals, was simultaneously a political and a religious act in the ancient Greek city. Performing – that is, sharing in – sacrifice whether public or private was a key demonstration of good citizenship, and it was the prime means of registering both one's communion with and one's distance from the gods. It was of the essence of Greek religious politics and political religion. Nonetheless, from Socrates' other main apologist, Plato, may perhaps be derived an idea of why the mere fact of Socrates' sacrificial participation might not have been considered an adequate response to the main religious charge against him. It seems that Socrates demanded an added ingredient from worshippers, over and above the mere fact of participation, for the act of sacrifice to be considered efficacious – namely a good mental disposition. It was not enough for him, apparently, that worshippers merely went through the motions, as it were. That added-value demand is somewhat reminiscent of Socrates' equally unconventional construction of the divine, of what it was truly to be a god: for him, a god properly so called had by definition to be morally good (*Euthyphro* 6a-c) – a view that would have astonished an audience brought up on Homer.

Perhaps, though, we are being too demanding. Maybe all Meletus needed to do to win over a majority of the jury was persuade them that Socrates was the sort of person who might have adopted such an unconventional stance, who might have cast doubt in words on the validity of what ordinary conventional Athenians assumed to be proper, efficacious, pious deeds. That assumption might indeed not only sufficiently account for the effectiveness of the charge; it might also explain why Plato in his *Apology* makes Socrates refer back to the *Clouds* of Aristophanes, staged in 423. The Athenians were generally very keen on the theatre, if not theatre-mad, and they had long memories – or, at any rate, effective gossip networks. The Socrates of the *Clouds* had been portrayed as an archetypal Sophist, and, as such, an atheist, in the sense that he wished to replace Zeus as divine governor of the cosmos with a god of his own fabrication, Dinos (Vortex or Whirlpool).

That, not coincidentally, takes us on to charge Ib, that of 'introducing *hetera kaina daimonia*'. Even if those three italicised Greek words were not in fact the actual words used by Meletus, they surely should have been, since they precisely capture the required nuances. Greek had two words for 'other': *heteron* and *allon*. *Heteron* means 'other of two', in this case two kinds of divinities, the good and the bad – a black–white polarisation thoroughly typical of Greek habits of thought, touching the most basic features of their culture (Cartledge 2002). The Greek language also had more than one word for 'new': the choice of *kainon* would have been designed to convey the sense of '*brand* new' – that is, unprecedented. To the Greeks' ways of thinking, any form of novelty was considered by itself to be potentially threatening to the established order. Their expressions for political 'revolution' were *neôterismos* (innovationism) and *neôtera pragmata* (*too* new affairs). The polar opposite of 'new' in these senses was 'traditional', and 'traditional' in Greek was *patrion*, literally 'pertaining to the (fore)fathers' or 'ancestral'. Greek or Athenian official religion could be glossed or even paraphrased as *ta patria*, 'the things of the fathers/ancestors'.

*Daimonia*, thirdly, meant supernatural powers generally. It was not in itself an unambiguously negative term, though the diminutive *-ion* termination was probably meant to imply a lower grade of divinity than *daimôn*, while *daimôn* was itself of a lower status than *theos* ('god'). So perhaps Meletus intended the jury to think of the sort of indistinct, unseen and potentially entirely harmful powers that frequented the Greek underworld and threatened to invade the upper world, rather than of the anthropomorphised gods who inhabited the lofty peak of Mount Olympus. At any rate, it is not at all certain that Meletus intended them to think of what Socrates himself, according to Plato's *Apology*, spoke of as his own personal *daimonion*. By that seems to have been meant a sort of hotline to the divine, an inner voice that Socrates said only ever told him when not to do something, and never positively urged him to any particular course of action. Even that negative force would not have been reassuring news to the jury, however, since it implied the existence of a power outside the regulatory control of the people, and that is just what was at stake in the verb used next by Meletus to describe what Socrates allegedly did with his *hetera kaina damonia*.

This was to 'introduce' (*eishêgoumenos*) them. Here perhaps was Meletus's most brilliant stroke, for there was nothing remotely odd or untraditional, let alone impious, in 'introducing' new divinities at Athens, provided the introduction was done properly – that is, formally, publicly and, above all, democratically (Garland 1992). In the course of the fifth century, indeed, several new official cults had been 'introduced' into the pantheon of divinities officially worshipped by the Athenian state: those of Pan, Asclepius and Bendis, among others, the last (a Thracian goddess) being moreover not only non-Athenian but non-Greek in origin. By implication, therefore, not only had Socrates' *daimonia* not received the seal of official approval, but they were not the sort of *daimonia* that would have been likely to receive it had Socrates attempted – as of course he had not – to 'introduce' them officially.

In short, the religious charges brought against Socrates were as weighty as they could have been, both in general terms – that is, as judged by the normal standards of Athenian piety and its official policing by the democracy – and specifically in the highly charged, highly unstable political circumstances of 399. They would, in my opinion, probably have been sufficient by themselves, if persuasively enough argued, to convince a majority of the 501 jurors to vote Socrates 'guilty'.

Just in case there happened to be a significant number of 'floating voters' on the jury, however, citizens who were either more tolerant of religious deviance on principle or more robust in the face of adversity, or who were not persuaded that Socrates had been impious in the past or that he constituted a genuine religious threat to the community for the future, charge II was, I believe, added as a supplementary for insurance purposes. This was possibly done at the instigation of one of Meletus's two *sunêgoroi* (supporting litigants), most likely the prominent politician Anytus (against whom Plato was to display unusual animus in the *Meno*).

Charge II was a 'political' charge in the narrow sense. It breached the 403 amnesty in spirit, if not formally, since its burden was to accuse Socrates of politically motivated anti-democratic behaviour in the lead-up to and during the regime of the Thirty. This was a breach that the prosecution team knew they would be able to get away with, however. Without accusing Socrates himself in so many words of being an anti-democratic traitor, it implied that Socrates was at the very least guilty by association. For 'corrupting the young' was a euphemistic, allusive way of saying that Socrates had been the teacher of corrupt young men, specifically both of Alcibiades, a proven traitor, and of Critias, leader of the virulently anti-democratic Thirty Tyrants; and it implied that what Socrates had taught them was precisely to be anti-democratic traitors. The syllogism – Socrates taught them, they were traitors; therefore Socrates taught them to be traitors – was logically false, but it would have been none the less persuasive for that. Even if jurors could not decide what 'impiety' exactly was, or whether Socrates was guilty of impiety as charged, they knew a traitor and an enemy of the *dêmos* when they saw one. What they knew, or thought they knew, of Socrates' views on majority rule and of his behaviour under the Thirty would have made him seem to be at the very least not a huge friend of the Athenian *dêmos* or of democratic government per se.

Nevertheless, although Socrates' admirers have been quick to claim that this political charge was the real charge against him, and the real reason why he was convicted, we should, I think, hesitate before leaping to assent to that reading. (It is a separate and massively controversial issue whether Socrates really was anti-democratic, either in theory or in practice.) In major Athenian political trials, the issue to be decided was typically not so much the defendant's guilt on technical grounds as charged but, rather, the good of the community as perceived by the majority of ordinary juror-citizens. Thus, by Athenian democracy's own lights, Socrates was indeed justly condemned by due legal process. Considered in broader religious terms, moreover, the outcome of the trial of Socrates, as of that of Andocides, would have performed something like the function of a collective civic rite of purification and reincorporation: purifying the citizen body by purging it of a cancerous irreligious traitor, and reincorporating it on a renewed, democratic basis.

Precise voting figures are uncertain, but it looks as though something like 280 out of the 501 jurors – a smallish but sufficiently clear-cut majority – voted him 'guilty' as indicted. All the same . . . need the jury also have condemned Socrates to death? This is a separate question, literally. For the kind of trial Socrates underwent (an *agôn timêtos*) was divided procedurally into two parts. In the first, the issue was the defendant's guilt or innocence. In the second, if the majority voted 'guilty', the issue was the nature of the convicted man's penalty (*timê*), and prosecutor and defendant again spoke to that.

Meletus, of course, argued strenuously for the death penalty. Impiety of this sort was, after all, a heinous political crime, and the Athenians had no scruples about inflicting the death sentence in cases in which they felt that major public crimes had been committed that threatened the good of the whole community. Socrates, not unnaturally, demurred. Instead of making a plausible counter-proposal of a truly heavy penalty (exile or a large monetary fine), however, it seems that at first he in effect claimed he ought to be treated as a public benefactor and feted (like an Olympic victor) with free dinners at the city's hearth for the rest of his days. This did not go down well. Nor was his eventual final offer (prompted perhaps by some residual respect for his friends' earnest wishes) of paying a substantial but by no means substantial enough monetary fine a winning move.

So, if Socrates would not himself offer either to pay a really seriously large fine or to remove himself into permanent exile, then he would have to be removed forcibly and irrevocably from the Athenian community by an act of the people. In the event, more jurors (perhaps 340 or so in all) voted for the death sentence than had voted for his guilt in the first place. Even then, though, Socrates need not have died as he did, by a self-administered draught of hemlock in the state prison. He could still have gone into exile, as his friends such as Crito urged.

To them, however, Socrates is said to have replied magnanimously, if also somewhat puzzlingly, that he owed it to the city under whose laws he had been raised to honour those laws to the letter. There is no denying his bravery. He can even be seen as a hero: a new kind of intellectual hero, a martyr to freedom of thought and conscience, who believed – in the famously ringing words attributed to him by Plato (*Apology* 38a) – that 'the unexamined life was not worth living for a human being'. He was in an important sense a voluntary martyr, though, and it is only in retrospect and, often enough, under very different political circumstances and from very different political standpoints from those obtaining at Athens in 399 that the guilt for the manner of his death has been transferred from Socrates to the Athenian people. Wrongly so, as I have tried to show, since the Athenians' democracy and ours are very differently constructed and construed. Whatever the rights or wrongs of 'l'affaire Socrates', however, through his conviction – and death – the Athenians' democracy had in their eyes been cleansed and reaffirmed.

# Narrative IV: The classical Greek world II,
## c. 400–300 BCE

Two of Socrates' former pupils, Xenophon and Plato, drew unambiguously negative lessons from the outcome of Socrates' trial: democracy, they believed, or at any rate democracy Athenian-style, was an irredeemably bad thing. In the real world, however, democracy achieved its widest reach and most powerful embrace precisely during the first half of the fourth century BCE. True, the democracies that were either now established for the first time, or re-established, perhaps after yet another bout of *stasis*, very rarely belonged to the species that Aristotle was to dub the 'last' or most extreme version of democracy. They were, instead, more or less 'moderate' democratic regimes, combining features of pure unfettered democracy, people-power, with more or less oligarchic features of government such as the imposition of a property qualification for eligibility to hold office or/and the use of election (not the lottery) to fill the highest executive offices.

Two of the most striking of the 'new', fourth-century democracies were the island state of Chios and the landlocked *polis* of Thebes, both of which would also become founder members of the Athenians' Second, mainly naval, League, which was established exactly a century after the First, in 378. Thucydides (8.24) had praised the Chian oligarchy of the fifth century for its self-restraint and stability amid prosperity; presumably by that he meant that the richest few Chiots had not abused their position of wealth and power by unduly exploiting or politically oppressing the masses. Thebes, as we have seen, thanks partly to its state of permanent confrontation with its near-neighbour Athens, had also remained resolutely oligarchic during the fifth century. Indeed, in 420, when other allies of Sparta broke temporarily away from their alliance leader and made an unholy pact with Argos, the leaders of the Thebans had refused to do so precisely because they were oligarchs by conviction and felt unable to hold hands, let alone get into bed, with democratic Argos (Thuc. 5.31). What changed the minds of both the Chians and the Thebans in the fourth century was, in a word, Sparta – that is, the way the Spartans had sought to exploit their crucially Persian-assisted victory over Athens by becoming, in the period between 404 and 386, an even more unpleasant and unacceptably interfering and domineering imperialist power than Athens had ever been.

The Second Athenian League of 378 was precisely an anti-Spartan alliance. It was not the smallest of the ironies surrounding it that the six Greek founder-allies proudly proclaimed they were entering upon it in order to enforce observance of the terms of an international agreement worked out by the Spartans conjointly with Persia in 386, the so-called King's Peace (the king in question being Artaxerxes II, who reigned from 404 to 359). In particular, they were proclaiming – accurately enough – that the Spartans were not observing the sworn obligation of every Greek city to respect the 'autonomy' of every other. 'Autonomy', freedom from external intervention and coercion, was the new watchword of fourth-century Greek interstate relations. At its most idealistic, or ideological, it found expression as a desire for the establishment of 'common peace'. Actually, common war of Greek against Greek was more usually the case – hence the need for repeated diplomatic renewals (375, 371, 362) of the supposedly established fact of 'common peace'.

Two of those renewals came hot on the heels of major pitched battles, which had the effect of reordering the precedence among the big three mainland powers, Thebes, Sparta and Athens. Between 382 and 379 Thebes had actually been occupied and garrisoned by Sparta. In 371 a newly democratic, militarily galvanised and expansionist Thebes put paid for good to Sparta's pretensions to big-power status on the battlefield of Leuctra. Thebes and Athens were then technically still allies, as they had been since 378, but the rise of Thebes pushed Athens back into the arms of Sparta, with which in 371 it concluded a lukewarm anti-Theban alliance.

In 362 Athens and Sparta sought ineffectually to cut fire-eating Thebes down to size at Mantinea in Arcadia – Mantinea, a former ally of Sparta, then being a free agent following the collapse of Sparta's Peloponnesian League in 365. Thebes, under the great Epaminondas and Pelopidas, won once again; but Epaminondas himself died, and after 362 Thebes was unable to maintain the kind of continental hegemony it had enjoyed during the decade since Leuctra. The result of the Battle of Mantinea, in the cynical words of Xenophon, was 'even more confusion in Greece than before', by which he really meant that no one mainland Greek state was able to establish a stable dominance – a state of affairs he found all the more regrettable because of the humbling of Sparta, which had done such a magnificent job for so long of propping up decent, right-minded oligarchies staffed by men of Xenophon's own right-wing stamp.

Athens remained a substantial democracy for another forty years, and some would argue more stably so and at least as vigorously, as compared with the supposed 'golden age' of 'Periclean' Athens. Politically speaking, however, the rest of the fourth century is essentially a story of strongman, one-man rule, an age of monarchy. Sicily fell almost entirely under the sway of Syracuse's tyrant Dionysius (405–367) – Dionysius I, as he became in retrospect, since he managed to establish a short-lived successor dynasty. Plato may have believed he might convert either father or son (Dionysius II) to Platonic philosophy, but the Sicilian dynasts themselves proved recalcitrant, and Syracuse experienced the all too prevalent fourth-century Greek pattern of *stasis*-induced instability until intervention in the 330s by Timoleon, a citizen of Syracuse's metropolis Corinth, restored a semblance of Hellenic order.

In Asiatic Greece oligarchy reasserted itself noiselessly under the impact of the dispensation ushered in by the King's Peace, and was reinforced by the machinations of the local despot Mausolus of Caria, who proclaimed his adopted Hellenism by transferring his capital from native Mylasa to Greek Halicarnassus and employing Greek artists and craftsmen. He also, however, engineered the revolts from Athens between 357 and 355 known as the Social War (War of the Allies), which effectively put paid to Athens' pretensions to being a power of any Aegean significance and reduced Greece's capacity to resist any new, external dynast.

In mainland Greece the big story was the rise to supremacy of the hitherto marginal northern kingdom of Macedon, under first King Philip II (359–336) and then his son Alexander III 'the Great' (336–323). Depending on how this is viewed, the triumph of Macedon represented alternatively the triumph of the *ethnos* state or the triumphant resurgence of the monarchic principle in Greek politics. *Ethnos* states are those based on some common principle of nationality or ethnicity. At least initially, they practised a less politicised, less civic, less articulated and sophisticated mode of governance than a typical *polis*. Nevertheless, an *ethnos* state such as the Thessalians could include *poleis* (Crannon and so on) or, like the Arcadians, not only include *poleis* but also coalesce into a federal state with a federal capital (Megalopolis, founded 368). Indeed, an *ethnos* state such as that of the Boeotians was capable both of developing a sophisticated form of oligarchic federalism (from 447) and transforming that (from 378 on) into a – moderately – democratic mode of federal self-governance dominated by a single *polis*, Thebes. In the second quarter of the fourth century, thanks to Epaminondas of Thebes, the federal principle gained a great boost in its moderately democratic form, and attracted the attention even of Aristotle (Huxley 1979). The great age of federal states as power units was yet to come, however, a century later (narrative V), when they proved the most effective means to resist the sovereign ambitions of hegemonic regimes, first of Macedon, then of Rome.

The *ethnos* state that was destined to exert the maximum political impact on all Greeks and Greek history was one that knew nothing of, and wanted to have nothing to do with, the *polis* within its own ethnic boundaries, namely Macedon. Here, too, was a classic case of autocracy tempered by assassination. Until the very end of the fifth century Macedon had been little more than a geographical expression, due chiefly to an extreme form of baronial regionalism. First Archelaus (413–399), however, then (after a nasty interlude of intra-dynastic bloodletting) Philip's father Amyntas III (393–369), had begun the necessary process of unification and centralisation – one that Philip himself developed to an unpredictably fast and vast degree. By 338, indeed, he was so far master of his own destiny in continental Greece that he could contemplate an expedition of Asiatic conquest and liberation at the expense of a by now somewhat enervated Achaemenid Persian monarchy. Philip put in place a Greek alliance system that we know as the League of Corinth, had himself declared its commander-in-chief and then got the tamed delegate council to vote as its first 'Hellenic' measure an expedition of conquest and liberation in Asia. In 336, though, an assassin's dagger put paid to Philip's ambitions, and, whether or not Alexander had had a hand in his father's death, it was certainly he who profited most massively from it.

There was never any doubt in Alexander's mind that he should complete his father's eastern project – whatever exactly that had been: only the advance force had been sent over to north-west Anatolia before the designated commander-in-chief was murdered. There was probably also never a shadow of doubt that from the first Alexander intended to conquer at least the existing Persian Empire, as far east as Afghanistan and western Pakistan today. Before that, though, he had to settle affairs in the Greek mainland and the northern fringes of Macedonia – strategically speaking, his rear – and that pacification cost him two whole years and much controversy, caused above all by his wholesale destruction of Thebes in 335. Partly this was done to punish Thebes for revolting from the League of Corinth, but mainly it served as an object lesson for any other would-be Greek dissenters. Officially, though, it was inscribed for propaganda purposes under the banner of 'Panhellenism', since the Thebans had 'medised' (taken the side of the Persians) in 480/79. Some Greeks had very long memories, others very short ones.

The other most controversial act of Alexander's reign – and there were many such – was the destruction in 330 of the Persian Empire's major symbolic centre, the palace complex at what the Greeks called Persepolis, 'the *polis* of the Persians' (though in fact it was anything but a *polis* in a Greek sense). In a way, Alexander had no choice but to burn Persepolis, in order for the Greeks' revenge for the Persians' sacrilegious sacking of Athens and other holy places in the early fifth century to be seen to have been piously carried out. By sacking Persepolis, however, Alexander was at the same time destroying one of his own capitals, since by then he was claiming to be, and beginning openly to act as if he really were, the legitimate successor to the former Persian dynasty. Indeed, here lies the peculiar genius – and, I would argue, the genuine political contribution – of Alexander: for he wished to become a new kind of Graeco-Oriental monarch, the king of Asia, on an unimaginably vast territorial scale. Just how practical such a wish might have been cannot fully be answered, since Alexander, like his father, was from this earth untimely ripped, more likely from natural causes than through an inevitably rumoured assassination. His early death, at the age of thirty-two in 323, launched a series of funeral games of prolonged competition for the royal and imperial succession among Alexander's family and former marshals and aides that continued until the Battle of Ipsus in 301 and beyond.

In his early teens Alexander had been taught by Aristotle at Mieza in Macedonia – a conjunction, engineered by Philip, of the Greek world's most powerful intellect with its future most powerful ruler. It remains an open question whether that conjunction had definite causal effects or was merely conjunctural. On the other hand, there is no doubt but that Alexander's quite extraordinary reign provoked a flurry of more or less theoretical writing on the subject of monarchy, picking up where the pro-monarchy speaker of Herodotus's imaginary 'Persian debate' and the fourth-century theroreticians such as Xenophon, Plato and Isocrates had left off.

CHAPTER 8

# Rule by one revisited: the politics of Xenophon, Plato, Isocrates, Aristotle – and Alexander the Great, c. 400–330 BCE

## THE TYRANNY OF THE *DÊMOS*

The ambiguity of the term *dêmos* noticed above (chapter 5) – meaning both the citizen body as a whole, and the poor majority of same – laid open *dêmokratia,* the *kratos* of the *dêmos*, to the charge of mob rule. The trope of the *dêmos* as tyrant recurs repeatedly in the non- or anti-democratic theorising of the fifth and fourth centuries, and indeed has recurred ever thereafter, from the fourth century BCE to the American founding father Alexander Hamilton and beyond (Roberts 1994). Plato, towards the end of the *Republic* (563c), enjoys playing with the magnificent conceit that under a regime of ultra-egalitarian democracy even the humblest dumb animals such as donkeys get puffed up with ideas above their proper station in life. Nonetheless, one of the cleverest illustrations of this strong countercurrent of oligarchic sentiment, theory and activity is to be found in a less predictable source, Xenophon of Athens, showing himself in this respect at least a worthy fellow pupil of Socrates (for whom the majority was pretty much always by definition wrong).

The earliest surviving example of Athenian prose, a vehemently anti-democratic 'Athenian constitution', was handed down from antiquity and subsequently printed as being a genuine work of Xenophon. That attribution is demonstrably false, however (see appendix II). The real Xenophon's own, highly derivative oligarchic political theory is to be found elsewhere, partly in the arguments he borrows from others or places in the mouth of his mentor in the work entitled *Memoirs of Socrates*, but more especially in the *Cyropaedia* (further, below, s.v. 'Xenophon').

The *Memoirs* is a collection of imaginary conversations in which Socrates (by then dead) talks with real Athenians about the practical business and the ethical underpinnings of contemporary Athenian politics. In one of these dialogues (I.2.40–6), Xenophon – borrowing no doubt from a much earlier source – gives his version of an imaginary dialogue within a dialogue;

96

supposedly, the original conversation had taken place in the 430s between the great Pericles and his then ward, the teenaged Alcibiades, who, ironically, would do more than any other individual to dissipate and destroy his guardian's political legacy. The subject of their discussion was the validity of laws; here follows an abbreviated translation.

Tell me, Pericles, can you explain to me what a law is?

Laws, Alcibiades, are what the mass of the citizens decree.

Do they think one ought to do good or evil?

Good, of course, my boy, not evil.

But if it's not the masses who come together and enact what is to be done, but – as happens under an oligarchy – a few, what do you call that?

Everything the ruling power in the city decrees is called a 'law'.

What, even if a *tyrant* makes decrees for the citizens, is that a 'law' too?

Yes, whatever a tyrant as ruler enacts, that too is called a 'law'.

But when the stronger compels the weaker to do what he wants, not by persuasion but by force, is that not negation of law?

Well, yes, I suppose so.

Then whatever a tyrant compels the citizens to do by decree, without persuading them, is the negation of law?

Yes, I agree – and I take back my earlier statement that whatever a tyrant enacts without persuasion is law.

Suppose the few make decrees, using force not persuasion – are we to call that coercion?

I should say that all forms of compulsion, whether by decree or otherwise, are a negation of law.

Alcibiades now has Pericles where he wants him, and can deliver the knockout anti-democratic argument (emphasis added):

Then everything the *masses* decree, not persuading but compelling the owners of property [i.e. the few richest citizens], would be coercion not 'law'?

Xenophon – or the oligarchic pamphleteering source from which he drew the original of this 'dialogue' – now permits himself a humorous coda:

Let me tell you, Alcibiades, I too was very clever at this sort of debating when I was your age.

Ah, Pericles, if only I had known you when you were in your prime!

Tyranny or autocracy of any kind was by the end of the fifth century considered to be an unambiguously bad thing (unless one was exercising it oneself . . .), and beautifully stigmatised as such both by Plato (for whom Dionysius I of Syracuse may well have served as the contemporary archetype) and by Aristotle. On the other hand, however, one-man rule in the form of kingship, legitimate monarchy, was by no means excluded from grace on principle. Far from it: indeed, something of a monarchist trend or at least tendency of political thought can be traced during the fourth century, from Isocrates, a younger contemporary of Socrates who outlived him by sixty years, through the 'Socratics' Plato, Xenophon and Aristotle, to, perhaps, the greatest ancient monarch of them all in political practice, Alexander of Macedon, and the intellectuals who buzzed around him.

## ISOCRATES (436–338)

Isocrates of Athens was perhaps aptly named: *isokratia*, though rare, was a term in use for a kind of moderate oligarchy (see chapter 5). Like his younger contemporary Plato, Isocrates set up shop and advertised his wares intellectually in an epideictic show of opposition to rival thinkers, whom he lumped together opportunistically and derogatorily as 'Sophists' (not that this saved him from being tarred with precisely that label himself). Unlike Plato, however, Isocrates was not uncomfortable with the notion and practice of rhetoric. Indeed, having started out as a *rhêtôr*, the ancient Athenian equivalent of a professional politician, he slipped back more into the shadows by becoming a forensic speechwriter, writing speeches, or drafts, for others to work up and deliver. Later still (he had a prodigiously long career) he specialised in the publication of political pamphlets, sometimes dressed up as if they were law-court speeches, sometimes as if they were letters addressed to potentates Greek and non-Greek. The latter career he combined seamlessly with establishing Athens' – and Greece's – first professional school of rhetoric-teaching. Throughout, he was always concerned more with the 'how' of political persuasion (or propaganda) than with the 'what' and the 'why' of moral-political philosophy, and he developed no known metaphysical system (Too 1995).

In his early *To Nicocles*, he foreshadowed a preoccupation with speaking truth to monarchical power, the monarch in question being a Cypriot Greek dynast. In his *Antidosis*, of the mid-350s, he issued a supposed clarion call for a return to the good old days of proper, decent democracy that was in fact a mask for more basic anti-democratic leanings and yearnings. It was in his epistolary 'advice' to King Philip of Macedon in the 340s, however, that Isocrates most nearly 'came out' as a monarchist thinker in all but name. His *Third Letter*, in particular, an 'open letter' designed for wide Greek consumption, points out that, were Philip to succeed in his project of conquering Asia, there would be nothing left for him to do but become a god – so clearly would he have scaled the heights of the possible for a mere mortal human. Whether that makes Isocrates a 'philippiser' who would have been happy for the Macedonian to occupy and rule Athens directly with him as special adviser is an unanswerable question, since Philip actually treated Athens with remarkable restraint after defeating it in 338, but that was what his democratic and arguably more patriotic opponents alleged.

PLATO'S PHILOSOPHER-KINGS

Far more interesting, theoretically, if also far more teasing, pedagogically, is the brand of monarchist thinking adumbrated by Plato through 'Socrates' in his *Republic*: until philosophers became kings and rulers, or rulers became (Platonic) philosophers, this Socrates opines, there would and could be no release for mankind from the manifold political troubles that afflicted it (473e). The real Socrates, however, seems never to have written down a word of his philosophy, thereby leaving *Republic* scholars forever knotted up in the problem of what in this work is Socrates' and what Plato's, a problem compounded by the existence of a very different – far more conventional – Socrates presented by Xenophon, and by Aristophanes' comic caricature (one assumes) of Socrates the Sophist in his *Clouds* of 423.

Even more so than Isocrates, Plato was intellectually committed to being anti-Sophist (see chapter 6). A further reinforcement of that commitment stemmed from the condemnation to death of Socrates in 399, on religious and political charges fuelled by a belief on the part of ordinary Athenians that Socrates was some kind of dangerous freethinking Sophist (chapter 7). If Plato was also politically anti-democratic, as there is every reason to believe, it is one of many ironies surrounding him that his own unfettered but politically ineffectual career as a teacher and writer, not least of the *Republic*, is the 'strongest proof of the *parrhesia* [freedom of speech] Athens so deplorably encouraged' (Brunt 1993: 389). There are some reasons for thinking that Plato did harbour ambitions to change as well as understand the world, and the career of a tyrant such as Clearchus of Heraclea Pontica in the 360s, supposedly a pupil of his, might be invoked in support of that supposition. Indeed, the Academy (shorthand for the school he established in the 380s within a public grove dedicated to the hero Academus) has even been viewed as a kind of proto-Rand Corporation (cf. Brunt 1993: ch. 10).

The usual and more plausible view, however, is that Plato's *Republic* and his political philosophy as a whole were good primarily for thinking with, not acting upon. The Platonic educational curriculum as adumbrated for his ideal rulers of the *Republic* – first, moral training; then mathematics, as a propaedeutic to ontology; and finally dialectic – probably shows his true order of priorities (Brunt 1993: 318 n. 74). Political philosophy and political practice on the basis of Platonic epistemology and ontology were only for those (very) few who possessed the right intellectual equipment, and had passed all the set tests, though for them they were an obligation not an option. All the same, the choice of the term 'kings' to describe the ideally trained Platonic philosopher-rulers is nicely eloquent of the fourth-century intellectualist trend towards monarchist thinking.

## XENOPHON (*c.* 428–355)

'The Socratics' is a technical doxographic term, but it can be extended to include Xenophon as well as Aristotle (below). Like Plato, Xenophon had been an associate and saw himself as a disciple of Socrates, and wrote profusely in defence of their shared mentor's memory and moral regimen. Xenophon's Socratic philosophy is on the whole a poor and etiolated thing by comparison to Plato's, however, despite flashes of (quite probably borrowed) brilliance such as the Pericles–Alcibiades dialogue quoted above.

There is little doubt that Xenophon was himself at best non-democratic in outlook, even if he did perhaps finally return to Athens after many years of exile (below). Among his first political actions as an adult was his presumably enthusiastic participation as a member of the elite cavalry under the infamous oligarchic regime of the Thirty Tyrants (404/3). Soon after the restoration of democracy at Athens he took off far abroad (as far as southern Mesopotamia) to serve as a mercenary under a Persian pretender supported by Sparta, and it was in the service of a Spartan king (Agesilaus II) that he fought at Coronea in Boeotia in 394, still as a mercenary, against his own native city. For that, or for his earlier service with Cyrus the Persian prince, he was formally exiled by popular decree, and watched the events culminating in the downfall of his Spartan benefactors in 371 from a retreat near Olympia.

One passage in his *Hellenic History* out of the several that could have been cited reveals particularly clearly where his political sympathies lay. The wheels of Sparta's Peloponnesian League had long been greased by Sparta's support of oligarchy among the member states of its alliance (Thucydides 1.19). Occasionally, however, a dissident member state might show signs of favouring democracy, or even openly embrace a democratic constitution in defiance of Spartan wishes or requests. One such was the city of Mantinea in Arcadia, always a peculiarly sensitive region for Sparta. In Asiatic Greece, as noted above (p. 93), oligarchy reasserted itself noiselessly under the impact of the dispensation ushered in by the King's Peace of 386. In mainland Greece, Sparta, its principal advocate and beneficiary, seized the moment to intervene forcibly to impose good – oligarchic – discipline and order on Mantinea, above all by demolishing its city walls and decentralising the formerly urbanised settlement pattern. Xenophon notes with relish how, although ordinary Mantineans did not like it, the 'owners of landed property' were delighted, because thanks to Sparta they had 'got rid of all the trouble they had had with the demagogues [one of Xenophon's only two uses of this pejorative term of abuse] and their government was now run on aristocratic lines' (*Hellenic History* 5.2.7). These landed property owners are just the sort of people Xenophon has in mind when he refers to right-minded souls who 'had the best interests of the Peloponnese at heart' (7.4.35, 5.1) – a Peloponnese made safe for more or less conservative oligarchy.

Xenophon's published and extant works cover a very broad spectrum, from historiography, hagiography and political memoirs to an early form of *Tendenzroman*. It is in the latter, the *Cyropaedia* or 'Education of Cyrus', that Xenophon most fully develops his governing idea(l) of benevolent monarchic despotism through the creatively reimagined figure of Cyrus the Great (d. 529), founder of the Achaemenid Persian Empire. Cyrus is characterised above all as a man of *kharis* (grace), a leader who knows how to dispense appropriately, as well as to attract, personal favours and blessings (Azoulay 2004, 2006). Xenophon goes considerably further than this somewhat traditional Greek portrait of an upper-class dynast, however, in making out Cyrus to be an embodiment of law. For Louis XIV 'L'état, c'est moi'. For Xenophon's Cyrus 'La loi, c'est moi'; more specifically, he was a 'seeing law' (*blepôn nomos: Cyropaedia* 8.8) preternaturally gifted with both insight and foresight. This is a far cry, and at the furthest possible remove, from the republican and especially democratic conception of *nomos* that we have explored earlier (chapters 5 and 6).

## ARISTOTLE

Aristotle was in a genealogical sense a Socratic, the best pupil of Socrates' best pupil Plato. Unlike Plato and Xenophon in their publicly expressed attitudes towards Socrates, however, he was not afraid explicitly to confront and confute the teachings of his master Plato. Indeed, he could be said to have turned Plato (at any rate the Plato of the *Republic*) on his head, as Karl Marx was to do to Hegel, in the sense that he chose to base his political theses and theories on empirically validated consensus among the *phronimoi* (practically wise men of experience and good sense) rather than axiomatic metaphysical postulates obscurely accessible only to a very few intellectuals. (Raphael's famous 'School of Athens' fresco neatly captures this antithetical stance of the two philosophers, showing Plato gesturing heavenwards, and Aristotle, ever the pragmatic idealist, pointing pointedly towards *terra firma* – and firmly *cognita*.) Aristotle, predictably, presented himself as the golden mediator between, on one hand, the 'ultimate democracy' exemplified by that of Athens, which he misrepresented as rule by an anarchic mob over – at the expense of – the laws, and, on the other, the extreme anti-democratic authoritarianism of Plato.

He was no more an ideological or intellectual democrat than Plato, however – unsurprisingly, since the known and certain exceptions to the rule that ancient Greek intellectuals were anti-democrats can be counted on the fingers of one hand: Pericles, Hippodamus, Protagoras, Democritus... Aristotle's ideal statesman was an idealised, and probably unrealisable, figure – 'exceptionally distinguished on account of virtue' (*Politics* 1284b28). It would be as unseemly and wrong for other, more ordinary citizens to rule over him as for humans to claim rule over Zeus – which is another, rather more rhetorically striking way of making the same sort of point as Isocrates in his open letter to Philip (above). It therefore seemed to Aristotle 'natural' for 'everyone to obey such a man gladly, so that men of that sort may be eternally *kings in the cities*' (1284b32–4; emphasis added). Pragmatism, though, swiftly kicks in, and this virtuous paragon of a kingly ruler is left on one side as Aristotle goes on to explore the pluses and minuses of the types of kings that did actually exist or had existed in the past.

Negatively, too, Aristotle went out of his way to denigrate the essence, or goal, of democratic sociability and self-government as merely a case of 'living as you please' (*Politics* 1317b10–14; cf. 1319b30). This was in accordance with his fundamental method of political-philosophical analysis and prescription, namely to proceed from the *phainomena* and *endoxa*, the reputable opinions of reputable persons, to what ideally and ideologically he thought should be the case, other things being equal (Cartledge 2002: index s.v. 'Aristotle, method of'). This method did enable him to give a much fuller and fairer appreciation of a democratic point of view than was normal among democracy's critics – indeed, to go so far as to concede that, in terms of a kind of social contract idea of decision-making, the opinions of the majority were likely on average and on the whole to be no worse in practice than those of an elite few. On the other hand, just as in his doctrine of the essence of natural slavery (Cartledge 2002: 135–41), so in his exposition of the essence of natural democracy (as it were), Aristotle allowed his prejudices to get the better of his intellect, so badly did he want and need the doctrines he was advocating – against democracy, for natural slavery – to be true. The telltale sign here is his overstatement of his case. For, he claims, so pre-eminently do all ideological democrats privilege their libertarian notion of freedom (freedom from, in Isaiah Berlin's terms) that they ideally wish there to be no constraints on their freedom of political action (freedom to) whatsoever. Thus, in effect, he accuses them of being anarchists, or would-be anarchists.

From there it was a relatively small step to identifying in all democracy by definition an innate predisposition to lawlessness, including the over-riding of the notionally permanent laws by temporary decrees, and even to classifying the 'last' or 'ultimate' democracy (by which Aristotle surely meant a democracy like that of his contemporary Athens) as precisely that in which the *dêmos* does not see itself as bound by the laws. That, indeed, is exactly what he means by the charge of 'living as you please'. 'Foul!' a genuine ideological democrat would surely – and legitimately – have objected.

So, if the thoroughly virtuous king was an ideal unattainable in practice, Plato's philosopher-kings unbelievable in theory, and mass rule undesir-able in both theory and practice, what for Aristotle was the 'best-case' constitutional scenario? A form of aristocracy – in practice, oligarchy – involving the rule of a few wealthy but morally admirable and imitable elites: a system that in its practically realisable form he very confusingly called *politeia* (usually transliterated 'polity'), and which represented a char-acteristically Aristotelian mixture or 'mean' between extremes, in which the preponderance of political power rested with the economically 'middling', hoplite-class citizens.

What gives particular poignancy to Aristotle's theorising about an ideal regime and to his brief indulgence in the dream of an all-virtuous king is that for a period in the late 340s he actually taught a future king, the thirteen-year-old Alexander of Macedon, and therefore potentially had the opportunity to influence decisively the thinking and practice of the ancient Greek world's future suzerain. Perhaps it was precisely his experience as both teacher and subject of Alexander that led him to his pragmatic rejection of the 'all-virtuous king' ideal (Rahe 1992: 908; Brunt 1993: 334–7).

## THEORISING AROUND ALEXANDER

The political-theoretical views of Alexander himself are impossible to dis-cern with any confidence, since he has left no personal writings, and reliable sources 'close' to him have not survived either. Clearly, he was no sort of ideological democrat, though for pragmatic purposes he could play the democratic card. Thus in Greek Asia Minor in 334 his public advocacy of democracy was merely a temporary expedient to foster the Asiatic Greeks' disaffection from a Persian imperial overlordship that systematically supported oligarchy, or even tyranny. Likewise, in an inscription of that same year (recorded by his best historian, Arrian, in his *Anabasis* 1.16), he could display a certain sensitivity towards the anti-monarchist sentiments of at any rate one of his subject Greek cities, democratic Athens – at least early on in his reign. For after his first victory over his Persian adversaries, at the battle of the river Granicus, he sent back to Athens 300 suits of armour as a trophy, accompanied by the following dedicatory inscription: 'Alexander and the Greeks, except the Spartans, dedicate these' – to Athena of the city of Athens. Spot the deliberate omission: no mention of the title 'king', which technically, of course, applied only to his immediate Macedonian subjects.

As the anti-Persian campaign proceeded, however, Alexander had no choice but to promote himself more and more as a king, indeed as a new-style king of Asia, to win the hearts and minds as well as the submissiveness of his new, non-Greek Asiatic subjects. Moreover, he promoted himself not just as a king but also as a living god, for the supposed benefit not only of his oriental but also his Greek subjects (see further below). That was a step too far for his Greek official historian, Callisthenes of Olynthus, a relative of Aristotle; but his all-too public opposition to what he saw as Alexander's unacceptably despotic orientalism cost him his own life.

Alexander included philosophers as well as a historian in his entourage, most prominently Anaxarchus of Abdera (city of Protagoras and Democritus). His philosophy has been aptly described as a mixture of 'skepticism, vigorous pursuit of personal happiness, and nihilism' (Roisman 2003: 305). One thing we may be sure of: he did not oppose Alexander's step up to living godhead, however it may have been justified. Indeed, a large number of more or less professional philosophers and writers from the last quarter of the fourth century BCE onwards adopted Alexander as their ideal embodiment of divine or divinely authorised kingship. Others, however, saw him as the ultimate warning counter-example of their pet political theories or programmes.

Cynicism as a lifestyle choice was traced back to Diogenes of Sinope, with whom Alexander was believed to have had a famous meeting – or, rather, stand-off – in Corinth in about 335 (Plutarch, *Life of Alexander* 14). The most serious of the extant Alexander historians, Arrian of Nicomedia, also thought this story worthy of inclusion in his generally sober, military-minded account (*Anabasis* 7.2). Both Plutarch and Arrian may have derived it from another Alexander historian, the contemporary Onesicritus of Astypalaea, who was a Cynic adept, and, as a participant in Alexander's expedition, journeyed as far east and south of his Aegean home as Taxila, where he met with Brahman sages.

Onesicritus predictably sought to depict Alexander as a philosopher in arms. It was less predictable, however, that he should have represented him as a Cynic philosopher, since at any rate the more extreme, 'hard' form of Cynicism (Moles 1995; Stoneman 2003: 332) taught that the material trappings of this world's civilised life, wealth and power, should be reckoned as naught. Onesicritus somehow squared the circle by making Alexander rule in accordance with 'Nature'. The Cynics were not strictly a philosophical 'school'. The Stoics, on the other hand, were precisely that, and had been founded as such in Athens (they took their name from the Painted Stoa in the Agora) by Zeno of Cypriot Citium around 300 BCE, in the wake of and with views tailored to suit the new globalised, post-Alexander Hellenic world. Zeno in his (lost) ideal *politeia* may well have expressed respect for what he took to be truly Spartan qualities of communalism, self-renunciation and indifference to material goods (Schofield 1999a). Neither he nor his followers had any truck with Alexander as a role model, however, and unambiguously judged him not to embody the ideal of the Stoic 'sage', who alone, according to Stoic doctrine, was truly free in all respects – that is, not just legally or politically free but morally free from enslaving passions and material trappings (Brunt 1993: 222–3).

### KINGSHIP AND THE MASSES

So far in this chapter the views on kingship that have been canvassed are very firmly those of elite Greek thinkers and writers, whose target audiences would have been a tiny minority of the late classical and early Hellenistic world's population. To discover the views of the Greek 'masses' one must look, rather, to public, official religious manifestations, and in particular to the new ruler cult, characteristic of the early Hellenistic age.

Apparently the first fully historical Greek person to be accorded divine religious worship in his lifetime was the Spartan Lysander, who was elevated to quasi-godhead by his fanatical oligarchic partisans on the island of Samos around 400 BCE but died soon afterwards (395). Further definite steps along the same path were taken first by Philip and then by his son Alexander of Macedon, and in the case of the latter democrats as well as oligarchs were prepared to – or perhaps had no realistic option but to – go along with him. Nonetheless, the ruler cult quickly sank roots deep enough for the post-Alexander successor 'kings' – once they had chosen so to title themselves (306–304; see narrative V) – to find it a useful prop to legitimise their would-be dynastic regimes. At once-democratic Athens a paroxysm of enthusiastic flattery saw Demetrius the Besieger hailed in 291 as on a par with the goddess Demeter – indeed, as a divinity whom, unlike Demeter, 'we can see present here' (Athenaeus, *Deipnosophistae* VI.253). This elevation and gross flattery are a measure of the distance Athens had travelled since the forcible suppression of democracy in the city by Macedon in 322.

# Narrative V: The Hellenistic Greek world,
## c. 300–30 BCE

It is a moot point whether Alexander was the first 'Hellenistic' ruler, or the last great monarch of the 'classical' age. At any rate, Alexander's reign both spanned the transition between the two epochs and hugely hastened the full flowering of the post-classical dispensation. 'Hellenistic' as a term of art carries a number of different notions and applications: a fusion of some sort between Greek and – especially oriental – non-Greek cultures; a culture that was Greek-ish, in which, though the language of government and high culture was Greek, 'native' cultures not only survived but actually contributed something positive to the mix; and, perhaps above all, an epoch of transition, during which Greeks were less and less masters of their own destiny, and within which indeed they succumbed ultimately to the imperial power of Rome.

The wars of the Alexandrine succession lasted at least twenty-two years, until the Battle of Ipsus in 301 or even the Battle of Corupedium in 281. The resulting 'Hellenistic' political pattern saw a vastly enlarged Greek world that now embraced Egypt on the continent of Africa and stretched as far east in Asia as Pakistan, parcelled up into a relatively small number of territorial monarchies. The two most considerable of these, the Seleucids and the Ptolemies, were based respectively in Syria and in Egypt, and more or less inevitably doomed to clash repeatedly. In the later third century a breakaway from the Seleucid Empire produced the Attalid royal house of Pergamon in north-west Anatolia, the last member of which, Attalus III, bequeathed his kingdom to the new power that had arisen from the west: Rome.

In due time what had been the Hellenistic kingdom of the Attalids was transmogrified into the wealthy Roman *provincia* of Asia. Alexander the Great would not have been impressed. The Antigonids, Alexander's nearest descendants, based themselves in old Macedonia, but by comparison not just with him but also with their contemporary Hellenistic rivals they were relatively small fry. Even so, they were normally more than a match for any individual Greek *polis* or federal state (a more characteristic phenomenon of the age) that cared to make a bid for independence. One might be tempted to think back to the situation in Mycenaean or Late Bronze Age Greece, except that this new Hellenistic world was not merely a rather pale imitation of something grander and non-Greek to the east. Rather, Hellenistic Greece (in the broadest sense) set the pattern for the next European superpower, Rome, to imitate, to embrace and to supersede (see narrative VI).

Modern political theories of Alexander as champion of such mighty notions as 'the brotherhood of mankind' or 'the fusion of races' have their ultimate origins in antique sources (much later than the time of Alexander himself, however); proximately, though, they owe far more to their proponents' rather overheated imaginings or longings – a model illustration of the persuasive thesis associated with Benedetto Croce that all history is contemporary history. The orthodox Jews of Judaea, for example, were not the only subject people of the Hellenistic world who did not see their Macedonian warlords, ruling as 'kings' from 306 to 304 regardless of their actual social origins, as cosmopolitanist humanitarians.

In the Chremonidean War of the 260s Athens and Sparta found themselves once again thrown together willy-nilly in alliance against a greater power, this time Antigonus II Gonatas of Macedon. In Seleucid Asia in the 210s there occurred what all dynastic regimes are by their fleshly nature heir to: a usurpation by a disgruntled member of the 'royal' family, in this case one Achaeus ('the Achaian' – possibly a dim and far distant homage to Homer's Greeks at Troy), who was probably a cousin of King Antiochos III 'the Great' (so titled in homage to Alexander). In the Egypt of the Ptolemies there is abundant and explicit evidence of endemic internal insecurity, even at the period of the country's greatest prosperity in the later third century BCE, reaching us with sometimes startling directness from the uniquely Egyptian source of documents on papyrus.

Probably the most extraordinary political phenomenon of the age, however, happened not at the centre of one or other of the mightier Hellenistic kingdoms but on the periphery of one of the least considerable, in Sparta (chapter 9). In the 240s and again in the 220s, by which date the city had become an almost forgotten backwater, political revolution did not merely occur 'under' but was actively promoted by two of its – hereditary – kings, one from each of Sparta's two hereditary royal houses. Tradition of immemorial antiquity met head-on the invention of tradition, with a very loud crash that reverberated both across the ancient world and well down into our own times. This is perhaps the supreme example of the continued vitality of the Greek *polis*, and its accompanying notions of freedom and autonomy, in the Hellenistic (and, indeed, Roman) period of Greek history.

CHAPTER 9

# (E)utopianism by design: the Spartan revolution, 244–221 BCE

The idea of a perfect and immortal commonwealth will always be found as chimerical as that of a perfect and immortal man. (David Hume, *History of Great Britain*, 1754–62)

## UTOPIANISM ANCIENT AND MODERN

Under the former Soviet-backed regime, the Hungarian writer György Konrád published in 1985 a stinging polemic against the intrusion of the State and of reason of state into every sphere of existence in 'Mitteleuropa'. He entitled it *Antipolitik*. The ancient Greeks too had their exponents of anti-politics, although their targets and attacks were, of course, radically different. Indeed, the critical and reflexive nature of the Greek tradition of political thought, from its inception in the poems of Homer and Hesiod onwards, had always encouraged resistance to the dominant constructions of politics as the true end of man and of the *polis* as the unique source of the truly good life. Broadly speaking, negative reactions took one of two forms: either advocacy of a total withdrawal from politics into a privatised existence beyond the reach of the *polis*, or the imagining of alternative political Utopias.

The surviving evidence for the withdrawal syndrome is largely Athenian, partly because ancient democracy was premised on endless open debate but also because Athens' radical form of democracy aroused fierce opposition from its articulate anti-democratic critics (Ober 1998). Virulently opposed to the ideal of democratic participation advocated famously in the Periclean funeral speech in Thucydides, they redescribed such participatory politics as *polupragmosunê* or 'meddlesomeness', an excess of engagement in *pragmata* (affairs of state) by the unfitted masses (Rahe 1992: 224 & n. 8). In its stead they advocated a life of *a-pragmosunê*, the 'alpha privative' nicely suggesting the privatised nature of this anti-political withdrawal.

Unlike some failed politicians in modern democracies, however, ancient oligarchs and other radical critics of democracy did not necessarily gloss their more or less enforced withdrawal from the public arena as a desire to spend more time with their families. Consider Socrates, or, at any rate, Plato's Socrates. In the *Republic* he is made to advocate nothing less than the abolition of the family for the ruling elites, the 'philosopher-kings' of the imaginary Callipolis ('Fair City'). Plato himself, moreover, seems to have wanted somehow to peg his 'philosopher-king' notion to the careers of actual fourth-century flesh-and-blood tyrants such as Dionysius I and II of Syracuse or Clearchus of Heraclea on the Black Sea, allegedly a pupil at the Academy (chapter 8). Such authoritarian imaginings could offer no long-term future for the renewal and enrichment of Greek politics, however, since the tyrant was by definition a marginal figure, ruling autocratically either outside or in defiance of any properly constituted *politeia*. There was, on the other hand, a great future for Utopia, or (E)utopia, both in theory and in practice.

To be sure, all political thought – all serious political thought, anyhow, that is seriously concerned with trying to alter as well as understand or explain the world as it is – is necessarily utopian in some way or degree or other: 'Unless we admit that the very notion is senseless, it demands at least an ounce of utopianism even to consider [political] justice . . .' (Shklar 1957: 272). Furthermore, to compose a utopia in writing, as Plato did more than once, is a peculiarly graphic way of asking whether and to what extent the categories that we typically use to understand and navigate our world can be rearranged. The word 'utopia' is not a genuine ancient Greek word, however, and, as invented by Thomas More in 1516, it is formally ambiguous. The prefix 'U' could stand either for Greek 'ou' ('not') or for Greek 'eu' ('well'), so that Utopia could in principle be either a No-place or a Place of Well-faring – that is, either a place that is good only, or primarily, to think with, or a place that might actually be good – or at least palpably better – to live in.

Some further distinctions have been usefully drawn by scholars work-ing with the genre of Utopia or Utopiography both ancient and modern. Lyman Tower Sargent, for example, in his introductory essay to a New York Public Library exhibition catalogue (2000), distinguishes first between 'Utopias brought about without human effort' and 'Utopias brought about by human effort'. The former category includes those utopias of the 'auto-matic life' in a mythic golden age that Greek comic poets, among others, were fond of imagining (what in mediaeval Europe came to be called the

land of Cockaigne). Of the latter category, Sargent mentions as early examples '[v]arious parts of the Old Testament, the Eloquent Peasant of Ancient
Egypt, Solon, the *Lycurgus* of Plutarch, the *Cyropaedia* of Xenophon,
Aristophanes and Plato'. This is probably too broad-brush, but Sargent
does then go on to distinguish between (e)utopias and dystopias of modern times and to assert, challengingly, that 'in the twentieth century there
has been a dialectic between eutopia and dystopia, with the eutopian hopes
of social movements being created as dystopias and then being overthrown
by the belief in a new utopia'. (His mention of Plutarch's *Lycurgus* we
return to below.)

A second relevant distinction is that made in 1967 by A. Giannini (and
drawn upon later by Moses Finley [1975]), between utopias 'd'evasione'
and utopias 'di ricostruzione'. Utopias of critical reconstruction, in their
turn, may be further subdivided (following Doyne Dawson [1992]) into
'high' and 'low' forms. 'Low' utopias aim merely at the amelioration of
existing political forms: a classic instance would be the theory of the
'mixture' (*krasis*), a 'mixed' constitution being either one that produces a
'moderate blending in the interests of both the few (rich) and the many
(poor)' citizens (Thucydides 8.97.2, on the 'Constitution of the 5000' at
Athens in 411) or one that harmoniously and equitably mixes elements of
the three principal constitutional types (rule by one, by some, or by all).
The underlying, mundanely political aim of all such 'mixture' theorists
was somehow to finesse, bypass or pre-empt the real-world class struggles
between the elite and the masses of the citizenries of the Greek *poleis*
that flourished especially between the fourth and second centuries BCE
(Fuks 1984).

Far more radical are Dawson's 'high' utopias, which theorised a root-
and-branch transcendence of existing politics. The classic instances of this
approach were Plato's *Republic* and *Laws*, both of which were, if in very
different ways, indebted to communalist ideal of social reconstruction
inspired or inflected by Sparta – or, rather, by Sparta's 'mirage', 'tradition'
or 'legend' (Ollier 1933–1943; Rawson 1969; Tigerstedt 1965–78). Thus it
was that Sparta, or variously idealised versions of the real but largely inac-
cessible polity of Sparta, became the fount and origin of all ancient Greek
utopiographic speculation (Hodkinson 2005), as indeed of the modern
tradition inaugurated by More (Africa 1979). In this chapter I explore
an episode of Spartan history, in the second half of the third century,
that both drew centrally upon and gave a huge boost to such utopian
imaginings.

THE SPARTAN REVOLUTION: THEORY AS WELL AS PRACTICE?

By the third century Sparta was but a shadow of its old great self, both externally weak and desperately in need of internal reconstruction, yet a prisoner of its own myth of immutability. Finally, in this innovative Hellenistic age, Sparta did actually undergo radical reform, and not only political but also economic and social reform – to such a degree, indeed, that the conventional and often loosely applied term 'revolution' (Finley 1986) does seem to have specific purchase on Spartan third-century BCE reality. Arguably, moreover, the Spartan revolution was at least tinged by political theory, however much its principal drivers were the underlying material conditions of life experienced by its increasingly divided and impoverished citizens. At any rate, it is certainly in the context of this third-century revolution that the theory of ancient Greek utopianism hit up against its – attempted – practical instantiation, through the careers of Kings Agis IV and Cleomenes III. Both appealed in their propaganda to the supposed example and precedent of Sparta's legislative founding father Lycurgus, but this was a strictly ritualistic and formulaic move.

For Lycurgus, if there had ever been a real Spartan reformer of that name (Plutarch's 'biography' hardly settles that issue), would have lived in a pre-theoretical age. By the middle of the third century BCE, however, Greek political theory was two centuries old, and even Sparta was producing thinkers and writers such as the antiquarian Sosibius, if not yet home-grown political theorists. In sharp contrast, the pre-Hellenistic Spartans had been notorious for being uncultivated boors, and Aristotle (*Politics,* 1338b12) claimed not implausibly that the type of state education that Sparta imposed on the young produced 'bestial' (*thêriôdeis*) characters (see Ducat 2006). Some outside observers (e.g. Isocrates in the *Panathenaicus*) even claimed the Spartans were all totally illiterate, but Aristotle's more measured 'least devoted to letters' (*hêkista philologoi, Rhetoric* 1389b) was nearer the mark. Many Spartans were at least functionally literate, as has been demonstrated in detail and at length (Cartledge 1978), and a couple of elite Spartans (King Pausanias, Thibron) are on reliable record as having composed written tracts. One, moreover (Lysander), is supposed to have employed a foreign rhetorician as a speechwriter (to make the case for a fundamental domestic political reform of the kingship), and in this respect, as in others, he seems to point forward to the Hellenistic epoch.

The prime candidate for the role of philosophical guru in third-century revolutionary Sparta is Sphaerus of Borysthenes (on the Black Sea). He was featured brilliantly in Naomi Mitchison's 1933 historical novel *The Corn King and the Spring Queen*, but is otherwise not widely known, mainly for lack of good contemporary evidence, alas. Whatever else he may have been or done, Sphaerus was a Stoic. This chapter therefore revisits the perennially absorbing general questions of the relationship between political theory and political practice, and the role of intellectuals in politics (Lilla 2001). It also reconsiders specifically Sphaerus's possible role in the Spartan revolution: were the reforms associated with Kings Agis IV and, especially, Cleomenes III significantly influenced by theoretical considerations, even perhaps by defined philosophical theory or doctrine, as introduced to Sparta by Sphaerus?

Any discussion of the political and social meaning of the reforms of Agis and Cleomenes has to begin with Plutarch (a key witness also for chapter 10). When this prolific intellectual sat down, in the decades on either side of 100 CE, to choose the subjects for his *Parallel Lives* of the great Greeks and Romans, he could hardly overlook the fame of the aristocratic Roman brothers Gracchi, Tiberius and Gaius. They had both been tribunes of the plebs (in 133 and in 123 and 122, respectively), and both had been murdered amid bitter civil strife, punished for trying to introduce necessary reforms into a Roman republican system of government that was still dominated by a deeply conservative and largely cohesive Senate. To which two Greeks – ideally a pair of brothers, but at any rate a pair in some sense – could Plutarch persuasively compare the stirring lives and even more stirring deaths of the brothers Gracchi? His answer was swift, unambiguous: Agis and Cleomenes of Sparta.

Plutarch's parallel was, at best, inexact. Agis and Cleomenes were not brothers, though they were at least related posthumously: Cleomenes married Agis's widow, Agiatis. Nor were Agis and Cleomenes official representatives of the people of Sparta in the way that Tiberius and Gaius Gracchus had been elected tribunes of the Roman plebs on reformist tickets. They were hereditary kings, succeeding to the thrones of the Eurypontid and Agiad royal houses and ruling from *c.* 244 to 241 and 236 to 222 BCE respectively. All the same, as Plutarch was surely not the first to see, there was indeed more than a little in common between the two Spartan kings and the two Roman republican tribunes. The Spartans too had explicitly espoused a radical, indeed revolutionary, social programme, which they had sought to implement through manipulation of the powers of their office, and both were killed in the course of bitter civil strife, victims of established power bases. The kingship at Sparta, moreover, was by no means absolute and could be quite naturally described as an 'office' (*arkhê*), like, for example, the archonship at Athens.

So, why did Agis IV and Cleomenes III live and die as they did? It is not enough, of course, simply to rely on Plutarch's joint *Life* for possible answers to that complex question. First, we must enquire into the nature and especially the reliability of the sources that Plutarch chose to follow. One writer above all, the contemporary third-century historian Phylarchus of Athens, was his preferred source. How reliable was his account, though? If we are to believe Phylarchus's fiercest critic, Polybius, we would have to say: 'Not at all.'

Phylarchus was indeed singled out by name by the great Arcadian historian of the rise of Rome as a paradigm of how not to write good history. What seems to have upset Polybius as much as anything was Phylarchus's style of writing, his categorical error of confusing pragmatic historiography with the fictional, emotion-ridden genre of tragic drama. There was also a serious ideological issue between them, however. Polybius of Megalopolis was born into the aristocratic elite that dominated the Achaean League in the later third and early second century. He was also of the view that patriotism justified favourable bias in the writing of the history of one's own country or city. Cleomenes III of Sparta was a determined, and for a considerable time very successful, enemy of the Achaean League, who had actually sacked and dealt very savagely with Polybius's own Megalopolis in 223, just a generation before the historian's birth. Polybius therefore could not accept, and indeed felt he had to demolish, the generally very favourable picture of Cleomenes that he found in the work of Phylarchus.

Where does the truth lie? Plutarch's choice to follow Phylarchus for interpretation as well as the facts is not, unfortunately, decisive. The most we can claim is that our modern account will not be inconsistent with such facts as Phylarchus, Polybius and Plutarch between them preserve relatively unadorned, and that our interpretation of those facts at least makes consistent sense of one of the most intriguing as well as most important episodes in Spartan history.

One further reason why this episode is so intriguing is that it is one of those very rare episodes in all ancient Greek (or Roman) history when we can say for sure that the role of women was not just unusually prominent but actually politically decisive. Aristotle in the *Politics* (1269b30–32) had written a century earlier that 'at the time of the Spartans' domination [404–371] many things were controlled by the women'. In the years between

244 and 221 that rather controversial claim acquires real substance and substantiation. I have mentioned already that Cleomenes III married the widow of Agis IV. Plutarch tells us that it was Agiatis, burning for revenge for the murder of her husband and no less keen to carry out the reform programme for which he had been murdered, who converted her second husband Cleomenes to the reformist cause. Then there were the mother and grandmother of Agis, Agesistrata and Archidamia, whom Plutarch confidently labelled 'the richest of all the Spartans' (including the men as well as the women), and who likewise gave Agis their unequivocal support; and, last but by no means least, Cleomenes' redoubtable mother Cratesicleia, who preceded her son into exile as a hostage at the court of Ptolemy III and was also murdered there in a bout of bloody faction fighting (*stasis*).

As noted above, *stasis* continued to rack the Greek world in the third century as it had in the fifth and fourth (Fuks 1984). What was new was that Sparta – the city once famed for its orderly good government, *eunomia*, its stability and its unanimity, *homonoia* – was now as disturbed by *stasis* as any other Greek city. The root of the condition here, as elsewhere, was extreme and increasing inequality in the distribution and ownership of landed property, although in Sparta this was given an extra twist by the myth that once upon a time and for a very long time thereafter Spartan land had been equally distributed among all the citizens. In fact, that had never been the case: there had always been rich and poor Spartans, as in other Greek cities (Hodkinson 2000). If a Spartan fell below the level at which he could contribute a legally fixed minimum of natural produce to a common mess (*suskanion, sussition*), however, he forfeited his status as a full citizen and became a member of the subclass of *hupomeiones* ('inferiors'). This process seems to have taken a vicious turn for the worse first of all towards the end of the fifth century, and had continued ever since.

Whatever exactly were the mechanisms causing this land concentration (modern scholars are as divided on this issue as the ancient sources), this was probably the main reason for Spartiate *oliganthrôpia* – that is, that between 400 and 250 BCE the citizen body fell from about 3,000 to only 700, of whom just 100 held a substantial stake in landed property ownership. It was this dire situation that Agis IV set out to remedy, by proclaiming a version of the characteristic rallying slogans of oppressed Greek peasantries everywhere: the cancellation of debts and the redistribution of land. With the exception of a handful of rich individuals who were his relatives or otherwise bound to him, the rich of Sparta as a group predictably combined to resist these measures, and turned equally predictably to the other king, Leonidas II, to champion their cause. Agis was initially a match for them. Leonidas was exiled, debts were indeed cancelled, and written mortgage deeds known as *klaria* (from *klaros*, meaning a lot or plot of land) were symbolically and publicly burned.

That was the extent of Agis's success, however. Before he could turn seriously to the planned land redistribution he suffered a humiliating reverse abroad, at the isthmus of Corinth, and on his return to Sparta he was murdered by his enemies, together with his immediate relatives. The cause of reform, as necessary pragmatically as it was justified ethically, had to be put on hold for almost fifteen years. It was taken up, somewhat surprisingly, by Leonidas's son Cleomenes, who succeeded to the Agiad throne in 236. Unlike Agis, Cleomenes realised that foreign policy mattered as much as domestic affairs, and he prepared the way for internal reform by a series of remarkable military successes abroad, most conspicuously against Aratus of Sicyon and the Achaean League that he dominated. The sack of Megalopolis in 223, mentioned above, was the culmination of this successful enterprise, which had made it look for a time as though Cleomenes might restore Sparta to something like the position of international dominance the city had enjoyed down to 371.

Cleomenes was not only a proficient military leader, however. He was also a highly effective domestic reformer, even possibly a social revolutionary. Agis had proposed a radical land redistribution: 4,500 lots for Spartans and 15,000 for Perioeci (free Laconians living in their own semi-autonomous communities within the borders of the Spartan state but not Spartan citizens) are mentioned as his ultimate targets. Agis got no further than proposing such a land reform, though. Cleomenes, however, beginning in 227, actually carried out a land redistribution on something like that scale. Moreover, he did not extend his scheme only to the Perioeci. He also set free some 6,000 of the remaining Laconian helots, Sparta's serf-like mainly agricultural workers, in exchange for a manumission fee payable by them in cash. These ex-helots presumably thus became the owners of some of the land on which they had previously worked under compulsion. Also included in the package were numbers of Cleomenes' foreign mercenary soldiers, for these recruits had formed a key part of Cleomenes' military reforms, whereby he tried to bring the decadent and outmoded Spartan army up to the best Hellenistic standards set by Antigonid Macedon and Ptolemaic Egypt.

To make absolutely sure that his entrenched political enemies could not prevent or overturn his reforms, he first had them murdered and then took decisive personal control of the political institutions and structures that might be used to thwart him. Ephors in office were killed, the Gerousia was finessed by the creation of the office of patronomos, and even the dual monarchy was effectively abolished when he placed his brother Eucleidas on the Eurypontid throne. Consistently with his image as a modernising Hellenistic king, Cleomenes became the first Spartan king to place an image of his head on Spartan coins (Palagia 2006: 209). Nor were Cleomenes' reforms restricted to the economic and political planes. He also embarked on major social reform, aiming to restore the supposedly 'Lycurgan' regime of comprehensive and uniform public education for all male potential citizens, and communal living in messes and constant training for the adult warriors, many of whom would have been newly enfranchised.

Might Cleomenes have been not just a (radical) reformer, however, but also a social revolutionary, and possibly an ideologically or even philosophically informed and motivated revolutionary? The fact that two followers of the Stoic school of philosophy, Sphaerus and Persaeus, are known to have written about Sparta in the third century suggests at least the possibility of direct Stoic influence. Moreover, the known personal association of Sphaerus with Cleomenes strengthens the possibility greatly. He is plausibly reported as having visited Sparta when Cleomenes was in power and conducting his reforms, and having fled with him to Egypt following their reversal. A noted Stoic philosopher with an unusually practical concern to change the world as it was and to see Stoic ideas implemented in practice, Sphaerus might well have seen in Cleomenes a potential Stoic 'wise man' and practical instrument of his ideas.

At all events, Andrew Erskine (1990: ch. 6) is only the most convinced and forceful recent exponent of the view that behind Cleomenes' practical social reform package, especially as regards the revived education system and the communal messing, lay the ideas and inspiration of Sphaerus. We may add that Sphaerus could well have been drawn to his practical Spartan involvement by the theoretical example of the Stoic school's founder, Zeno, who arguably had propounded a notably Spartanising utopia of his own (Schofield 1999b). Nor would it have been inconsistent with the massive cultural changes that Sparta had undergone since the heyday of, for example, King Agesilaus II (*c.* 445–360), if a consciously innovative Spartan king such as Cleomenes really had been so philosophically motivated and inspired.

In practice, however, the reforms, however well formulated, were destined to have only a very short shelf life for reasons beyond either
Cleomenes' or Sphaerus's control. In 222 Cleomenes was decisively defeated
at Sellasia by Antigonus III of Macedon; his reforms were reversed, and,
three years later, he met a less than glorious death in exile, at the Ptolemaic
capital Alexandria. Thus ended a remarkable and unrepeatable political
and social experiment.

# Narrative VI: 'Graecia capta' ('Greece conquered'), c. 146 BCE – CE 120

Polybius (*c.* 200–120 BCE) is the major extant Greek historian of the middle Hellenistic period. He was a citizen of Megalopolis, literally the 'Great City', which had been created in the early 360s, out of some forty pre-existing communities, as both a consequence and a perpetuation of Sparta's humiliation at the hands of Thebes. He spent a good deal of his adult life in futile pursuit of his city's independence from the federal Achaean League, until, by a stroke of irony, he was forcibly removed to Rome as a hostage precisely for the good behaviour of the Achaeans – who had had the temerity to try to escape from under Rome's ever-lengthening and ever-strengthening grip on the Greek peninsula. Rome's victory in the Achaean War, following on a generation after its victory at Pydna in 168 over the last of the Antigonids, meant that from 146 BCE mainland Greece south of Macedonia was a Roman protectorate, a province in everything but name. (The name and formal status were imposed in 27 BCE, under the new Roman emperor Gaius Julius Octavianus Caesar, known to us by his adopted surname of Augustus – in Greek 'Sebastos', 'the Revered One'.)

Polybius, who in effect 'crossed the floor of the House' (that is, went over to the Roman side) during his loose captivity, sealed his conversion by writing a pro-Roman Greek history in forty books (most of which do not survive). In it he gave a characteristically Greek type of explanation for what he considered to be the most extraordinary and explanation-worthy phenomenon of recent world history: the rise of Rome to suzerainty over most of the circum-Mediterranean world and hence most of the Greek world between 220 and 145. His explanation, in one word, was the Romans' *politeia*. This Polybius interpreted as 'mixed', in the sense that it included in a condition of fruitful tension or balance elements of all the three fundamental constitutional types identified as such by Greek political theory since the fifth century BCE: rule by one (monarchy – though actually republican Rome abhorred kingship and had two joint consuls per annum), by some (aristocracy – the Senate), and by all (popular rule – the People's Assemblies).

Polybius indeed devoted an entire book (six) to a description and analysis of the structure and function of the Roman *politeia*, insofar as he, a Greek outsider, could gain knowledge of it through privileged personal contacts such as the younger Scipio. He positioned this discussion artfully in the context of the narrative of 216 BCE, the date of Rome's worst ever defeat up to then (by Hannibal of Carthage at Cannae), and the gravest thereafter until the Battle of Adrianople in CE 378. His explanatory point was that not even such a massive defeat as Cannae could overthrow Rome's political system. The same mixed *politeia* that had enabled Rome to grow great in the first place also enabled her to recover triumphantly from the Cannae disaster and to go on to even bigger and better imperial things.

More controversially, but again probably thanks to his thoroughly Greek political outlook, Polybius interpreted the popular element of the Romans' *politeia* as 'democratic', and he assigned to it a powerful, causative force in the development of what from another point of view is the 'late republican' epoch of Roman history (following on from the 'early republic', 509–287, and the 'middle republic', 287–146). In truth, although there have been a few modern defenders of a 'democratic' interpretation (notably Fergus Millar; e.g. 2002), the republic was a funny sort of aristocratic oligarchy with important popular but not strictly democratic components. For example, to cut a very long story short, the Roman conception of citizenship always treated some citizens structurally as more equal than others, and, never advancing as far as the quintessentially democratic notion of one citizen one vote, operated various systems of group voting in which wealth and residence played distinctly undemocratic roles. This republican political system, such as it was, fell apart between 133 (the tribunate of Tiberius Gracchus) and 49 BCE (Julius Caesar's illegal invasion of Italy). It yielded to the pressure exerted chiefly by freebooting politician-generals with devoted veterans at their back (devoted more to their generals than to the republic), whom the often modified but still quite rudimentary – fundamentally, city state – institutions of Rome were no longer able to contain.

From the prolonged bloodbath of the civil wars (49–31 BCE) Caesar Augustus emerged the victor both *domi* and *militiae* – both in the domestic civilian sphere and in the expanded empire at large. An elaborate fiction of legitimacy was maintained not only during his very long reign (27 BCE to CE 14) but also after his death – via the text of his self-penned *Res Gestae* ('Accomplishments') inscribed on bronze sheets set up outside his pharaonic-style dynastic mausoleum. This fiction held that he was merely the '*princeps*', or 'boss', whose unique position of unparalleled authority rested on the universal consent and acclaim of the empire's subjects. In harsh reality, he was the *capo di capi*, the boss of bosses – or, as Edward Gibbon acutely phrased it, a 'subtle tyrant', hypocritically obeying the decrees of the Senate, the supposed ruling power, that he had himself dictated to it. A remarkable chapter at the end of the *Life of Augustus* written by Suetonius (a well-informed imperial servant under a much later emperor, Hadrian) lets the cat out of the bag. In his will Augustus not only in effect appointed his successor – a contradiction in terms, if he had really been only an informal *princeps* – but also coolly told the Senate that information as to the finances and military dispositions of the empire could be had on application to one of his own imperial freedmen. These ex-slaves, often of Greek origin, had legally belonged to Augustus's own personal household, the *familia Caesaris*, and de facto they still did belong to him personally even after manumission. These imperial servants in effect wielded more power even than any senator, which led to enormous clashes in the reign of a weaker if no less intelligent emperor such as Claudius (CE 41–54). By no means all the early emperors were that intelligent, however, and not a few of them were quite seriously deranged. The suicide of Nero (CE 54–68) provoked a general civil war, and the period from 68 to 69 was known as 'the year of the four emperors'.

Stability at the centre was restored only when the Flavian house headed by Vespasian (69–79) occupied the throne; for what Augustus had in fact succeeded in founding and bequeathing was a dynastic monarchy. It was, furthermore, in the reign of Vespasian, one of Augustus's few relatively sane early successors, that the logical and honest step was taken by the Senate of legally enshrining the emperor's position, above the law(s), in a formal document. As Polybius was the great historian of Rome's rise to 'world' domination under the republic, so Tacitus was the great historian of the supersession – or rather annihilation – of the republic by a principate-cum-dynastic monarchy. 'How few,' Tacitus laments, writing of those who witnessed Augustus's funeral in CE 14, 'had seen the Republic.' It was not until the reign of Nerva (96–98), so he optimistically proclaimed in his posthumous laudation of his father-in-law Agricola (a former governor of Britain), that 'liberty' – as understood by a Roman senator – and the principate were finally united. It was a precarious and one-sided liberty, though, weighted very heavily on the side of the emperor. In Tacitus's own heyday, the later first century and early second, the most and best that could be hoped for, he intimated, was that the *princeps*/emperor of the day would observe the laws more or less.

That was the insider's point of view of a Roman senator and imperial governor (Tacitus's top posting had been the wealthy province of Asia, the summit of a senatorial career), who was also a 'new' man (the first of his family to enter the Senate). Actually, Tacitus had done remarkably well out of the new imperial dispensation for someone without senatorial ancestors and – possibly – of provincial, not Italian, let alone Roman, origins. Quite different again was the outsider perspective of a Greek provincial subject, even a relatively privileged one, as expressed in our final case study. Plutarch of Chaeronea, in Boeotia in central Greece, was a slightly older contemporary of Tacitus and shared his literary pretensions and skills, but came from and lived out his days in a genuinely provincial backwater. His political treatise on the art of the possible as he saw it provides us with an invaluable worm's-eye view of the early Roman imperial dispensation, as well as a peculiarly illuminating retrospective on Greek political thought since the time of Homer.

# The end of politics? The world
# of Plutarch, c. CE 100

Greek political thought (and theory) did not die with the early Stoics of the third century BCE. After Panaetius of Rhodes (2nd century) and Poseidonius of Apamea in Seleucid Syria (1st century BCE), however, the torch passed firmly to Rome, in the massy shape of Cicero. His writings, thanks to his golden style, were preserved in bulk and have come down to us more or less intact – minus, somewhat ironically, his treatise *De Re Publica*, which survives only fragmentarily.

Cicero actually translated Xenophon's *Oeconomicus* and other more or less philosophical Greek works into Latin, and was in other ways heavily indebted to Greek thinkers for the development of his own brand of philosophising, which, in accordance with Roman pragmatic norms, retained a very close connection indeed to political actuality. For example, in one of his many private letters to Titus Pomponius, nicknamed Atticus ('the Athenian'), his publisher as well as friend, he made a sneering reference to Cato the Younger – a figure whom he in many ways deeply admired and probably envied for his unbending moral rectitude. Cato spoke, he wrote, as though he were living in the ideal utopian state of Plato's *Republic* (the Latin translation of *Politeia*), whereas actually he lived in the Sin City (literally 'dregs', *faex*, plural *faeces*) of Romulus! Even more than Aristotle, Cicero based his political philosophy on his perception of the world as it really was, and perhaps we should be grateful to him for the unblinking and unflinching manner in which he explicitly identified his personal class interest with the moral welfare of the entire Roman world. The state, in the sense of political community, he regarded as a law-based framework for the social control of the unruly as well as for the advancement of human civilisation. This state, so Cicero affirmed in a foundational treatise (*De Officiis*, 'On Duties') that was to have a massive influence in the eighteenth-century Enlightenment, was invented for the sake of the preservation of the private ownership of property, especially real estate, no matter how massively unequal or inequitable its distribution might be.

Roman Stoics too revealingly bent the precepts of the original Greek founders to accommodate the material interests of an elite ruling class that possessed – by ancient Greek standards – simply enormous material assets in both land and movables (see Duncan-Jones 1982: ch. 1 on the extensive property of the Younger Pliny). Wealth, which had started out as a Stoic 'indifferent', morally speaking, was transmuted alchemically into a positive Roman good. Aristotle had indeed argued that it was not possible to be fully virtuous unless one possessed a (considerably large) sufficiency of material wealth – enough, for example, to exhibit the virtue of *megalophrosunê*, magnanimity (which involved by no means altruistic outlays of lavish hospitality and more basic material aid to those less fortunate). Nonetheless, Aristotle was not constrained by having to work within a system of thought whose founders had, so far from privileging the possession of wealth, rather scanted it.

Plutarch, the main subject of this final substantive chapter, straddled both the ancient Greek and the modern Roman worlds. He was born about CE 46 in Chaeronea, a small town or village in central Greece not far from Delphi, where he served as a loyal and devoted priest. He was also a Roman citizen, however, and had powerful intellectual friends with metropolitan connections. He was thus heir to both the Greek and the Roman philosophical traditions, and, being a voracious reader and writer, placed on exhibition his various debts to that heritage to the fullest extent imaginable. A couple of youthful works well illustrate 'where he was coming from', as the saying goes.

In *On the Mean-spiritedness* (or *Malignity*) *of Herodotus* he castigates the great historian of the Graeco-Persian Wars for his many errors of both commission and omission. On the latter side, two obtruded. He was, so the Boeotian patriot Plutarch felt, unfairly disparaging of his fellow Boeotian Thebans. True, the ruling elite of Thebes had blatantly 'medized' (that is, taken the Persian side), but those Thebans who did fight under Leonidas of Sparta at Thermopylae did so as liberationist Greek patriots, not (*pace* Herodotus) as unwilling hostages. That complaint of ungenerosity pales beside the more heinous accusation that Herodotus was a *philobarbaros*, however, a really nasty word conveying something of the abusive flavour of 'wog-lover' or 'nigger-lover' today. By that Plutarch meant that Herodotus had systematically underplayed the Persians' and other barbarians' vices and exaggerated their virtues, to such an extent that one might even call his Hellenic patriotism into question. Sadly, this is not Plutarch at his best, since Herodotus, for example, did nothing to disguise the far from panhellenist dissensions within the ranks of the few unquestionably loyalist cities led by Sparta.

Another of Plutarch's youthful works, an explicitly literary-rhetorical exercise, was a pair of model speeches discussing the *tychê* ('luck', 'fortune') of Alexander the Great. As in the Herodotus essay, Plutarch was again homing in on one of those crisis moments in the history of Hellenism, another decisive showdown between West and East, on which the survival of the Hellenic cultural tradition to which Plutarch was heir depended. Here, though, he took an unambiguously positive line, defending Alexander against the charge that he had been merely lucky, a chance favourite of the fickle goddess Fortune. Alexander, as we have seen (chapter 8), had been much more than a practical politician and general. He had served to crystallise and focus a debate on the merits or demerits of kingship that had been going on discontinuously since Homer. In the Roman era of Pompey and Caesar, however, Alexander's very name and title 'the Great' had become talismanic, and the major Roman historians (Livy to the fore) and philosophers had debated the case for and against Alexander as a philosopher in arms. Plutarch was thus doing more than just flexing his literary muscles by weighing in on Alexander's side.

The major works of his maturity fall into two distinct but overlapping and interconnecting halves. On the one hand, there was his series of 'parallel lives' of the great Greeks and Romans, biographies whose influence was so enormous that eventually they would affect even the work of a dramatist with notoriously little Greek: one William Shakespeare. On the other hand, there were Plutarch's many philosophical essays, known conventionally by their collective Latin name as the *Moralia*. Among the latter is the *Politika Parangelmata*, a work usually referred to by its Latin title, *Praecepta Rei Gerendae*, 'Precepts for Statecraft' or 'Advice on Public Life' (*Moralia* 798a–825f).

Had he been writing it a century and a half earlier, before Caesar crossed the Rubicon in 49 BCE, say, then these might well have been precepts for how to conduct oneself politically under the unique constitution known as the Roman Republic. Despite some rather desperate modern pleas to the contrary, this was never a democracy in any sense that Greek political theory or practice would have recognised. In actuality, as we have seen, Greek democracy had died out in the Hellenistic era, during the second century BCE. That death coincided, not coincidentally, with the rise of Rome to supremacy in what had been the Hellenistic Greek world. For the rulers of the Roman Republic never showed much sympathy even for the ideals of Greek democracy, let alone its practice; and, wherever they could, they played an active role in opposing it or stamping it out (de Ste. Croix 1983: 386, with 300–26 & app. IV). Some few Roman radical politicians such as Gaius Gracchus seem to have been willing to appeal to Greek democratic concepts, but they were soon brutally suppressed, and the system itself remained stubbornly non- or anti-democratic, for all the outward show of ultimate power residing with the *populus* or people (by which was meant the combined Roman-status citizenry of the hugely enlarged Roman world numbering several hundreds of thousands, way more than the 10,000 that Aristotle considered the very upper limit of workable *polis*-style democracy). The very existence of a genuine urban-proletarian 'Roman mob' (Brunt 1966) is testimony to the disempowerment of the mass of what the Greeks would have called the *dêmos*. Indeed, arguably it was precisely because it did not and could not democratise itself that the Republic ultimately fell, with a resounding crash, in the latest round of the civil war initiated by Julius Caesar's transit of the little river Rubicon.

What replaced the Republic was a new kind of monarchy, a 'dictatorship disguised by the forms of a commonwealth', as Gibbon brilliantly puts it. Monarchy in various forms had imbued Greek political history and culture from the time of the Mycenaean, Homeric and Hesiodic kings onwards. Its most recent incarnation was Mark Antony's assumption of a quasi-pharaonic position in the last of the Hellenistic territorial monarchies, the Ptolemaic dynasty of Egypt, as consort of Queen Cleopatra VII. Since the title of *rex* ('king') was anathema in Roman political parlance, however, Augustus was cleverly able to exploit Antony's monarchism as a powerful propaganda weapon. For himself, though de facto a monarch, he claimed disingenuously to have merely re-established the old order. Insofar as the new regime had an acknowledged name beyond 'Republic restored', it was a *principatus* or 'chiefdom'. It was this new Principate with which Plutarch's Greek readers in *c.* 100 CE had to contend – or, rather, to which, as his treatise taught, they had to learn to accommodate themselves.

Plutarch was an ornament of what is now perhaps a little misleadingly known as the 'Second Sophistic', an era of considerable intellectual and literary achievement from the mid-first to the early third century CE that stood consciously in the shadow of the first such era – the 'age of the Sophists' of the mid-fifth to mid-fourth century BCE centred on Athens as the 'City-Hall of Wisdom' (Plato's nice phrase). Plutarch stood at a small – though significant – distance apart from what has been construed as the dominant current of ethical thought represented by the 'Roman-Greek Socratics', however: their exclusive concern and focus, unlike Plutarch's, was 'the inner self, not any external identity as a citizen' (Whitmarsh 2004: 154). Plutarch, however, firmly within the tradition of Greek political thought stretching back at least to Protagoras, aimed to be his compatriots' teacher and guide in this brave newish world of monarchist imperial power. The Romans were, he believed (on good personal authority), 'very eager to promote the political interests of their friends' (814c), and it was therefore in the interests of the Romans' friends to know what the Romans wanted them to do.

Needless to spell out, only the rich among the subject Greek provincials would qualify for such friendship status. As the Spartan tyrant ruler Nabis was reported by Livy (34.31.17, following Polybius) to have said to Roman proconsul Titus Quinctius Flamininus in 195 BCE, the Romans' wish is that 'a few excel in wealth, and that the common people be subjected to them'. Ostensibly, the *Praecepta* is addressed to a young friend from the long Hellenised Lydian city of Sardis, a man of wealth, though (on the model of Solon, perhaps) not one to wish to flaunt it. It is written by a Roman citizen desperately proud of his Greek descent and local affiliation as a citizen of Chaeronea in Boeotia, where he occupied positions of authority – involving such relatively humble tasks as supervising the transport of stones or concrete, or the measuring of tiles (811bc).

Rather as his younger contemporary Tacitus (*Annals* 4.32–3) had lamented the loss of scope under the Principate to write up great and glorious public deeds such as the Roman Republic had accomplished, so Plutarch begins by asking what scope there might be for a conspicuously splendid career 'when the affairs of the [Greek] cities do not include leadership in war or the overthrow of tyrannies or the concluding of alliances' (805ab). At least, he answers, 'there remain public lawsuits and conducting embassies to the Emperor', for which tasks there are required persons of ardour, courage and intelligence. There are, moreover, various ways in which one may still fulfil the time-honoured Greek ethical imperative to 'help one's friends' (809a). The rub comes, though, when such a man (as his Sardian addressee) takes up an official magistracy in his home city: for then

> [y]ou must say to yourself: 'You who rule [at home] are a
> subject [of imperial Rome], and the city you rule is
> dominated by proconsuls, the agents of [the Emperor]
> Caesar.'

In two memorably graphic images Plutarch first points out that above his head his young Sardian friend sees the proconsul's boots, and then advises him to play his role as if he were the sort of actor on stage who takes no liberties with rhythms and metres 'beyond those permitted by those in authority' and listens carefully to the prompter. In the past, failure to do so, stepping out of line, it is drily noted, has resulted in banishment to islands or, at the limit, summary execution.

What Plutarch understands by stepping out of the right line is then made abundantly clear. Playing the demagogue with the masses is to be avoided like the plague. Inappropriate 'imitation of the deeds and aims and actions of their ancestors' – or encouragement to same, in the manner of the contemporary Sophists (who harp on the glories of Marathon, etc.) – is likewise to be eschewed. It is not enough, though, for the aspiring Greek provincial politician merely to avoid irritating his Roman superiors; he should also take care to ingratiate himself with some Roman bigwig who is in a position to do him a favour. Not, however, at the cost of neglecting the interests of his community: 'when the leg has been fettered' he should not then 'go on to place the neck under the yoke' – as happens when the Romans are kowtowed to excessively, on small matters as well as great. Then – and here Plutarch recurs to the oldest political slogan of all, the battlecry of freedom, traceable back at least to 500 BCE – the Greeks would be no better off than slaves, having deprived themselves of all claims to self-government (814ef); and of their rulers they would be making masters (*despotai*; 814f).

In the next main section Plutarch reverts to the necessity of avoiding old-style, classical-era Greek demagoguery. 'The statesman will not allow to the masses . . . any confiscation of the property of others, or distribution of public funds' (818cd). That Plutarch is here consciously echoing the old slogans of the enfranchised Greek citizen poor – the cancellation of debts, the redistribution of lands (see chapter 9) – is suggested by his further admonition to avoid the evil of *stasis*. In 338 Philip of Macedon had outlawed precisely those three things within the framework of his League of Corinth. To that end, Plutarch prescribes, the prudent statesman of *c.* 100 CE should aim to produce unanimity (*homonoia*) and mutual friendship (*philia*). Nothing original there, just conventional conservative politics as usual, apart perhaps from the – pragmatic – stress on the prudent statesman's ideal gentleness (*praotês*). Plutarch even has the nerve to claim that any more freedom than the masses are already granted by their Roman rulers would be harmful to them (824bc). Above all, though, and more accurately, Plutarch reiterates the sheer powerlessness of the Greeks in the Roman Empire, imprisoned in a world in which '[f]ortune has left us no prize for which to compete' (824def).

A generation or so after Plutarch, *c.* 150 CE, a Greek professional *rhêtôr* (orator, speechwriter, declaimer) coined a masterpiece of doublespeak – and perhaps doublethink. The Roman imperial system, wrote Publius Aelius Aristides (a neat combination of Roman and Greek names), who came from the new city of Hadrianotherae in Mysia (north-west Turkey), was 'a perfect democracy...under one man' (sp. 26.60, cf. 90). If we were to assume, however, that that must surely be the ultimate debasement of the noble word *dêmokratia*, our assumption would easily be proved false. In CE 330 the Roman Empire was divided formally into a predominantly Greek-speaking east and a Latin-speaking west, both parts dominated at first by Emperor Constantine the Great (r. 312–337) ruling from the new Rome known now as Constantinople (formerly Byzantium). By the time of Byzantine emperor Justinian (527–565), when old Rome had long since had to cede premier political status even in the Italian peninsula, *dêmokratia* could even be used to mean 'riot'. *Sic transit gloria democratiae.*

# CHAPTER II

# *The Greek legacy and democracy today*

It has been said that democracy is the worst form of government, except all those other forms that have been tried from time to time.
(Winston Churchill, speech of 11 November 1947 to the House of Commons)

Nous vivons à une époque où l'on peut tout discuter mais, étrangement, il y a un sujet qui ne se discute pas, c'est la démocratie.
(José Saramago [Nobel laureate 1998], interview in *Le monde*, 24 November 2006)

After thesis and antithesis, what else but synthesis? If there has been a single underlying theme running through this book, it is the difference – or, rather, the alterity (otherness) – of the Greek city. Whatever the ancient Greek *polis* and its politics were, they were emphatically *not* 'liberal' as that term is today understood in mainstream Western political theory. Any attempt to detect even a quasi-metaphorical 'liberal temper' in Greek politics is deeply misguided (Havelock 1957; cf. Brunt 1993: 389–94); but does that inevitably entail that the ancient Greek political experience has nothing to teach us today?

A reading of Nietzsche in sombre mood would indeed suggest so: 'The classicist is *the great skeptic* in our cultural and educational circumstances', since 'if we understand Greek culture, we see that it is gone for good' ('Wir Philologen', as cited by Williams 1993: 171 n. 10; emphasis in original). Not even the sceptical Nietzsche ruled out of court all dialogue between ancients and moderns, however, although he typically preferred a rather more lurid, Homer-derived image than that of the exchange of mere words. 'It is only if we give them [the works of earlier times] our soul that they can go on living: it is *our* blood that makes them speak to us' (*ap.* Williams 1993: 174–5 n. 36; emphasis in original). Moreover, as Bernard Williams himself aptly remarked, applying the characteristically modern emphasis on power rather than morality, 'We need a politics, in the sense of a coherent set of opinions about the ways in which power should be exercised in modern societies, with what limitations and to what ends' (10–11).

Even if not all Western philosophy is but a series of footnotes to Plato, ancient Greek political thinkers and theorists do still arguably have much to teach us. Indeed, in the present crisis of legitimacy confronting Western democracy, due chiefly to a widening chasm between formally sovereign electorates and actually non-responsible executives, there is an increasing number who think the Greeks may yet have something to teach us, even about the practicalities of democratic self-government. In a brilliant little dissection of Western political theory, conducted with an eye to the future of Western politics, John Dunn has commented on the poignant irony of our all seeming to be democrats today: 'If we are all democrats today, it is not a very cheerful fate to share. Today, in politics, democracy is the *name* for what we cannot have – yet cannot cease to want' (Dunn 1993: 28; emphasis in original).

That is surely too pessimistic. Dunn, familiar as he is theoretically with the world of the ancient Greek democratic polity, correctly sees that two of the absolutely key elements in the modern democratic equation are popular participation in decision-making at the national or central as well as the local levels, and the responsibility of office-holders to those whom they claim to represent. Rightly, too, he dismisses current Western democratic representative politics in their electoral aspect ('one day's rule in four years') as having 'very much the air of a placebo – or at best of an irregular modern Saturnalia' (Dunn 1993: 17, 28 n. 69; see also Dunn 1992a: 239–66). Rather than pressing for strong democracy at the centre as well, however, Dunn merely advocates, for supposedly pragmatic reasons, the injection of some tincture of ancient Greek democracy at the local level. Others are prepared to go considerably further, especially those who regard new technology as a potential friend rather than foe to the process of a more radical democratisation (e.g. Chadwick 2006 and McLean 1989).

No one doubts that the advent of the mass media, especially the insinuation of television images into the heart and hearth of voters' private homes, has transformed our political culture, probably irreversibly. Politicians have had to alter their style even more significantly than their content in order to take advantage of this communications revolution, resorting to talk-show campaigning and the photo-opportunity no less assiduously than to the old-style party political broadcast. Is this all necessarily just more bad news, though? Why should not the media – not only television, but also interactive computer networks in the home or workplace – be exploited further in order to generate genuine dialogue between rulers and ruled? Why confine participatory politics to electoral politics, or to local government only? Why not extend 'deliberative responsibility' – the best available opportunity for thought and discussion with others about the important options they face – as widely as is technologically feasible, so as to further the satisfaction of the needs and the success of the projects of the least advantaged as well as the most advantaged citizens, thereby moving towards ensuring recognition and status as political equals for all (see Beitz 1991)? Vladimir Lenin was fond of saying that communism was a combination of the most advanced technology of electrification with the most advanced institution for democratic (as he understood it) decision-taking, namely the soviets of workers and peasants: might we not claim, *mutatis mutandis*, that democracy should be the sum of mass communications media *plus* an equal say for all citizens?

Objections or obstacles will spring readily to mind. The principal of these are of two kinds. First, as any ancient Greek oligarch would hasten to tell us, educational: in order to make such an enriched participatory democracy feasible, the '*dêmos* previously disdained' (Herodotus's phrase, 5.69.2, applied to Cleisthenes' supporters 2,500 years ago: chapter 5) must be allowed and enabled to enjoy the fruits of the most extensive available critical *paideia*, directed towards moral ends as well as technical means (see Euben, Wallach and Ober 1994). Without such *paideia* the sort of mass-media electronic 'voting' that has become commonplace for televisual 'reality' (talent-spotting) shows can be no substitute – or harbinger of a brighter, politically informed future. Practical difficulties have to be discussed philosophically, since philosophical arguments may have practical conclusions. Then, if mistakes are made, as they will be, at least they will not be due to sheer factual ignorance or evaluative inexperience (see further, on deliberative democracy, Gutmann and Thompson 2004).

The second objection or obstacle is both chronological and chronic: participatory politics takes – or, rather, consumes – time. 'The price of liberty', it has been well said (Crick 1992: 272), is 'eternal commitment to political activity'. If large numbers of modern citizens are to be willing to pay that price, however, there will need to be, over and above some sort of more or less egalitarian distribution of social affluence, a serious change in popular political attitudes. Such change would constitute not a minor rejigging but a major structural alteration of the systems of democratic politics currently on offer.

BACK TO THE FUTURE?

A third obstacle is historical. The dominant tradition of Western political thought or theory from Plato onwards, at least until the later nineteenth century, has been 'anti-democratic' (Roberts 1994). I have sketched above the unhappy fate of (the word) 'democracy' (see end of chapter 10). Pragmatically speaking, the relatively newly founded city of Rhodes (408 BCE) functioned perhaps as a genuine democracy into the second century BCE, but thereafter, when the term was used, it is normally best translated into English as 'republic'. The major philosophies of the Hellenistic era (the last three centuries BCE) for the most part shed any significant political emphasis: after 300 BCE 'the schools themselves virtually ceased to discuss political questions' (Brunt 1993: 300). This was reasonable enough, in that 'when it was clear that the *polis* was outdated in practice' political theory advanced beyond the relatively narrow confines of the *polis* (Brunt 1993: 393; see also Walbank 1944). Even so, a number of individual men of action (e.g. Persaeus) were both Stoics and writers, and a number of Stoic philosophers do arguably seem to have attempted to influence the course of practical affairs, not least Sphaerus (chapter 10; see Vatai 1984 and Erskine 1990).

Hellenistic and then Greek-influenced Roman political philosophy, in so far as it was civic and republican, was certainly not democratic, however. In fact, it manifested itself as predominantly monarchist, if not actually absolutist – a few isolated gestures towards (non-economic) egalitarianism notwithstanding. Moreover, even the more politicised variants tended to share the general post-Platonic displacement of emphasis from public civic morality onto a privatised morality of the soul. One might note, for conspicuous instance, the Stoic view that every bad man is a slave – which managed the tricky feat of both collapsing the crucial, real-world legal distinction between slave and free man and eliding the important function played by slavery thitherto in the Greek civic imaginary (see Cartledge 1993 and de Ste. Croix 2004: 347).

The eventual rise of various forms of Christianity reinforced the theoretical concentration on the (now *ex hypothesi* immortal) soul in two ways. First, the life hereafter – eternal life, as it was hopefully viewed – became considered vastly more important than earthly life in this miserable vale of tears. What, as the third-century African Christian Tertullian memorably asked, has Athens to do with Jerusalem? Second, the instruction credited already to Jesus himself – 'Render unto Caesar that which is Caesar's' – anticipated the institutionalised separation of Church and State, and the triumph of the Church (or, rather, of the one particularly favoured brand of Catholic orthodox dogma), under the first Christian emperor Constantine. As Geoffrey de Ste. Croix (1983) well observed, although Christianity had much that was pertinent to say on relations between man and man, it had but little to say – and that little not very enlightening – on relations between men and men.

All the same, there was nevertheless a legacy – a legacy of Greek political *logos*: from Christian late antiquity, through early mediaeval Byzantium, down eventually to its reception in the southern European Renaissance, especially in the city republic of Venice. Transmission and reception were eased somewhat by the intermittent republicanism of certain mediaeval city states, with Venice, again, prominently to the fore; though this was hardly (*pace* Nelson 2005) marked by any strongly Hellenic ancestry. In the early modern era two opposing views took hold. On the one side, there developed the tradition of 'civic republicanism' from Machiavelli onwards, somewhat anciently inflected in aspiration as well as inspiration, though (again, *pace* Nelson 2005) more Roman than Greek. On the other side, there was the liberal, state-based republicanism of John Locke that can then be traced on down, more or less directly, as far as the American Revolution. The latter trend comported a downsizing – and downgrading – of the political and civic in favour of the social and, especially, the economic/commercial (Rahe 1992).

Both traditions rejected the tripartite typology of regimes inherited ultimately from Herodotus (3.80–2: monarchy, aristocracy, democracy), because it was felt to be inappropriate to the seventeenth-/eighteenth-century world. Thus Montesquieu's schema comprised tyranny, constitutional monarchy and the republic (Rahe 1992: 722), reflecting France's emergence from Louis-XIV-style absolutism. More idiosyncratically, Montesquieu also approved the British Glorious Revolution of 1688 (see Rahe 1992: 1056 n. 55, on Jeremy Bentham), but most 'progressive' thinkers favoured versions of non-monarchical – though not democratic – government. The originally English Tom Paine, a participant and shaper of both the American and then the French Revolutions, was in good company in denouncing 'the monster aristocracy'. The question remained, though: what was to be put in place of it, or of absolutism?

One answer, as discovered by the American Revolution after much error as well as trial and some theory, was a combination of 'representative democracy' and federalism. The theory was mainly Hamilton's (Rahe 1992: 1049 n. 9 – 'democracy'; 1055 n. 51 – representation; 1056 n. 55 – Hamilton), and it was he too who specifically rejected the classical Athenian democratic model and opposed modern American federalism and representation positively to 'the commonwealths of Greece'. Another answer, excogitated by the French Revolution, was the discovery of the rights of man and citizen; this in its proto-democratic, Jacobin form espoused a model much closer than the American Revolution to ancient Greek democratic thinking and practice but still separated from it by crucial imaginative and institutional gulfs (Cartledge and Edge 2009). Nevertheless, this French model both failed in political practice and was soon countered by Benjamin Constant's intellectually persuasive (if empirically shaky) distinction between ancient and modern liberty (Constant 1819 [1988]).

One key effect of the radical separation of 'ancient' from 'modern' was to make democracy once again acceptable in principle, although the 'radical' versions advocated by George Grote and John Stuart Mill carried less favour and support than the tamed forms of democracy, made safe for rule by the State and party, that were eventually institutionalised from the third quarter of the nineteenth century onwards on both sides of the Atlantic. This progressive – or, rather, regressive – etiolation of ancient Greek democracy in practice has been countered in theory by historians and thinkers of various stripes (e.g. Williams 1993), who claim to see merit, indeed superior merit, in some Greek moral-political theory, especially in so far as modern moral-political theory is Christianising. Other historians, historians of philosophy and political theorists with a crusading bent (especially Barber 1984) see practical value in going back to the Greeks in order to rejuvenate tired modern 'democracy'. They thereby betray a hankering for 'strong' – that is, reconstructed and participatory – democracy, but a democracy that is inclusive and not exclusive (of women and other minorities), and not natal but contractual.

For them, the resolution of major national and local issues by communal debate is a desideratum, as opposed to the dominant obsession with the 'reason' of so-called experts, who advocate technocratic solutions to all social problems, and give preference to financially measured efficiency over qualitative moral and ethical judgement. Not that high-tech and democracy are incompatible – in principle: the problem, as noted above, is instead one of culture and education. A hopeful sign of the times, perhaps, is a recent tract entitled *A People's Parliament: A (Revised) Blueprint for a Very English Revolution* (Sutherland 2008).

To be realistic, however, we must conclude, as we began, with contrast. In the world of the male-dominated, small-scale polities of ancient Greece, Simonides (epigraph to chapter 2) could unself-consciously, accurately and, not least, laconically observe that 'the *polis* teaches a man' – that is, instructs him (male gender) both that, and how, he should be a citizen. Within the purview of the enlarged political vision sketched above, the citizen of the future – female now, of course, as well as male – will have to be taught (how) to become a different kind of political animal, environmentally adapted to the new ecology of a more or less cosmopolitanist democratic politics.

## Selected texts and documents

### I.I LAW OF ELIS, 6TH CENTURY BCE (TRANS. DILLON AND GARLAND 1994: 307, NO. 10.29, SLIGHTLY MODIFIED)

[the first tablet is lost]

If he commits fornication [?] in the sacred precinct, he shall pay the penalty by sacrificing an ox and by total purification, and the *thearos* [official] the same. If anyone gives judgement contrary to what is written, the judgement shall be invalid, and the *rhêtra* of the People shall be final in judging. Anything of what is written may be amended if it seems better with regard to the God [Zeus], by withdrawing or adding with [the approval of] the whole Council of 500 and the People in full assembly. Changes may be made three times, adding or withdrawing.

### I.2 FROM THE 'PERSIAN DEBATE' IN HERODOTUS (3.80–2)

The speech of 'Otanes' (3.80):

To me it seems best that no single one of us should henceforth be ruler, for that is neither pleasant nor profitable. [. . .] [H]ow should the rule of one alone be a well-ordered thing, given that the monarch may do as he desires without rendering any account for his acts? Even the best of all men, were he to be placed in this position, would change from his accustomed outlook. For insolence is engendered in him by the good things that he possesses and envy is implanted in man from the beginning; and, having these two things, he has all vice. For he does many reckless wrongs, partly motivated by insolence arising from excess, and partly by envy... Towards his subjects, however, he displays exactly the opposite temper. For he begrudges the nobles their life and livelihood, but delights in the basest of the citizens, and he is more ready than any other man to entertain calumnies. Then, of all things he is the most inconsistent. For if you express admiration of him moderately he is offended that no very great court has been paid him, whereas if you flatter him extravagantly he is offended that you are a flatterer. Most important of all, he transgresses the customs handed down from our ancestors. He ravishes women. He puts men to death without trial.

Over against that, the rule of the Many has, first, the fairest of names – equality under the laws [*isonomia*]. Next, the multitude does none of those things the monarch does. Offices are filled by sortition. All officials are obliged to render accounts for their actions. Finally, all matters of deliberation are decided by the public Assembly.

I therefore propose that we abandon monarchy and increase the power of the multitude, for in the Many is contained All.

### 1.3 FROM THE 'ATHENIAN LAW ON TYRANNY', 337/6 (*see* ARNAOUTOGLOU 1998: 75–7, NO. 65)

[preamble omitted]

[I]f anyone revolts in order to establish a tyranny or aids to this end or abolishes the democracy or deprives the Athenian People of their constitution, whoever kills this person shall not require purification; and it is not permitted to members of the Areopagus Council while the democracy is abolished in Athens to go to the Areopagus hill, to sit together in council, to take any decision on any affair; if any member of the Areopagus while the democracy is abolished in Athens goes to the Areopagus hill or sits in session or takes any decision, he will be disfranchised, himself and his descendants, and his property will be confiscated and a tithe shall belong to the Goddess . . .

[clauses providing for the inscribing of the law have been omitted]

# The 'Old Oligarch': a close reading

Ah, how the cold sea, friendless of old, stretches all round us!
That mildew democracy has filled our city now,
Rots its green shoots, tough root-stock. Oh, I have found it
More hateful and sore to me than to raw hill-side the plough!
(from Naomi Mitchison, 'The exiled oligarchs are driven out
of the city', in *Black Sparta* [1928])

Like the work itself, its conventional English title – due to Gilbert Murray –
is distinctly odd. It has been handed down wrongly attached to Xenophon's
completely extant corpus, but, though certainly Attic (Athenian) in dialect,
it is not Xenophontic in style. Possibly already in antiquity, it was given
the same title as other works on Athens' constitution (*politeia*), but this
can be very misleading, because it is very different in both approach and
content from the Aristotelian *Athenaiôn Politeia* of the 330s. So different is
it, in fact, that it has been seen as a work of *epideixis*, a purely rhetorical
display piece, glorying in both the discovery and the incipient codification of rhetoric by mid-fifth-century BCE Sicilian rhetoric masters, and
in the clever-clever proto-philosophical sophistical reasoning that takes its
name precisely from the movement associated with the rhetoricians (and
other skills-mongers) labelled collectively – and pejoratively – Sophists,
with a capital 'S', who also began to make their presence felt at Athens
and elsewhere in the Greek world from the mid-fifth century on (see
chapter 6).

There is not space here to go deeply into the questions of genre and
purpose, but the 'Old Oligarch' should in my view be read, as I believe it
was written, as a serious pragmatic political pamphlet, a very early example indeed of the sometimes pro- but mainly anti-democratic pamphlet
literature that sprang up in the third quarter of the fifth century BCE
and reached a climax in the flurry of pamphleteering asociated with the
oligarchic counter-revolution of the '400' at Athens in 411 (Cartledge 2008,
ch. 2). For various reasons, both intratextual and contextual, I believe it

is most plausibly dated in the mid-420s, about the same time – not coincidentally – that the leading oligarchic theorist and politician Antiphon began to 'publish' versions of his lawcourt speeches for agitational and propaganda purposes (see Cartledge 1990). This would make it probably the earliest extant example of Attic prose, and interesting on that account if no other. As it happens, though, it's full of other sorts of interest, not least for its admittedly rather crude and not altogether contradiction-free practical application of oligarchic political theory. It is not certain that the author was 'old'; I'm inclined to think he's more likely to have been relatively young and inexperienced. He was certainly an oligarch, though – if a perhaps unusually flexible and pragmatic one. Josiah Ober (1998) reasonably enough takes this work as his starting point in an acute examination of 'political dissent in democratic Athens', but the author himself, with deliberate paradox, makes out the 'worst' constitution to be the best for the Athenian *dêmos*, and apparently can envisage no possibility of the democracy's being either overthrown from without or reformed from within.

The argument of his short work goes, in summary, like this. Democracy is no good absolutely, but at and for Athens it makes sense, and is secure from attack (both from within and from without). The Athenians use the elite when they require skills, but the common people take paying political office and make the final decisions in their own interest. Unusually cosmopolitan Athens allows slaves and metics (resident aliens) great freedom because it requires their economic services. The Athenians control the elite at home through compulsory, legal financial exactions, and their allies abroad by sequestering their assets through the Athenian People's Courts, as well as by the naval skill that ruling the allies generates. Athens' naval power and geographical location enable it to force its will upon others, to enjoy the fruits of resources originating elsewhere and to raid the territory of others without the risk of suffering raids on its own. Democracy blames elite individuals while protecting the common people from their due share of any blame. Blameworthy are those of the elite who take an actively positive part in the democracy. Democracy is inefficient, and better constitutions exist, but nothing can be done to remedy that without endangering the whole democratic system. Moreover, the democratic Athenians deprive few enough citizens of their civic rights not to be in danger of overthrow from such disfranchised people.

After Herodotus – or perhaps, indeed, before Herodotus – the Old Oligarch is the first writer on record to use the abstract noun *dêmokratia*. It is easy to overlook or underestimate the significance of this. Comparison with the pro- and anti-democratic arguments of Herodotus's 'Persian debate' is entirely fruitful. *Dêmokratia* is in effect analysed here into its two constituent parts. The *dêmos* bit is always taken to mean the majority, the mass, aka the mob, the (*ex hypothesi*) ignorant, stupid, uneducated, fickle poor who made up the bulk of the citizen body of the Athenians, both in the abstract and concretely at any particular decision-taking meeting of either Assembly or Lawcourts. The writer's main argument throughout is the one stated at the outset – namely that democracy is a bad thing absolutely, but democracy at Athens makes sense both for the selfish, sectarian interests of the *dêmos* (mob), who exercise their *kratos* both *for* themselves and *against* their (variously described) elite few 'betters', and also for the city of Athens as such, which – despite democracy's inherent moral flaws – exercises great power abroad thanks to the fact that the mob is precisely a naval mob: that is, it is the *dêmos* that supplies the rowers who power the fleets that enable Athens to exercise *arkhê,* empire or hegemony, abroad over allies who are in fact subjects.

It is this latter dimension of the writer's argument that has given rise to the – to me persuasive – hypothesis that he is either literally or figuratively writing from outside Athens, addressing himself specifically to those allied subjects who were of the same oligarchic disposition and outlook as he but who, unlike him, were suffering from rather than unfairly exploiting the economic, political and psychological advantages offered by the Athenians' empire.

FURTHER READING

I was fortunate to be able to take advantage of the admirable recent edition of this text – including introduction and commentary as well as translation – by Robin Osborne (2004). Since I first wrote this appendix, a new, and very useful, commentary has appeared, by Vivienne Gray (2007): 49–58 (introd.), 187–210 (comm.). See also Ober 1994, 1998.

# *Bibliographical essay*

## LEVEL OF THIS BOOK

Somewhere between those of, on the one hand, Ampolo 1997, Finley 1983 or Vatai 1984, in which discussion of political thought and theory is implicit or secondary to analysis of political institutions, and, on the other, of Sinclair 1951, still a standard textbook in use (for example) at the University of Athens, or the first volume of Coleman 2000, which are quite abstractly philosophical and unconnected dialectically to practical developments in the real world of Greek politics. A model comparandum, for its level rather than its approach, would be Balot 2006; see also Camassa 2007 (comprehensive in the range of 'forms' treated, and it adds chapters on Argos, Corinth and Syracuse to the 'usual suspects', Sparta and Athens). For my approach, compare, rather, Wood and Wood 1978 or Ober 1989.

## NARRATIVE HISTORIES

No one-volume history quite covers all the ground from late prehistory to the early Roman-imperial period in Greek history, though Freeman 2004 makes a good fist of putting these 'civilizations of the ancient Mediterranean' in a genuinely interactive context. Cartledge 1997a may be found a useful (profusely illustrated) companion as well as compendium. The best monograph series are those edited respectively by Oswyn Murray and Fergus Millar, of which the most relevant volumes are Murray 1993, Osborne 1996, and Hornblower 2002. See also now – in the Blackwell History of the Ancient World – Rhodes 2006 and Hall 2007. For the more disjointed Hellenistic period, I recommend – besides Walbank 1992 – Shipley 2000, Erskine 2003 and Bugh 2006; see also Cartledge 1997a.

### I  MEANING IN CONTEXT: HOW TO WRITE A HISTORY
### OF GREEK POLITICAL THOUGHT

For the '*indispensability' of political theory*: MacIntyre 1983; see also Miller and Siedentop 1983; Pocock 1962, 1980. Further on *contemporary political theory*: Ball, Farr and Hanson 1989; Beck 1995; Held 1991; Richter 1980, 1986; Skinner 1985; Waldron 1989. For the '*Cambridge School' approach* (of P. Laslett, W. G. Runciman,

J. Pocock, Q. Skinner, R. Geuss, J. Dunn, R. Tuck and their followers), see, in addition to works by or edited by those, Ball, Farr and Hanson 1989, Tully 1988 and, most recently, Brett and Tully 2006 (which contains among many excellent contributions a remarkable attempt by Richard Tuck to save the early Thomas Hobbes for 'democracy'). For a sketch of *how to write a history of political thought in the archaic period* (*c.* 700–500 BCE), see Cartledge 1998. I also preface my 'Comparatively equal' (1996b) with some methodological remarks and try to provide a fairly full documentation of *equality studies* (e.g. Beitz 1991; but note that in the past four decades well over 200 books, and many more articles, have been published on the subject in English alone). For ancient notions of *equality*, see especially Harvey 1965 and Raaflaub and Wallace 2007. On ancient Greek *freedom/liberty*: Cartledge and Edge 2009; Mulgan 1984; Patterson 1991; Raaflaub 1983, 1985, 1990–1991; Rosen and Sluiter 2004; Saxenhouse 2006; Wallace 1994.

### 2  THE GREEK INVENTION OF THE *POLIS*, OF POLITICS AND OF THE POLITICAL

Nature *of the Greek 'state', politics and 'the political'*: Cartledge 1996c, 2000a; see also Ampolo 1997 (*further bibliography*), Balot 2006, Berent 1994, 1996, 2000, 2004 (*a rejoinder to Hansen 2002*), Detienne 1988, Ehrenberg 1969, Farrar 1988, Finley 1981, 1985, Hansen 1983, 2006, Murray and Price 1990, Rahe 1984, Rhodes 1994, Runciman 1990 and Sakellariou 1989. For the *Greek city as 'city of reason'*: Murray 1990, 1991. An *inventory of poleis*: Hansen and Nielsen 2005; see also Hansen 2006. *Politeia* (*qua 'constitution'*): Bordes 1982. *Religion*: Bruit Zaidman and Schmitt Pantel 1992; Connor 1988; Parker 1996, 2005 (*Athens*); de Polignac 1995a, 1995b; Price 1999; Sourvinou-Inwood 1988, 1990.

### 3  RULE BY ONE: THE POLITICS OF HOMER, C. 750 BCE

Gagarin and Woodruff 1995 (*sourcebook*); Latacz 1991 (*scholarship*); see also Calhoun 1934 (*early attempt to read Homer politically*), Carlier 1991 (*acute survey of political decision-making from the Mycenaean to the archaic ages of Greece*), Greenhalgh 1972 (*patriotism*) and Schofield 1986 (*euboulia*). Finley 1978, Hammer 2002, Haubold 2000, Morris 1986, Raaflaub 1991, 1993, Scully 1990 and Snodgrass 1974 offer contrasting perspectives on *the 'world' of Homer*; see also the sensible remarks in Dickinson 2006: esp. 248–51. *Hesiod*: Clay 2003.

### 4  RULE BY SOME: THE POLITICS OF SOLON, C. 600 BCE

A flurry of important recent work includes Blok and Lardinois 2006, Irwin 2005, Lewis 2006, de Ste. Croix 2004: chs. 1–3 (originals go back to the 1960s) and Wallace 2007; see also Anhalt 1993, Larsen 1949, endorsed by de Ste. Croix 2004: 73–5 (*counting of votes*), Loraux 1988, Oliva 1988 and Vlastos 1946. *Solon as mythical democratic founding father*: Hansen 1989a. *Archaic lawgiving*: Eder 1986;

Gagarin 1986, with Hölkeskamp 1990; Gehrke 1993; Gehrke and Wirbelauer 1994; Hölkeskamp 1992, 1993, 1994, 1995, 1999; Szegedy-Maszak 1978. For *Sparta* in the same period: Cartledge 1980.

### 5 RULE BY ALL: THE ATHENIAN REVOLUTION, C. 500 BCE

*Political background*: Andrewes 1982; Forrest 1966; Lavelle 1993; McGlew 1993. *Intellectual/ideological background*: Detienne 1965; Donlan 1970; Dougherty and Kurke 1993; Gagarin and Woodruff 1995 (*sourcebook*); Griffiths 1995; Lloyd 1979; Meier 1986, 1990; Morris 1996; Raaflaub 2000; Raaflaub and Müller-Luckner 1993; Vernant 1957, 1965. On *Cleisthenes*, I give a full bibliography in Cartledge 2008: ch. 1; see especially Anderson 2003, Lévêque and Vidal-Naquet 1996, Manville 1990, Ober 1993, 2007, Ostwald 1969, 1988 and Raaflaub 1995, 2007. *Early democratic ideology*: Brock 1991; Vlastos 1964. *Early democracy illustrated*: Hedrick and Ober 1993. On *political revolution (not) in Aristotle*: Yack 1993: 209–41, esp. 239–41; on '*revolution' in antiquity generally*: Finley 1986; Meier 1984.

### 6 THE HUMAN MEASURE: THE GREEK INVENTION OF POLITICAL THEORY, C. 500–400 BCE

Farrar 1988 is fundamental, especially for *Protagoras*; see also Cole 1967 (*Democritus*), Euben 1986a (with caution), 1986b, Gagarin and Woodruff 1995 (*sourcebook*), Goldhill 2000, Griffith 1995, Henderson 1998, Meier 1993, Miralles 1996, Ostwald 2000 (*oligarchia*), Pelling 2002 (*Herodotus's 'Persian debate'*), Raaflaub 1988a, 1988b, 1989, 1992, Schubert 1993, Stanton 1973, Thompson 1996, Vlastos 1945–1946 (*Democritus*) and Winton 2000. *Sophists*: see also Gibert 2003, Kerferd 1981, Ostwald 2005 and Poulakos 1995.

### 7 THE TRIAL OF SOCRATES, 399 BCE

The bibliography on Socrates is inexhaustible; Ahbel-Rappe and Kamtekar 2006 and Prior 1996 are useful reference points for modern approaches; see also Cartledge 2008: ch. 3, citing a selection seen from my own viewpoint. *Ancient sources*: Giannantoni 1971. *Modern receptions*: Lane 2001. Other worthwhile work includes, in particular, Allen 1996, Blank 1985 (*payment for teaching*), Brickhouse and Smith 1995, 2002, Burnyeat 1997, Cataldi 2005, Connor 1991, Desirée and Smith 2005, Euben 1997, Finley 1977, Garland 1992 ('*introducing new gods*'), Giordano-Zecharya 2005, Gower and Stokes 1992, Hansen 1995, Irwin 1989, Kraut 1984, Lenfant 2002 (cf. Dover 1976), McPherran 1996, 2002, Muir 1985, Nichols 1987, Ober 2000, Ostwald 1999, Stone 1988 (with Todd 1989), Villa 2001, Vlastos 1983, 1991, Winiarczyk 1990, Winton 2000, Yunis 1988 and Zuckert 2004. Burkert 1985: ch. 7 may exaggerate the generality of a religious 'crisis' in the Greek world as a whole.

8  RULE BY ONE REVISITED: THE POLITICS OF XENOPHON,
PLATO, ISOCRATES, ARISTOTLE — AND ALEXANDER
THE GREAT, C. 400–330 BCE

*Xenophon*: Azoulay 2006 (also *Isocrates*); Waterfield 2005; Gray 2007 is a most helpful commentary on some of the basic works, as well as the pseudonymous 'Old Oligarch'. *Plato*: Schofield 2006 is the best recent overview of Plato's political philosophy. *Isocrates*: Azoulay 2006 (also *Xenophon*); at 141 he nicely notes that, ideologically, 'les chefs deviennent le pivot autour duquel s'organise la *politeia*' ('the leaders become the pivot around which the *politeia* is organised'); Too 1995. *Aristotle*: Cartledge 2002, *passim*; see also Fuks 1984, Gehrke 1985 (*stasis*), Nippel 1980, de Ste. Croix 1983, von Fritz 1954 (*mixed constitution*), Walbank 1969 and Yack 1993: ch. 8 (209–41, 'Class conflict and the mixed regime', with an appendix on why Aristotle lacks the category 'political revolution'). On *Boeotian federalism*, see Cartledge 2000b. *Agesilaus*: Cartledge 1987 is both a general history of Aegean Greece and a case study of a Spartan king (Agesilaus II) from the Peloponnesian War to *c.* 360. *Alexander's legacy*: Stoneman 2003.

9  (E)UTOPIANISM BY DESIGN: THE SPARTAN
REVOLUTION, 244–221 BCE

*Utopia, comparative*: Claeys and Sargent 1999; Schaer, Claeys and Sargent 2000, esp. Sargent 2000. *Utopianism, ancient Greek*: Cartledge 1987: 414–16; 1996a; Dawson 1992, with Schofield 1998; Dubois 2006; Finley 1967; Giannini 1967; Hansen 2005; Schofield 2006: ch. 5 (*Plato*). *General Hellenistic context*: Fuks 1984; see also Brown 1995, Martinez Lacy 2005 and Walbank 1957 (*Polybius*). *Spartan political, social and economic context*: Cartledge and Spawforth 2002: ch. 4; Hodkinson 2000, 2005; Mossé 1991; Oliva 1971; Shimron 1972. *Legend of Lycurgus as lawgiver*: Szegedy-Maszak 1978. *Image of Spartan royalty*: Palagia 2006. *Spartan myth*: Hodkinson 2005; Ollier 1933–1943; Rawson 1969; Tigerstedt 1965–1978; see also Africa 1979 (*More's Utopia*). *Stoicism and politics*: Brunt 1993: 210–33, 'Aspects of the social thought of Dio Chrysostom and the Stoics' (originally 1978), and 234–43, 'Appendix: Panaetius and Cicero, *de Officiis*, 1.150f.' (originally 1973); Schofield 1999b (*Stoicism in Hellenistic politics*, *Zeno as proponent of Spartan-style ideal city*). *Sphaerus*: Erskine 1990: ch. 6; with Green 1994; see also Martinez Lacy 2003, Schofield 1999a: 42 and Scholz 1998: 369 (noting *closeness of relationship of Sphaerus and other Stoics to Hellenistic kings*). *Cynics*: Moles 1995. '*Revolution' in antiquity generally*: Finley 1986; Meier 1984.

10  THE END OF POLITICS? THE WORLD OF PLUTARCH, C. CE 100

*Roman Republic*: Brunt 1966 (*mob rule*); Millar 2002 (with caution). *Early imperial*: Hahn 1989; Walbank 1944. *Plutarch in the round*: Lamberton 2001; *as ethicist*: Pelling 2002: esp. ch. 10, 'The moralism of Plutarch's lives' (originally 1995);

Whitmarsh 2004. *Politico-cultural context*: Stadter and van der Stockt 2002 (a very wide-ranging collection); Swain 1996.

## 11  THE GREEK LEGACY AND DEMOCRACY TODAY

*Anti-democratic Western tradition from Greek antiquity* BCE *to the end of the twentieth century*: Roberts 1994. *Pro-democratic recuperations*: Barber 1984; Cartledge and Edge 2009; Chadwick 2006; Duncan 1983; Dunn 1992a, 1992b, 1993, 2006; Euben, Wallach and Ober 1994; Finley 1985; Hansen 1989b; Lieber 1994, esp. Nippel 1994b; Lilla 2001; McLean 1989; Nippel 1994a; Ober and Hedrick 1996; Rahe 1992; Stüwe and Weber 2004 (*sourcebook*); Vidal-Naquet 1990; Vidal-Naquet and Loraux 1990; West 2004. *Lottery*: Dowlen 2008. *Parliamentary/representative democracy more generally*: Manin 1997: ch. 1, 'Direct democracy and representation: selection of officials in Athens'; Sutherland 2008.

# References

Africa, T. W. (1979) 'Thomas More and the Spartan mirage', *Historical Reflections/ Réflexions historiques* 6: 343–52.

Ahbel-Rappe, S., and R. Kamtekar (eds.) (2006) *A Companion to Socrates*. Oxford.

Allen, R. E. (1996) 'The trial of Socrates: a study in the morality of the criminal process', in W. J. Prior (ed.) *Socrates: Critical Assessments*, vol. II, *Issues Arising from the Trial of Socrates*. London and New York: 1–14.

Ampolo, C. (1997) *La Politica in Grecia*, 2nd edn. Milan.

Anderson, G. (2003) *The Athenian Experiment: Building an Imagined Political Community in Ancient Attica, 508–490 BC*. Chicago.

Andrewes, A. (1982) 'The growth of the Athenian state' and 'The tyranny of Pisistratus', in J. Boardman, I. E. S. Edwards, E. Sollberger and N. G. L. Hammond (eds.) *The Cambridge Ancient History*, vol. III, *The Assyrian and Babylonian Empires and Other States of the Near East, from the Eighth to the Sixth Centuries BC*, 2nd edn. Cambridge: 360–391, 392–416.

Anhalt, E. K. (1993) *Solon the Singer: Politics and Poetics*. Lanham, MD.

Arendt, H. (1958) *The Human Condition: A Study of the Central Dilemmas Facing Modern Man*. Chicago and Garden City, NY.

Arnaoutoglou, I. (1998) *Ancient Greek Laws: A Sourcebook*. London and New York.

Aron, R. (1972) *Progress and Disillusion: The Dialectics of Modern Society*. Harmondsworth.

Azoulay, V. (2004) *Xénophon et les grâces du pouvoir: De la charis au charisme*. Paris.
 (2006) 'Isocrate, Xénophon et le politique transfiguré', *Revue des Etudes Anciennes* 108: 133–53.

Ball, T., J. Farr and R. L. Hanson (eds.) (1989) *Political Innovation and Conceptual Change*. Cambridge.

Balot, R. (2006) *Greek Political Thought*. Malden, MA, and Oxford.

Barber, B. (1984) *Strong Democracy: Participatory Politics for a New Age*. Berkeley and Los Angeles [repr. with new preface 2004].

Beck, U. (1995) *Ecological Politics in an Age of Risk*. Oxford.

Beitz, C. (1991) *Political Equality: An Essay in Democratic Theory*. Princeton, NJ.

Berent, M. (1994) 'Stateless polis', unpublished PhD dissertation, University of Cambridge.
 (1996) 'Hobbes and the "Greek tongues"', *History of Political Thought* 17: 36–59.

148

(2000) 'Anthropology and the Classics: war, violence and the stateless *polis*', *Classical Quarterly new series* 50: 257–89.

(2004) 'In search of the Greek state: rejoinder to M. H. Hansen', *Polis* 21: 107–46.

Blank, D. L. (1985) 'Socratics versus Sophists on payment for teaching', *Classical Antiquity* 4: 1–24 (testimonia, 25–49).

Blok, J., and A. Lardinois (eds.) (2006) *Solon of Athens: New Historical and Philological Approaches*. Leiden.

Bordes, J. (1982) *Politeia dans la pensée grecque des origines jusqu'à Aristote*. Paris.

Brett, A., and J. Tully (eds.) (2006) *Rethinking the Foundations of Modern Political Thought*. Cambridge.

Brickhouse, T. C., and N. D. Smith (1995) *Plato's Socrates*. New York and Oxford.

(2002) *The Trial and Execution of Socrates: Sources and Controversies*. New York.

Brock, R. (1991) 'The emergence of democratic ideology', *Historia* 40: 161–9.

Brown, B. R. (1995) *Royal Portraits in Sculpture and Coins: Pyrrhos and the Successors of Alexander the Great*. New York.

Bruit Zaidman, L., and P. Schmitt Pantel (1992) *Religion in the Ancient Greek City* (ed. and trans. P. A. Cartledge). Cambridge [repr. with add. bibl. 1997] [French original 1989].

Brunt, P. A. (1966) 'The Roman mob', *Past and Present* 35: 3–22.

(1993) *Studies in Greek History and Thought*. Oxford.

Bugh, G. R. (ed.) (2006) *Cambridge Companion to the Hellenistic World*. Cambridge.

Buitron-Oliver, D. (ed.) (1993) *The Greek Miracle: Classical Sculpture from the Dawn of Democracy, the Fifth Century BC*. Washington, DC.

Burkert, W. (1985) *Greek Religion: Archaic and Classical*. Oxford [German original 1977].

Burnyeat, M. F. (1997) 'The impiety of Socrates', *Ancient Philosophy* 17: 1–12.

Calhoun, G. M. (1934) 'Classes and masses in Homer, I–II', *Classical Philology* 29: 192–208, 301–16.

Camassa, G. (2007) *Forme della vita politica dei Greci in età arcaica e classica*. Bologna.

Campbell, D. A. (ed.) (1991) *Greek Lyric*, vol. III: *Stesichorus, Ibycus, Simonides and Others*. Cambridge, MA.

Carlier, P. (1991) 'La procédure de décision politique du monde mycénien à l'époque archaïque', in D. Musti (ed.) *La transizione del miceneo all'alto arcaismo*. Rome: 85–95.

Cartledge, P. A. (1978) 'Literacy in the Spartan oligarchy', *Journal of Hellenic Studies* 98: 25–37 [rev. repr. in P. A. Cartledge (2001) *Spartan Reflections*. London and Berkeley, CA: ch. 4].

(1980) 'The peculiar position of Sparta in the development of the Greek city-state', *Proceedings of the Royal Irish Academy* 51: 91–108 [rev. repr. in P. A. Cartledge (2001) *Spartan Reflections*. London and Berkeley, CA: ch. 3].

(1985) 'Rebels and *sambos* in classical Greece: a comparative view', in P. A. Cartledge and F. D. Harvey (eds.) *Crux: Essays Presented to G. E. M. de Ste.*

*Croix on His 75th Birthday.* Exeter and London: 16–46 [rev. repr. in P. A. Cartledge (2001) *Spartan Reflections.* London and Berkeley, CA: ch. 10].

(1987) *Agesilaos and the Crisis of Sparta.* London and Baltimore.

(1990) 'Herodotus and "the Other": a meditation on empire', *Echos du Monde Classique/Classical Views* 9: 27–40 [Greek translation in A. Melista and G. Sotiropoulou (eds.) (2005) *Herodotos: Dekatessara Meletimata.* Athens].

(1993) '"Like a worm i' the bud"? A heterology of classical Greek slavery', *Greece and Rome* 40: 163–80.

(1996a) 'Utopie et critique de la politique', in J. Brunschwig and G. E. R. Lloyd (eds.) *Le Savoir grec: Dictionnaire critique.* Paris: 200–17 [repr. in English as 'Utopia and the critique of politics', in J. Brunschwig and G. E. R. Lloyd (eds.) (2000) *Greek Thought: A Guide to Classical Knowledge.* Cambridge, MA, and London: 163–79].

(1996b) 'Comparatively equal', in J. Ober and C. W. Hedrick (eds.) *Demokratia: A Conversation on Democracies, Ancient and Modern.* Princeton, NJ: 175–85 [rev. repr. in P. A. Cartledge (2001) *Spartan Reflections.* London and Berkeley, CA: ch. 6].

(1996c) 'La politica', in S. Settis (ed.) *I Greci: Storia-Cultura-Arte-Società*, vol. I, *Noi e I Greci.* Rome: 38–75.

(ed.) (1997a) *The Cambridge Illustrated History of Ancient Greece.* Cambridge [corr. repr. 2002].

(1997b) '"Deep plays": theatre as process in Athenian civic life', in P. E. Easterling (ed.) *The Cambridge Companion to Greek Tragedy.* Cambridge: 3–35.

(1997c) 'Introduction', in P. A. Cartledge, P. Garnsey and E. Gruen (eds.) *Hellenistic Constructs: Essays in Culture, History, and Historiography.* Berkeley, CA: 1–19.

(1998) 'Writing the history of Archaic Greek political thought', in N. Fisher and H. van Wees (eds.) *Archaic Greece: New Approaches and New Evidence.* Swansea and London: 379–99.

(2000a) 'The historical context', in C. Rowe and M. Schofield (eds.) *The Cambridge History of Greek and Roman Political Thought.* Cambridge: 11–22.

(2000b) 'Boeotian swine f(or)ever? The Boeotian superstate, 395 BCE', in P. Flensted-Jensen, T. H. Nielsen and L. Rubinstein (eds.) *Polis and Politics: Studies in Ancient Greek History.* Copenhagen: 397–418.

(2002) *The Greeks: A Portrait of Self and Others*, 2nd edn. Oxford.

(2003) 'Raising hell? The helot mirage – a personal re-view', in N. Luraghi and S. E. Alcock (eds.) *Helots and Their Masters in Laconia and Messenia: Histories, Ideologies, Structures.* Washington, DC: 12–30.

(2007) 'Democracy, origins of: contribution to a debate', in K. A. Raaflaub, J. Ober and R. Wallace (eds.) *Origins of Democracy in Ancient Greece: Interpretations and Controversies.* Berkeley, CA, and London: 155–69.

(2008) *Eine Trilogie über die Demokratie.* Stuttgart.

Cartledge, P. A., and M. Edge (2009) '"Rights", individuals, and communities in ancient Greece', in R. Balot (ed.) *A Companion to Greek and Roman Political Thought.* Oxford: ch. 10.

Cartledge, P. A., and A. Spawforth (2002) *Hellenistic and Roman Sparta: A Tale of Two Cities*, rev. edn. London and New York.

Castriota, D. (1992) *Myth, Ethos and Actuality: Official Art in Fifth-century B. C. Athens.* Madison, WI.

Cataldi, S. (2005) 'Filosofi e politici nell'Atene del V secolo a.C.', in L. Breglia and M. Lupi (eds.) *Da Elea a Samo: Filosofi e politici di fronte all'impero ateniese.* Naples: 95–150.

Chadwick, A. (2006) *Internet Politics: States, Citizens, and New Communication Technologies.* Oxford.

Claeys, G., and L. T. Sargent (eds.) (1999) *The Utopia Reader.* London.

Clay, J. S. (2003) *Hesiod's Cosmos.* Cambridge.

Cole, A. T. (1967) *Democritus and the Sources of Greek Anthropology.* Cleveland, OH.

Coleman, J. (2000) *A History of Political Thought from Ancient Greece to Early Christianity* (2 vols.). Oxford.

Connor, W. R. (1988) '"Sacred" and "secular": *Hiera kai Hosia* and the classical Athenian concept of the state', *Ancient Society* 19: 161–88.

  (1991) 'The other 399: religion and the trial of Socrates', in M. A. Flower and M. Toher (eds.) *Georgica: Greek Studies in Honour of G. L. Cawkwell.* London: 49–56.

Constant, B. (1819 [1988]) 'The liberty of the ancients compared to that of the moderns', in B. Fontana (ed. and trans.) *Constant: Political Writings.* Cambridge: 308–28.

Crick, B. (1992) *In Defence of Politics*, 4th edn. London.

Dawson, D. (1992) *Cities of the Gods: Communist Utopias in Greek Thought.* New York.

De Polignac, F. (1995a) *Cults, Territory, and the Origins of the Greek City-state*, 2nd edn. Chicago.

  (1995b) 'Repenser la "cité"? Rituels et société en Grèce archaïque', in M. H. Hansen and K. A. Raaflaub (eds.) *Studies in the Ancient Greek Polis.* Stuttgart: 7–19.

De Ste. Croix, G. E. M. (1983) *The Class Struggle in the Ancient Greek World: From the Archaic Age to the Arab Conquests*, rev. impr. London and Ithaca, NY.

  (2004) (eds. D. Harvey and R. Parker) *Athenian Democratic Origins: And Other Essays.* Oxford.

Desirée, P., and N. D. Smith (eds.) (2005) *Socrates' Divine Sign: Religion, Practice, and Value in Socratic Philosophy.* Kelowna, BC.

Detienne, M. (1965) 'En Grèce archaïque: géométrie, politique et société', *Annales: Economies, Sociétés, Civilisations* 20: 425–41.

  (1988) 'L'espace de la publicité, ses opérateurs intellectuels dans la cité', in M. Detienne (ed.) *Les savoirs de l'écriture en Grèce ancienne.* Lille: 29–81.

  (2007) *The Greeks and Us: A Comparative Anthropology of Ancient Greece.* Cambridge [French original 2005].

Dickinson, O. T. P. K. (2006) *The Aegean from Bronze Age to Iron Age*. London and New York.

Dillon, M., and L. Garland (1994) *Ancient Greece: Social and Historical Documents from Archaic Times to the Death of Socrates*. London and New York.

Donlan, W. (1970) 'Changes and shifts in the meaning of *demos* in the literature of the archaic period', *Parola del Passato* 135: 391–5 [repr. in W. Donlan (1999) *The Aristocratic Ideal in Ancient Greece: Attitudes of Superiority from Homer to the End of the Fifth Century BC*. Wauconda, IL: 225–36].

Dougherty, C., and L. Kurke (eds.) (1993) *Cultural Poetics in Archaic Greece: Cult, Performance, Politics*. New York.

Dover, K. J. (1976) 'The freedom of the intellectual in Greek society', *Talanta* 7: 24–54 [repr. in K. J. Dover (1987) *The Greeks and Their Legacy: Collected Papers*, vol. II, *Prose Literature, History, Society, Transmission, Influence*. Oxford: 135–58].

Dowlen, O. (2008) *The Political Potential of Sortition: A Study of the Random Selection of Citizens for Public Office*. Exeter and Charlottesville, VA.

Dreher, M. (trans.) (1993) *Aristoteles: Der Staat der Athener*. Stuttgart.

DuBois, P. (2006) 'The history of the impossible: ancient utopia', *Classical Philology* 101: 1–14.

Ducat, J. (2006) *Spartan Education: Youth and Society in Classical Sparta*. Swansea.

Duncan, G. (ed.) (1983) *Democratic Theory and Practice*. Cambridge.

Duncan-Jones, R. P. (1982) *The Economy of the Roman Empire: Quantitative Studies*, 2nd edn. Cambridge.

Dunn, J. (ed.) (1992a) *Democracy: The Unfinished Journey 508 BC to AD 1993*. Oxford.

(1992b) 'Democracy: the politics of making, defending and exemplifying community: Europe 1992', in J. Dunn (ed.) *Democracy: The Unfinished Journey 508 BC to AD 1993*. Oxford: ch. 11.

(1993) *Western Political Theory in the Face of the Future*, 2nd edn. Cambridge.

(2006) *Democracy: A History*. New York.

Eder, W. (1986) 'The political significance of the codification of law in archaic societies: an unconventional hypothesis', in K. A. Raaflaub (ed.) *Social Struggles in Archaic Rome: New Perspectives on the Conflict of the Orders*. Berkeley, CA: 262–300.

Ehrenberg, V. (1969) *The Greek State*, 2nd edn. London.

Erskine, A. W. (1990) *The Hellenistic Stoa: Political Thought and Action*. London and Ithaca, NY.

(ed.) (2003) *Blackwell Companion to the Hellenistic World*. Oxford.

Euben, J. P. (1986a) 'The battle of Salamis and the origins of political theory', *Political Theory* 14: 359–90.

(ed.) (1986b) *Greek Tragedy and Political Theory*. Berkeley, CA, and London.

(1997) *Corrupting Youth: Political Education, Democratic Culture, and Political Theory*. Princeton, NJ.

Euben, J. P., J. R. Wallach and J. Ober (eds.) (1994) *Athenian Political Thought and the Reconstruction of American Democracy*. Princeton, NJ.

Farenga, V. (2006) *Citizen and Self in Ancient Greece: Individuals Performing Justice and the Law*. Cambridge.

Farrar, C. (1988) *The Origins of Democratic Thinking: The Invention of Politics in Classical Athens*. Cambridge.

Finley, M. I. (1967) 'Utopianism ancient and modern', in K. H. Wolff and B. Moore (eds.) *The Critical Spirit: Essays in Honor of Herbert Marcuse*. Boston: ch. 1 [repr. in M. I. Finley (1975) *The Use and Abuse of History*. London: ch. 11].

  (1971) *The Ancestral Constitution*. Cambridge [rev. repr. in M. I. Finley *The Use and Abuse of History*. London: 34–59].

  (1975) *The Use and Abuse of History*. London.

  (1977) 'Socrates and Athens', in M. I. Finley *Aspects of Antiquity*, rev. edn. Harmondsworth: ch. 7.

  (1978) *The World of Odysseus*, 2nd edn. London.

  (1981) 'Politics', in M. I. Finley (ed.) *The Legacy of Greece: A New Appraisal*. Cambridge: 22–36.

  (1983) *Politics in the Ancient World*. Cambridge.

  (1985) *Democracy Ancient and Modern*, 2nd edn. London.

  (1986) 'Revolution in antiquity', in R. Porter and M. Teich (eds.) *Revolution in History*. Cambridge: 47–60.

Fisher, N. R. E. (1992) *Hybris: A Study in the Values of Honour and Shame in Ancient Greece*. Warminster.

Forrest, W. G. (1966) *The Emergence of Greek Democracy*. London.

Freeman, C. (2004) *Egypt, Greece and Rome: Civilizations of the Ancient Mediterranean*, 2nd edn. Oxford.

Fuks, A. (1984) *Social Conflict in Ancient Greece*. Jerusalem and Leiden.

Gagarin, M. (1986) *Early Greek Law*. Berkeley, CA, Los Angeles and London.

Gagarin, M., and P. Woodruff (eds.) (1995) *Early Greek Political Thought from Homer to the Sophists*. Cambridge.

Garland, R. (1992) *Introducing New Gods*. London.

Garnsey, P. (1996) *Ideas of Slavery from Aristotle to Augustine*. Cambridge.

Gehrke, H.-J. (1985) *Stasis: Untersuchungen zu den inneren Kriegen in den griechischen Staaten des 5. und 4. Jh.s v. Chr.* Munich.

  (1993) 'Gesetz und Konflikt: Überlegungen zur frühen Polis', in J. Bleicken and K. Bringmann (eds.) *Colloquium aus Anlass des 80. Geburtstages von A. Heuss*. Kallmünz, Germany: 49–67.

Gehrke, H.-J., and E. Wirbelauer (eds.) (1994) *Rechtskodifizierung und soziale Normen im interkulturellen Vergleich*. Tübingen.

Giannantoni, G. (1971) *Socrate: tutte le testimonianze da Aristofane e Senofonte ai Padri cristiani*. Rome and Bari.

Giannini, A. (1967) 'Mito e utopia nella letteratura greca prima di Platone', *Rendiconti del Istituto Lombardo: Classe di Lettere* 101: 101–32.

Gibert, J. (2003) 'The Sophists', in C. Shields (ed.) *The Blackwell Guide to Ancient Philosophy*. Oxford: 27–50.

Giordano-Zecharya, M. (2005) 'As Socrates shows, the Athenians did not believe in gods', *Numen* 52: 325–55.

Golden, M. (1992) 'The uses of cross-cultural comparison in ancient social history', *Echos du Monde Classique/Classical Views* new series 11: 309–31.

Goldhill, S. D. (1988) *Reading Greek Tragedy*, corr. edn. Cambridge.
   (2000) 'Greek drama and political theory', in C. J. Rowe and M. Schofield (eds.) *The Cambridge History of Greek and Roman Political Thought*. Cambridge: ch. 3.

Goody, J. (2006) *The Theft of History*. Cambridge.

Gower, B. S., and M. C. Stokes (eds.) (1992) *Socratic Questions: The Philosophy of Socrates and Its Significance*. London and New York.

Gray, V. J. (ed.) (2007) *Xenophon on Government*. Cambridge.

Green, P. (1994) 'Philosophers, kings, and democracy, or, how political was the Stoa?', *Ancient Philosophy* 14: 147–56 [review of Erskine 1990].

Greenhalgh, P. (1972) 'Patriotism in the Homeric world', *Historia* 21: 528–37.

Griffith, M. (1995) 'Brilliant dynasts: power and politics in the Oresteia', *Classical Antiquity* 14: 62–129.

Griffiths, A. (1995) 'Non-aristocratic elements in archaic poetry', in A. Powell (ed.) *The Greek World*. London: 85–103.

Grote, G. (1846–1856) *A History of Greece* (12 vols.). London.

Gutmann, A., and D. Thompson (2004) *Why Deliberative Democracy?* Princeton, NJ.

Hahn, J. (1989) *Der Philosoph und die Gesellschaft: Selbstverständnis, öffentliches Auftreten und populäre Erwartungen in der höhen Kaiserzeit*. Stuttgart.

Hall, J. M. (2007) *A History of the Archaic Greek World ca. 1200–479 BCE*. Oxford.

Hammer, D. (2002) *The Iliad as Politics: The Performance of Political Thought*. Norman, OK.

Hansen, M. H. (1983) *Initiative und Entscheidung: Überlegungen über die Gewalt-enteilung im Athen des 4.Jh.s.* Konstanz, Germany.
   (1989a) 'Solonian democracy in fourth-century Athens', *Classica et Mediaevalia* 40: 71–99.
   (1989b) *Was Athens a Democracy? Popular Rule, Liberty and Equality in Ancient and Modern Political Thought*. Copenhagen.
   (1995) *The Trial of Sokrates – from the Athenian Point of View*. Copenhagen.
   (2002) 'Was the *polis* a state or a stateless society?', in T. H. Nielsen (ed.) *Even More Studies in the Ancient Greek Polis*. Stuttgart: 17–47.
   (ed.) (2005) *The Imaginary Polis*. Copenhagen.
   (2006) *Polis: An Introduction to the Ancient Greek City-state*. Oxford.

Hansen, M. H., and T. H. Nielsen (eds.) (2005) *An Inventory of Archaic and Classical Poleis*. Oxford.

Hanson, V. D. (1995) *The Other Greeks: The Family Farm and the Roots of Western Civilization*. New York.

Harvey, F. D. (1965) 'Two kinds of equality', *Classica et Mediaevalia* 26: 101–46.

Haubold, J. (2000) *Homer's People: Epic Poetry and Social Formation*. Cambridge.

Havelock, E. A. (1957) *The Liberal Temper in Greek Politics*. London.

Hedrick, C. W., and J. Ober (eds.) (1993) *The Birth of Democracy* [exhibition catalogue]. Washington, DC.

Held, D. (1991) 'Editor's introduction', in D. Held (ed.) *Political Theory Today*. Oxford: 1–22.

Henderson, J. (1998) 'Attic Old Comedy, frank speech, and democracy', in D. Boedeker and K. A. Raaflaub (eds.) *Democracy, Empire, and the Arts in Fifth-century Athens*. Cambridge, MA: 255–73.

Hesk, J. (2000) *Deception and Democracy in Classical Athens*. Cambridge.

Hodkinson, S. J. (2000) *Property and Wealth in Classical Sparta*. London.

(2005) 'The imaginary Spartan politeia', in M. H. Hansen (ed.) *The Imaginary Polis*. Copenhagen: 222–81.

Hölkeskamp, K.-J. (1990) 'Review of M. Gagarin, *Early Greek Law*, Berkeley etc., 1986', *Gnomon* 62: 116–28.

(1992) 'Written law in archaic Greece', *Proceedings of the Cambridge Philological Society* 38: 87–117.

(1993) 'Demonax und die Neuordnung der Bürgerschaft von Kyrene', *Hermes* 121: 404–21.

(1994) 'Tempel, Agora und Alphabet. Die Entstehungsbedingungen von Gesetzgebung in der archaischen Polis', in H.-J. Gehrke and E. Wirbelauer (eds.) *Rechtskodifizierung und soziale Normen im interkulturellen Vergleich*. Tübingen: 135–64.

(1995) 'Arbitrators, lawgivers and the "codification of law" in archaic Greece: problems and perspectives', *Métis* 7 (offic. 1992, but publ. 1995): 49–81.

(1999) *Schiedsrichter, Gesetzgeber und Gesetzgebung im archaischen Griechenland*. Stuttgart.

Hornblower, S. (2002) *The Greek World 479–323 BC*, 3rd edn. London and New York.

Huxley, G. L. (1979) *On Aristotle and Greek Society*. Belfast.

Irwin, E. (2005) *Solon and Early Greek Poetry: The Politics of Exhortation*. Cambridge.

Irwin, T. H. (1989) 'Socrates and Athenian democracy', *Philosophy and Public Affairs* 18: 184–205 [review of Stone 1988].

(1998) 'Mill and the Classical world', in J. Skorupski (ed.) *The Cambridge Companion to Mill*. Cambridge: 423–63.

Keane, J. (2003) *Global Civil Society?* Cambridge.

Kerferd, G. B. (1981) *The Sophistic Movement*. Cambridge.

Kraut, R. (1984) *Socrates and the State*. Princeton, NJ.

Lamberton, R. (2001) *Plutarch*. New Haven, CT.

Lane, M. S. (2001) *Plato's Progeny: How Socrates and Plato Still Captivate the Modern Mind*. London.

Larsen, J. A. O. (1949) 'The origin and significance of the counting of votes', *Classical Philology* 44: 164–81.

Latacz, J. (ed.) (1991) *Zweihundert Jahre Homer-Forschung: Rückblick und Ausblick*. Stuttgart.

Lavelle, B. M. (1993) *The Sorrow and the Pity: A Prolegomenon to a History of Athens under the Peisistratids, c. 560–510 BC*. Stuttgart.

Lenfant, D. (2002) 'Protagore et son procès d'impiété: peut-on soutenir une thèse et son contraire?', *Ktéma* 27: 135–54.

Lévêque, P., and P. Vidal-Naquet (1996) *Cleisthenes the Athenian: An Essay on the Representation of Space and Time in Greek Political Thought*. Atlantic Highlands, NJ [French original 1964].

Lewis, J. (2006) *Solon the Thinker*. London.

Lieber, H.-J. (ed.) (1994) *Politische Theorien von der Antike bis zur Gegenwart*. Bonn.

Lilla, M. (2001) *The Reckless Mind: Intellectuals in Politics*. New York.

Lloyd, G. E. R. (1979) *Magic, Reason and Experience: Studies in the Origins and Development of Greek Science*. Cambridge.

Loraux, N. (1988) 'Solon et la voix de l'écrit', in M. Detienne (ed.) *Les savoirs de l'écriture en Grèce ancienne*. Lille: 95–129.

  (2002) *The Divided City: On Memory and Forgetting in Ancient Athens*. New York.

McGlew, J. F. (1993) *Tyranny and Political Culture in Ancient Greece*. Ithaca, NY.

MacIntyre, A. (1983) 'The indispensability of political theory', in D. Miller and L. Siedentop (eds.) *The Nature of Political Theory*. Oxford: 17–33.

McLean, I. (1989) *Democracy and New Technology*. Cambridge.

McPherran, M. L. (1996) *The Religion of Socrates*. University Park, PA.

  (2002) 'Does piety pay? Socrates and Plato on prayer and sacrifice', in T. C. Brickhouse and N. D. Smith (eds.) *The Trial and Execution of Socrates: Sources and Controversies*. New York: 162–89.

Manin, B. (1997) *The Principles of Representative Government*. Cambridge.

Manville, P. B. (1990) *The Origins of Citizenship in Ancient Athens*. Princeton, NJ.

Manville, P. B., and J. Ober (2003) *A Company of Citizens: What the World's First Democracy Teaches Leaders about Creating Great Organizations*. Cambridge, MA.

Martinez Lacy, R. (2003) 'Esfero en Sparta', *Nova Tellus* 21: 17–22.

  (2005) 'La constitución mixta de Polibio como modelo político', *Studia Historica, Historia Antigua* 23: 373–83.

Meier, C. (1984) '"Revolution" in der Antike', in O. Brunner, W. Conze and R. Koselleck (eds.) *Geschichtliche Grundbegriffe*. Stuttgart: 656–70.

  (1986) 'The emergence of an autonomous intelligence among the Greeks', in S. N. Eisenstadt (ed). *The Origins and Diversity of Axial Age Cultures*. New York: 65–91 [German version repr. in C. Meier (1989) *Die Welt der Geschichte und die Provinz des Historikers*. Berlin: 70–100].

  (1990) *The Greek Discovery of Politics*. Cambridge, MA, and London.

  (1993) *The Political Art of Greek Tragedy*. Oxford [German original 1988].

Mill, J. S. (1859) *On Liberty*. London.

Millar, F. (2002) *The Roman Republic in Political Thought*. Hanover, NH, and London.

Miller, D. (1990) 'The resurgence of political theory', *Political Studies* 38: 421–37.

Miller, D., and L. Siedentop (eds.) (1983) *The Nature of Political Theory*. Oxford.

Miralles, C. (1996) 'Poeta, saggio, sofista, filosofo: l'intellettuale nella Grecia antica', in S. Settis (ed.) *I Greci: Storia-Cultura-Arte-Società*, vol. I, *Noi e I Greci*. Turin: 849–82.

Moles, J. L. (1995) 'The Cynics and politics', in A. Laks and M. Schofield (eds.) *Justice and Generosity*. Cambridge: 129–58.

More, T. (1516 [1989]) *Utopia*, ed. G. M. Logan and R. M. Adams. Cambridge.

Morgan, K. A. (ed.) (2003) *Popular Tyranny: Sovereignty and Its Discontents in Ancient Greece*. Austin, TX.

Morris, I. (1986) 'The use and abuse of Homer', *Classical Antiquity new series* 5: 81–138.

(1996) 'The strong principle of equality and the archaic origins of Greek democracy', in J. Ober and C. W. Hedrick (eds.) *Dēmokratia: A Conversation on Democracies, Ancient and Modern*. Princeton, NJ: 19–48.

Mossé, C. (1991) 'Women in the Spartan revolutions of the third century BC', in S. Pomeroy (ed.) *Women's History and Ancient History*. Chapel Hill, NC, and London: 138–53.

Muir, J. V. (1985) 'Religion and the new education', in P. E. Easterling and J. V. Muir (eds.) *Greek Religion and Society*. Cambridge: 200–18.

Mulgan, R. G. (1984) 'Liberty in ancient Greece', in Z. Pelcynski and J. Gray (eds.) *Conceptions of Political Liberty in Political Philosophy*. New York: 7–26.

Murray, O. (1990) 'Cities of reason', in O. Murray and S. Price (eds.) *The Greek City: From Homer to Alexander*. Oxford: 1–27.

(1991) 'History and reason in the ancient city', *Proceedings of the British School of Rome* 59: 1–13.

(1993) *Early Greece*, 2nd edn. Glasgow.

Murray, O., and S. Price (eds.) (1990) *The Greek City: From Homer to Alexander*. Oxford.

Myres, J. L. (1958) *Homer and His Critics*, completed and edited by D. H. F. Gray. London.

Nafissi, M. (2005) *Ancient Athens and Modern Ideology. Value, Theory and Evidence in Historical Sciences: Max Weber, Karl Polanyi and Moses Finley*. London.

Neer, R. M. (2002) *Style and Politics in Athenian Vase-painting: The Craft of Democracy, circa 530–460 BCE*. Cambridge.

Nelson, E. (2005) *The Greek Tradition in Republican Thought*. Cambridge.

Nichols, M. P. (1987) *Socrates and the Political Community: An Ancient Debate*. Albany, NY.

Nippel, W. (1980) *Mischverfassungstheorie und Verfassungsrealität in Antike und früher Neuzeit*. Stuttgart.

(1994a) 'Ancient and modern republicanism', in B. Fontamara (ed.) *The Invention of the Modern Republic*. Cambridge: 6–26.

(1994b) 'Politische Theorien der griechisch-römischen Antike', in H.-J. Lieber (ed.) *Politische Theorien von der Antike bis zur Gegenwart*. Bonn: 17–46.

(1995) *Public Order in Ancient Rome*. Cambridge.

Ober, J. (1989) *Mass and Elite in Democratic Athens: Rhetoric, Ideology and the Power of the People*. Princeton, NJ.

(1993) 'The Athenian revolution of 508/7 BCE. Violence, authority, and the origins of democracy', in C. Dougherty and L. Kurke (eds.) *Cultural Poetics in Archaic Greece: Cult, Performance, Politics*. New York: 215–32 [repr. in J. Ober (1996) *The Athenian Revolution: Essays on Ancient Greek Democracy and Political Theory*. Princeton, NJ: ch. 4].

(1994) 'How to criticize democracy in late fifth- and fourth-century Athens', in J. P. Euben, J. R. Wallach and J. Ober (eds.) *Athenian Political Thought and the Reconstruction of American Democracy*. Princeton, NJ: 149–71 [repr. in J. Ober (1996) *The Athenian Revolution: Essays on Ancient Greek Democracy and Political Theory*. Princeton, NJ: ch. 10].

(1998) *Political Dissent in Democratic Athens*. Princeton, NJ.

(2000) 'Living freely as a slave of the law: why Socrates lives in Athens', in P. Flensted-Jensen, T. H. Nielsen and L. Rubinstein (eds.) *Polis and Politics: Studies in Greek History*. Copenhagen: 541–52 [repr. in J. Ober (2005) *Athenian Legacies: Essays on the Politics of Going on Together*. Princeton, NJ: 157–70].

(2007) ' "I besieged that man": democracy's revolutionary start', in K. A. Raaflaub, J. Ober and R. Wallace (eds.) *Origins of Democracy in Ancient Greece: Interpretations and Controversies*. Berkeley, CA, and London: 83–104.

Ober, J., and C. W. Hedrick (eds.) (1996) *Dēmokratia: A Conversation on Democracies, Ancient and Modern*. Princeton, NJ.

Oliva, P. (1971) *Sparta and Her Social Problems*. Amsterdam and Prague.

(1988) *Solon: Legende und Wirklichkeit*. Konstanz, Germany.

Ollier, F. (1933–1943) *Le mirage spartiate*, 2 vols. Paris.

Osborne, R. G. (1996) *Greece in the Making 1200–479 BC*. London and New York.

(2004) *The Old Oligarch*. London.

Ostwald, M. (1969) *Nomos and the Beginnings of the Athenian Democracy*. Oxford.

(1988) 'The reform of the Athenian state by Cleisthenes', in J. Boardman, N. G. L. Hammond, D. M. Lewis and M. Ostwald (eds.) *The Cambridge Ancient History*, vol. IV, *Persia, Greece and the Western Mediterranean, c. 525 to 479 BC*, 2nd edn. Cambridge: 303–46.

(1999) 'Atheism and the religiosity of Euripides', in T. Breyfogle (ed.) *Literary Imagination, Ancient and Modern: Essays in Honor of David Grene*. Chicago and London: 33–49.

(2000) *Oligarchia: The Development of a Constitutional Form in Ancient Greece*. Stuttgart.

(2005) 'The Sophists and Athenian politics', in U. Bultrighini (ed.) *Democrazia e antidemocrazia nel mondo greco: Atti del convegno internazionale di studi, Chieti 9–11 Aprile 2003*. Alessandria, Italy: 35–51.

Palagia, O. (2006) 'Art and royalty in Sparta of the 3rd century BC', *Hesperia* 75: 205–17.

Parker, R. (1996) *Athenian Religion: A History*. Oxford.

(2005) *Polytheism and Society at Athens*. Oxford.

Pelling, C. B. R. (2002) 'Speech and action: Herodotus' debate on the constitutions', *Proceedings of the Cambridge Philological Society* 48: 123–58.

Pocock, J. G. A. (1962) 'The history of political thought: a methodological enquiry', in P. Laslett and W. G. Runciman (eds.) *Politics, Philosophy and Society: A Collection.* Oxford: 183–202 [repr. in J. G. A. Pocock (2009) *Political Thought and History: Essays on Theory and Method.* Cambridge: 3–19].

(1980) 'Political ideas as historical events', in M. Richter (ed.) *Political Theory and Political Education.* Princeton, NJ: 139–58.

Poulakos, J. (1995) *Sophistical Rhetoric in Classical Greece.* Columbia, SC.

Price, S. R. F. (1999) *Religions of Ancient Greece.* Cambridge.

Prior, W. J. (ed.) (1996) *Socrates: Critical Assessments* (4 vols.). London and New York.

Raaflaub, K. A. (1983) 'Democracy, oligarchy, and the concept of the "free citizen" in late fifth-century Athens', *Political Theory* 11: 517–44.

(1985) *Die Entdeckung der Freiheit: Zur historischen Semantik und Gesellschaftsgeschichte eines politischen Grundbegriffes der Griechen.* Munich [Eng. trans., 2004, 2nd edn, Chicago].

(1988a) 'Die Anfänge des politischen Denkens bei den Griechen', in I. Fetscher and H. Münkler (eds.) *Pipers Handbuch der politischen Ideen*, vol. I, *Frühe Hochkulturen und die europäische Antike.* Munich: 189–271.

(1988b) 'The beginnings of political thought among the Greeks', *Boston Area Colloquium in Ancient Philosophy* 4: 1–25 [slightly diff. version of Raaflaub 1989].

(1989) 'Die Anfänge des politischen Denkens bei den Griechen', *Historische Zeitschrift* 248: 1–32.

(1990–1991) 'I Greci scoprono la libertà', *Opus* 9–10: 7–28.

(1991) 'Homer und die Geschichte des 8.Jhs. v. Chr.', in J. Latacz (ed.) *Zweihundert Jahre Homer-Forschung: Rückblick und Ausblick.* Stuttgart: 205–56.

(1992) *Politisches Denken und Krise der Polis: Athen im Verfassungskonflikt des späten 5. Jahrhunderts v. Chr.* Munich.

(1993) 'Homer to Solon: the rise of the polis (the written evidence)', in M. H. Hansen (ed.) *The Ancient Greek City-state.* Copenhagen: 41–105.

(1995) 'Einleitung und Bilanz: Kleisthenes, Ephialtes und die Begründung der Demokratie' [written 1992], in K. Kinzl (ed.) *Demokratia: Der Weg zur Demokratie bei den Griechen.* Darmstadt: 1–54 and 451–2.

(1996) 'Equalities and inequalities in Athenian democracy', in J. Ober and C. W. Hedrick (eds.) *Dēmokratia: A Conversation on Democracies, Ancient and Modern.* Princeton, NJ: 139–74.

(2000) 'Poets, lawgivers, and the beginnings of political thought in archaic Greece', in C. J. Rowe and M. Schofield (eds.) *The Cambridge History of Greek and Roman Political Thought.* Cambridge: 23–59.

(2007) 'The breakthrough of *dēmokratia* in mid-fifth-century Athens', in K. A. Raaflaub, J. Ober and R. Wallace (eds.) *Origins of Democracy in Ancient Greece: Interpretations and Controversies.* Berkeley, CA, and London: 105–54.

Raaflaub, K. A., and R. Wallace (2007) '"People power" and egalitarian trends in archaic Greece', in K. A. Raaflaub, J. Ober and R. Wallace (eds.) *Origins of Democracy in Ancient Greece: Interpretations and Controversies*. Berkeley, CA, and London: 22–48.

Raaflaub, K. A., and E. Müller-Luckner (eds.) (1993) *Anfänge politischen Denkens in der Antike: Die nahöstlichen Kulturen und die Griechen*. Munich.

Rahe, P. A. (1984) 'The primacy of politics in Classical Greece', *American Historical Review* 89: 265–93.

(1992) *Republics Ancient and Modern*, two vols. Chapel Hill, NC.

Rawls, J. (1999) *A Theory of Justice*, rev. edn. Cambridge, MA.

Rawson, E. D. (1969) *The Spartan Tradition in European Thought*. Oxford.

Rhodes, P. J. (trans.) (1984) *Aristotle: The Athenian Constitution*. Harmonsdworth.

(1994) 'The polis and the alternatives', in D. M. Lewis, J. Boardman, S. Hornblower and M. Ostwald (eds.) *The Cambridge Ancient History*, vol. VI, *The Fourth Century BC*, 2nd edn. Cambridge: 589–91.

(2006) *A History of the Classical Greek World 478–323 BC*. Oxford.

Richter, M. (ed.) (1980) *Political Theory and Political Education*. Princeton, NJ.

(1986) 'Conceptual history (Begriffsgeschichte) and political theory', *Political Theory* 14: 604–37.

Roberts, J. T. (1994) *Athens on Trial: The Anti-democratic Tradition of Western Thought*. Princeton, NJ.

Robinson, E. W. (1997) *The First Democracies: Early Popular Government outside Athens*. Stuttgart.

(ed.) (2003) *Ancient Greek Democracy: Readings and Sources*. Oxford.

Roisman, J. (2003) 'Honor in Alexander's campaign', in J. Roisman (ed.) *Brill's Companion to Alexander the Great*. Leiden: 279–321.

Rosen, R. M., and I. Sluiter (eds.) (2004) *Free Speech in Classical Antiquity*. Leiden.

Rowe, C. J., and M. Schofield (eds.) (2000) *The Cambridge History of Greek and Roman Political Thought*. Cambridge.

Runciman, W. G. (1990) 'Doomed to extinction: the *polis* as an evolutionary dead-end', in O. Murray and S. Price (eds.) *The Greek City: From Homer to Alexander*. Oxford: 347–67.

Sakellariou, M. B. (1989) *The Polis-state: Definition and Origins*. Athens.

Sargent, L. T. (2000) 'Utopian traditions: themes and variations', in R. Schaer, G. Claeys and L. T. Sargent (eds.) *Utopia: The Search for the Ideal Society in the Western World*. New York: 8–17.

Saxenhouse, A. (2006) *Free Speech and Democracy in Ancient Athens*. Cambridge.

Schaer, R., G. Claeys and L. T. Sargent (eds.) (2000) *Utopia: The Search for the Ideal Society in the Western World*. New York.

Schofield, M. S. (1986) '*Euboulia* in the Iliad', *Classical Quarterly* 36: 6–31.

(1998) 'Zeno of Citium's anti-utopianism', *Polis* 15: 139–49 [review of Dawson 1992].

(1999a) *Saving the City: Philosopher-kings and Other Paradigms*. London.

(1999b) *The Stoic Idea of the City*. Chicago.

(2006) *Plato: Political Philosophy*. London.

Scholz, P. (1998) *Der Philosoph und die Politik: Die Ausbildung der philosophischen Lebensform und die Entwicklung des Verhältnisses von Philosophie und Politik im 4. und 3. Jh. v. Chr.* Stuttgart.

Schubert, C. (1993) *Die Macht des Volkes und die Ohnmacht des Denkens: Studien zum Verhältnis von Mentalität und Wissenschaft im 5. Jahrhundert.* Stuttgart.

Scully, S. (1990) *Homer and the Sacred City.* Ithaca. NY.

Shimron, B. (1972) *Late Sparta: The Spartan Revolution 243–146 BC.* Buffalo, NY.

Shipley, G. (2000) *The Greek World after Alexander 323–30 BC.* London and New York.

Shklar, J. (1957) *After Utopia: The Decline of Political Faith.* Princeton, NJ.

Sinclair, T. A. (1951) *History of Greek Political Thought.* London.

Skinner, Q. R. D. (1969) 'Meaning and understanding in the history of ideas', *History and Theory* 8: 3–53 [repr. in J. Tully (ed.) (1988) *Meaning and Context in the Greek World.* London and New York: 26–67].

   (ed.) (1985) *Return of Grand Theory in the Human Sciences.* Cambridge.

Skocpol, T. (2003) *Diminished Democracy: From Membership to Management in American Civic Life.* Norman, OK.

Snodgrass, A. M. (1974) 'An historical Homeric society?', *Journal of Hellenic Studies* 94: 114–25 [repr. with new introduction in A. M. Snodgrass (2006) *Archaeology and the Emergence of Greece.* Edinburgh and Ithaca, NY: 173–93].

Sourvinou-Inwood, C. (1988) 'Further aspects of *polis* religion', *Annali dell'Istituto Universitario Orientale di Napoli: archaeologia e storia antica* 10: 259–74.

   (1990) 'What is *polis* religion?', in O. Murray and S. Price (eds.) *The Greek City: From Homer to Alexander.* Oxford: 295–322.

Stadter, P. A., and L. van der Stockt (eds.) (2002) *Plutarch, Greek Intellectuals, and Roman Power in the Time of Trajan (98–117 AD).* Leuven, Belgium.

Stanton, G. R. (1973) 'Sophists and philosophers: problems of classification', *American Journal of Philology* 94: 350–64.

Starr, C. G. (1992) *The Aristocratic Temper of Greek Civilization.* New York.

Stone, I. F. (1988) *The Trial of Socrates.* London and Boston.

Stoneman, R. (2003) 'The legacy of Alexander in ancient philosophy', in J. Roisman (ed.) *Brill's Companion to Alexander the Great.* Leiden: 325–45.

Stüwe, K., and G. Weber (eds.) (2004) *Antike und Moderne Demokratie: Ausgewählte Texte.* Stuttgart.

Sutherland, K. (2008) *A People's Parliament: A (Revised) Blueprint for a Very English Revolution.* Exeter and Charlottesville, VA.

Swain, S. (1996) *Hellenism and Empire: Language, Classicism, and Power in the Greek World, AD 50–250.* Oxford.

Szegedy-Maszak, A. (1978) 'Legends of the Greek lawgivers', *Greek, Roman, and Byzantine Studies* 19: 199–209.

Thomas, C. G. (2005) 'The birth of the author', in C. G. Thomas *Finding People in Early Greece.* Columbia, MO, and London: 88–127.

Thompson, N. S. (1996) *Herodotus and the Origins of the Political Community: Arion's Leap.* New Haven, CT.

Tigerstedt, E. N. (1965–1978) *The Legend of Sparta in Classical Antiquity*, 2 vols. + index vol. Göteborg and Stockholm.

Todd, S. C. (1989) 'The journalist, the academic and the trial of Socrates', *Polis* 8: 28–48 [review of Stone 1988].

Too, Y. L. (1995) *The Rhetoric of Identity in Isocrates: Text, Power, Pedagogy.* Cambridge.

Tsetskhladze, G. R. (ed.) (2006) *Ancient Greeks East and West.* Leiden.

Tuck, R. (1991) 'History of political thought', in P. Burke (ed.) *New Perspectives on Historical Writing.* Oxford: 193–205.

Tully, J. (ed.) (1988) *Meaning and Context: Quentin Skinner and His Critics.* Princeton, NJ.

Vatai, F. L. (1984) *Intellectuals in Politics in the Greek World.* London and New York.

Vernant, J.-P. (1957) 'La formation de la pensée positive dans la Grèce archaïque', *Annales: Economies, Sociétés, Civilisations* 12: 183–206 [trans. J. Lloyd (1983) *Myth and Thought in Ancient Greece.* Baltimore: 343–74].

(1965) 'Espace et organisation politique en Grèce ancienne', *Annales: Economies, Sociétés, Civilisations* 20: 576–95 [repr. in J.-P. Vernant (1985) *Mythe et pensée chez les Grecs.* Paris: 238–60].

Vernant, J.-P., and P. Vidal-Naquet (1988) *Myth and Tragedy in Ancient Greece* (two vols. in one). New York.

Vidal-Naquet, P. (1990) *La démocratie grecque vue d'ailleurs.* Paris.

Vidal-Naquet, P., and N. Loraux (1990) 'La formation de l'Athènes bourgeoise', in Vidal-Naquet 1990: ch. 7.

Villa, D. (2001) *Socratic Citizenship.* Princeton, NJ.

Vlastos, G. (1945–1946) 'Ethics and physics in Democritus', *Philosophical Review* 54: 578–92 and 55: 53–64.

(1946) 'Solonian justice', *Classical Philology* 41: 65–83.

(1953) 'Isonomia', *American Journal of Philology* 74: 337–66.

(1964) 'Isonomia politike', in J. Mau and E. G. Schmidt (eds.) *Isonomia: Studien zur Gleichheitsvorstellung im griechischen Denken.* Berlin: 1–35.

(1983) 'The historical Socrates and Athenian democracy', *Political Theory* 11: 495–516 [repr. in *Socratic Studies*, ed. M. F. Burnyeat. Cambridge: 87–108.]

(1991) *Socrates: Ironist and Moral Philosopher.* Cambridge and Ithaca, NY.

Von Fritz, K. (1954) *The Theory of the Mixed Constitution in Antiquity: A Critical Analysis of Polybius' Political Ideas.* New York.

Walbank, F. W. (1944) 'The cause of Greek decline', *Journal of Hellenic Studies* 64: 10–20.

(1957) *A Historical Commentary on Polybius*, vol. I. Oxford.

(1969) 'Review of G. J. D. Aalders *Die Theorie der gemischten Verfassung in der Antike* (1968)', *Classical Review new series* 19: 314–17.

(1992) *The Hellenistic World*, 2nd edn. Glasgow.

Waldron, J. (1989) 'Political philosophy', in J. O. Urmson and J. Rée (eds.) *The Concise Encyclopedia of Western Philosophy and Philosophers.* London.

Wallace, R. W. (1994) 'Private lives and public enemies: freedom of thought in Classical Athens', in A. L. Boegehold and A. C. Scafuro (eds.) *Athenian Identity and Civic Ideology*. Baltimore: 127–55.

(2007) 'Revolutions and a new order in Solonian Athens', in K. A. Raaflaub, J. Ober and R. Wallace (eds.) *Origins of Democracy in Ancient Greece: Interpretations and Controversies*. Berkeley, CA, and London: 49–82.

Waterfield, R. (2005) 'Xenophon's Socratic mission', in C. J. Tuplin (ed.) *Xenophon and His World*. Stuttgart: 79–113.

West, C. (2004) *Democracy Matters: Winning the Fight against Imperialism*. New York.

Whitmarsh, T. (2004) *Ancient Greek Literature*. Cambridge.

Williams, B. A. O. (1993) *Shame and Necessity*. Berkeley and Oxford.

Winiarczyk, M. (1990) 'Methodisches zum antiken Atheismus', *Rheinisches Museum* 55: 1–15.

Winton, R. I. (2000) 'Herodotus, Thucydides and the Sophists', in C. J. Rowe and M. Schofield (eds.) *The Cambridge History of Greek and Roman Political Thought*. Cambridge: 89–121.

Wolin, S. (2004) *Politics and Vision: Continuity and Innovation in Western Political Thought*, 2nd edn. Princeton, NJ.

Wood, E. M., and N. Wood (1978) *Class Ideology and Ancient Political Theory*. Oxford.

Yack, B. (1993) *The Problems of a Political Animal*. Berkeley, CA, and London.

Yunis, H. (1988) *A New Creed: Fundamental Religious Beliefs in the Athenian Polis and Euripidean Drama*. Göttingen, Germany.

(1997) *Taming Democracy: Models of Political Rhetoric in Classical Athens*. Ithaca, NY.

Zuckert, C. (2004) 'The Socratic turn', *History of Political Thought* 25: 189–219.

# Index